THE SHAKESPEARE PARALLEL TEXT SERIES

OTHELLO

Edited by
Wim Coleman

Cover illustration by
Heather Cooper

THE PERFECTION FORM COMPANY
Logan, Iowa

The Past is Prologue

Shakespeare lives! So writes his most eminent biographer, S. Schoenbaum, in the prologue to *Shakespeare: The Globe and the World* (New York: Oxford University Press, 1979). And the evidence is all around us.

We find it in the language we use. When we lament that "the course of true love never did run smooth," whether we are conscious of it or not, we are quoting from *A Midsummer Night's Dream.* When we observe that a well-intended law or regulation is "more honor'd in the breach than the observance," we are applying — or perhaps misapplying — a phrase from *Hamlet.* When we inscribe "What's past is prologue" on the National Archives building in our nation's capital, we are dignifying a minor line from *The Tempest.* Often without realizing it, we find ourselves speaking, if only momentarily, in the accents of a Portia or a Polonius, a Macbeth or a Mercutio. And when we *do* realize it — when we are conscious of the Shakespearean idiom embedded in so much of our daily speech — we take pleasure in those subtle turns of phrase that continue to enrich our discourse. A veteran gardener recently observed, for example, that anyone who calls a rose by any other name has probably been pruning.

Alongside the Greek classics and the King James version of the Bible, Shakespeare's words and works offer a cultural treasure chest from which English-speaking peoples have been drawing, in one way or another, for more than three and a half centuries. Folks have been

following the advice given in *Kiss Me Kate* — brushing up on their Shakespeare — for quite some time.

But Shakespeare's presence is also reflected in a number of other ways. Consider, for example, the more than 800 operatic and symphonic compositions deriving from such plays as *The Merry Wives of Windsor*, *The Taming of the Shrew*, and *Othello*. Or Broadway musicals, such as *The Boys from Syracuse* (a take-off on *The Comedy of Errors*) and *West Side Story* (Leonard Bernstein's New York gang-war updating of *Romeo and Juliet*). Or literary works such as William Faulkner's *The Sound and the Fury*, a sustained allusion to Macbeth's "tomorrow and tomorrow and tomorrow" speech. Here in the United States, Shakespeare has been part of our lives since the earliest days of the republic — even on the frontier, where spinoffs and parodies of Shakespeare helped while away many an hour in the nineteenth century. We've all delighted in the fractured Shakespeare offered up by the Duke and the King in Mark Twain's *Huckleberry Finn*. Ah yes, numerous — but not always sweet — are the uses of Shakespeare.

Nor is there any reason to think that Shakespeare's influence will be any less vital in the future than in the past. In most of the countries of the world, Shakespeare continues to maintain his position as the most frequently performed playwright. Every summer in the United States, for example, Shakespeare festivals highlight the vacation map from Maine to Texas, from Alabama to Oregon.

Ben Jonson was right, then, when he prefaced the first collected edition of Shakespeare's plays with the words "he was not of an age, but for all time!"

The Stratford Years

But if Shakespeare was a man for all time, he was also very much a man of his own age. Christened at Holy Trinity Church in Stratford-upon-Avon in April, 1564, he grew up, the son of illiterate parents, in a small Warwickshire town more noted for its wool and leather goods than for its literary cultivation. His mother, Mary Arden, was the daughter of a well-to-do farmer. His father, John Shakespeare, was a successful glovemaker who held several important borough offices in Stratford before he suffered financial reverses during William's teen years. The birthplace house still stands.

It seems all but certain that young Shakespeare spent most of his weekdays at the nearby Stratford grammar school, where, having learned his ABCs and the Lord's Prayer from a hornbook, he would have gone on to study Latin

Holy Trinity Church, Stratford-on-Avon

Shakespeare's House, Stratford-on-Avon

under the supervision of a stern schoolmaster.
Sundays he would have attended religious
services, studying the catechism of the newly
re-established Church of England and worshiping
in accordance with *The Book of Common Prayer*.

It was a rigorous upbringing, and it equipped
Shakespeare with enough background to become
one of the most widely educated men who ever
lived — despite the fact that he never attended a
day at a college or university.

Judging from his plays and poems, we may
infer that Shakespeare was interested in virtually
every aspect of human life — in professions such
as law, medicine, religion, and teaching; in everyday occupations such as farming, sheepherding,
tailoring, and shopkeeping; in skills such as
fishing, gardening, and cooking. Much of what
Shakespeare knew about these and countless
other subjects he would have acquired from
books. He must have been a voracious reader.

But he would have learned a great deal, also, from simply being alert to all that went on around him. He would have observed the plant and animal life of the nearby woods that he would later immortalize, in *As You Like It*, as the Forest of Arden. While there, he may have hunted from time to time; one legend has it that he left Stratford because he had been caught poaching deer from the estate of a powerful squire four miles upstream. He probably learned to swim as a youth, skinny-dipping in the river Avon. He may have participated in the kinds of athletic competition that were popular in the Elizabethan equivalent of the Olympics, the Cotswold Games. Chances are, too, that he would have been familiar with indoor recreations such as hazard (a popular dice game), or chess, or any of a number of card games. His works make it clear that he was fully at home with a broad spectrum of pastimes characteristic of the daily life of Elizabethan England.

Once his schooldays ended, Shakespeare married, at the age of eighteen, a woman who was eight years his senior. Anne Hathaway was pregnant when the wedding vows were solemnized. That it was a forced marriage is unlikely. But we shall never know how close the couple were. What we do know is that a daughter, Susanna, was baptized in Holy Trinity in May of 1583, followed less than two years later by the christening of twins, Hamnet and Judith. Sometime thereafter, certainly by the late 1580s, the father was in London.

The London Years

London was approximately a hundred miles distant. Shakespeare may have traveled there by way of the spires of Oxford, as do most visitors returning from Stratford to London today. But why he went, or when, history does not tell us. It has been plausibly suggested that he joined an acting troupe that was one player short when it toured Stratford in 1587. All we know for certain is that by 1592 Shakespeare had established himself as an actor and had written at least three plays. One of these — the third part of *Henry VI* — was alluded to in that year in a testament by a dying poet and playwright. Robert Greene warned his fellow playwrights to beware of the "upstart crow" who, not content with being a mere player, was aspiring to a share of the livelihood that had previously been the exclusive province of professional writers such as "the University Wits."

If we look at what Shakespeare had written by the early 1590s, we see that he had already become thoroughly familiar with the daily round of what was rapidly developing into one of the great capitals of Europe. Shakespeare knew St. Paul's Cathedral, famous not only as a house of worship but also as the marketplace where books were bought and sold. He knew the Inns of Court, where aspiring young lawyers studied for the bar. He knew the river Thames,

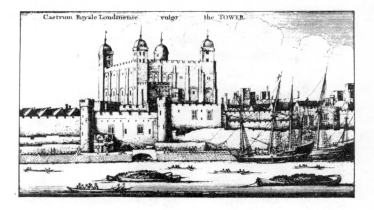

spanned by the ever-busy, ever-fascinating
London Bridge. He knew the Tower, where so
many of the characters he would depict in his
history plays had met their deaths, and where in
his own lifetime, such prominent noblemen as the
Earl of Essex and Sir Walter Raleigh would be
imprisoned prior to their executions. He knew
Westminster, where Parliament met when summoned by the Queen, and where the Queen
herself kept her court at Whitehall Palace. He
knew the harbor, where English ships, having
won control of the seas by defeating the "invinci-
ble" Spanish Armada in 1588, had begun in
earnest to explore the New World.

In Shakespeare's day, London was a vigorous
city of approximately 160,000. If in its more
majestic aspects it was dominated by the court of
Queen Elizabeth — the sovereign most historians
regard as the greatest monarch in English
history — in its everyday affairs it was accented
by the hustle-bustle of getting and spending. Its
Royal Exchange was one of the forerunners of
today's stock exchanges. Its many marketplaces
offered a variety of goods for a variety of tastes.

Its crowded streets presented a colorful pageant of Elizabethan modes of transport and dress, ranging from countrywomen in homespun to elegant ladies in apparel as decorative as their husbands' wealth — and the Queen's edicts on clothing — would allow. Its inns and taverns afforded a robust diversity of vivid personalities—eating, drinking, talking, and enjoying games of all kinds.

London was, in short, a stimulating social and cultural environment for the poet whose works would later be praised as the very "mirror of life." And the young playwright took full advantage of the opportunity to observe humanity in all its facets. Without the broadening that London provided, it is doubtful that Shakespeare could ever have created such breathtakingly real characters as Falstaff, Prince Hal, and "all the good lads in Eastcheap."

Not that all was always well. Like any major city, London also had its unpleasant aspects. For one thing, it was riddled with conflict. Preachers were constantly denouncing the excessive use of cosmetics by women of the period. Even Hamlet speaks out against "your paintings," telling Ophelia "God has given you one face, and you make yourselves another."

In a similar vein, the city's Puritan authorities, regarding the theatres as dens of iniquity, closed them down on any available pretext, particularly during periods when the plague was rampant.

But even with the theatres closed, London was not free of vice and crime. In the Bankside district, prostitution abounded, as did gambling and drunkenness. Pickpockets, vagabonds, and other members of the fraternity of urban lowlife lay in wait for "conies" or unsuspecting victims. With so many "notorious villainies" for the "Belman of London" to bring to light, it is not surprising that some of the most interesting pamphlets of the period were muckraking tracts from reformers outraged by the sinfulness of the modern metropolis.

In such a setting did Shakespeare write and perform the greatest dramatic works the world has ever seen. And he did so in an area of the city that was accustomed to entertainments we would regard as the very antithesis of the sweet Swan of Avon's poetic sublimity. For if Bankside was to blossom into the finest theatrical center of that or any other age, it was also, for better or worse, the seedbed for such crude and cruel spectator sports as bear-baiting, bull-baiting, and cock-fighting. This may help account for the blood and violence one often sees on the Elizabethan stage, even in such Shakespearean works as *Titus Andronicus*, *Julius Caesar*, and *King Lear*.

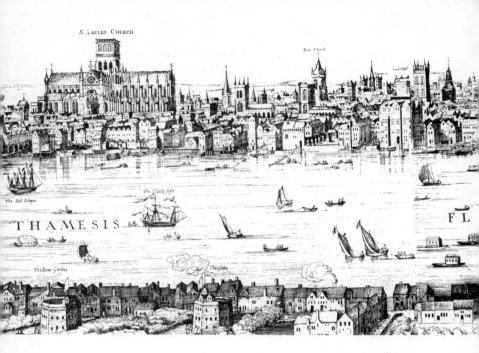

S. i AULES CHURCH

Bow Church

Guild Hall

The Ball Schmas

THAMESIS

FL

The Globe fight

The Bear Gardine

The Globe

But of course there was more than murder and mayhem in the "wooden O" that served as amphitheatre for Shakespeare's works. On a stage largely devoid of scenery, the playwright and the actor made splendid use of language and gesture to establish locale, atmosphere, and meaning. And because the stage was surrounded on three sides by nearby spectators, the playwright and the actor benefited from a more intimate relationship with the audience than is customary in present-day theatres fitted with a curtain and a proscenium arch. For Shakespeare, this meant that he could allow a character to confide in the audience through asides, as does Iago in *Othello*, or to be overheard as he meditates in solitude, as does Hamlet in his celebrated "To be or not to be" soliloquy.

The limitations of the Globe and similar Elizabethan theatres are obvious to us today. For one thing, they were exposed to the sky and thus could not operate comfortably in inclement weather or in darkness. For another, lacking spotlights and other modern paraphernalia, they could not achieve some of the special effects we have come to take for granted in the theatre of our own day. What we sometimes forget, however, is that these limitations could be liberating for the playwright and the actor, making possible a kind of dramatic invention and flexibility difficult to duplicate in the more "advanced" theatre of the twentieth century.

The same was probably true in the Blackfriars and other private indoor theatres of the period, not to mention the halls at Court or the great palaces of the nobility. For it is well to remember that many of Shakespeare's plays were performed in theatrical settings other than the Globe, or its predecessor, the Theatre, or other amphitheatres of the period. Shakespeare's company was known as the Lord Chamberlain's Men from 1594 to 1603, when Queen Elizabeth died; after the accession of King James I, from 1603 on, it was known as the King's Men. Both designations implied a special relationship with the Court, and Shakespeare and his colleagues were invited to perform before the monarch more often than all the other acting troupes in the realm combined.

Shakespeare's real bread and butter, however, came from the immense cross section of the English populace who thronged to Bankside to see his plays performed. Despite the occasional caviling of such rival playwrights as Ben Jonson (whose admiration for Shakespeare was at times "this side idolatry"), we have reason to believe

Interior of Holy Trinity Church

that Shakespeare's dramatic works were immediately recognized for their artistic merits. By 1598, a critic named Francis Meres was comparing Shakespeare's genius to that of the greatest poets of antiquity — Ovid, Plautus, and Seneca — and finding the contemporary playwright superior to his classical predecessors. But unlike many great writers, Shakespeare was also a popular success in his own lifetime. He earned a generous amount of money, invested it wisely in real estate, both in London and in Stratford, and around 1613, eased into a gentleman's retirement — the owner of New Place, the second largest house in his native town.

There, three years later, he died. Fittingly, his death date, like the date tradition has agreed upon for his birth date, was April 23, the day England celebrated its patron saint. In the four centuries since the poet's birth, it seems no exaggeration to say that he has eclipsed even the heroic St. George in glory.

Epilogue

Shakespeare was laid to rest where fifty-two years earlier he had been christened. Shortly thereafter, a monument to his memory was erected above the tomb in Holy Trinity, and that monument is still in place for Shakespeare admirers to see today. But an even greater monument to his memory was produced several years later, when his theatrical colleagues assembled a large volume of his plays. The First Folio of 1623 was a labor of love, compiled as "an office to the dead, to procure his orphans' guardians" and "to keep the memory of so worthy a friend and fellow alive as was our Shakespeare." To that end, it was an unparalleled success, a publication that has aptly been summed up as "incomparably the most important work in the English language."

Among other things, the First Folio preserves what is generally considered the most reliable portrait of Shakespeare, the title-page engraving by Martin Droeshout. In dedicatory verses opposite the portrait, Ben Jonson attests to its authenticity. But quite properly, he then goes on to observe that though the engraver has "hit his face," he has been unable to draw "his wit." For that — for the mastery of language, of character, of poetic drama, of all that reminds us that, after all is said and done, "the play's the thing" — Jonson tells the reader, "look not on his picture but his book."

And so, for more than three and a half centuries, we have. We have read, and studied, and memorized, and performed — and yes, we have worshiped — the man Jonson praised as "Soul of the Age! The applause, delight, the wonder of our stage!"

Bardolatry — the word we use to refer to Shakespeare-worship — has had many manifestations over the intervening centuries. It has animated hundreds of Shakespeare festivals and celebrations, of which undoubtedly the most famous was the great Shakespeare Jubilee of 1769. On that occasion, thousands braved rainy Stratford weather to participate in ceremonies presided over by the principal actor of the eighteenth century, David Garrick. In a somewhat inverted form, Bardolatry has given rise to the notion that someone other than the son of ill-educated, small-town parents wrote the plays

we attribute to William Shakespeare. Hence
Francis Bacon, the Earl of Oxford, and other
members of the nobility have been proposed as
the "true" author of the works we still securely
hold to be Shakespeare's. And Bardolatry has
also occasioned an unceasing cavalcade of
Shakespearean curios and knickknacks:
everything from ceramic figurines and mulberry-
wood chests to Shakespeare-lovers' poker cloths
and Superbard T-shirts.

On the more serious side, appreciation of
Shakespeare has inspired notable works of art by
painters as diverse as Thomas Rowlandson,
George Romney, Henry Fuseli, Eugene Delacroix,
George Cruikshank, Arthur Rackham, Pablo
Picasso, Salvador Dali, and David Hockney. His
works have provided the basis of hundreds of
musical tributes, by composers ranging from
Beethoven to Mendelssohn, Tchaikovsky to
Verdi. And of course his plays continue to be
performed in theatres, in movie houses, and on
television screens.

The Bard is in our bones. Shakespeare lives.

John F. Andrews
Former Editor Shakespeare Quarterly
Folger Shakespeare Library

GOOD FREND FOR IESVS SAKE FORBEARE,
TO DIGG THE DVST ENCLOASED HEARE.
BLESE BE Y MAN Y SPARES THES STONES
AND CVRST BE HE Y MOVES MY BONES

LORDS ROOMS or private galleries. Six pennies let a viewer sit here, or sometimes on stage.

FLAG
A white flag above the theater meant a show that day.

HUT
A storage area that also held a winch system for lowering characters to the stage.

MIDDLE GALLERY
The seats here were higher priced.

TRAP DOOR
Leading to the Hell area where a winch elevator was located.

THE HEAVENS
So identified by being painted with the zodiac signs.

WARDROBE
An essential storage area.

ENTRANCE
Point leading to the staircase and upper galleries.

GALLERY
Located above the stage to house musicians or spectators.

CORRIDOR
A passageway serving the middle gallery.

DRESSING ROOMS
Rooms where actors were 'attired' and awaited their cues.

MAIN ENTRANCE
Here the doorkeeper collected penny admission.

INNER STAGE
A recessed playing area often curtained off except as needed.

THE PIT
Sometimes referred to as 'The Yard' where the 'groundlings' watched.

TIRING-HOUSE DOOR
The rear entrance or 'stage door' for actors or privileged spectators.

TIRING-HOUSE
Backstage area provided space for storage and business.

STAGE
Major playing area jutting into the Pit, creating a sense of intimacy.

HELL
The area under the stage, used for ghostly comings and goings or for storage.

STAIRS
Theatergoers reached the galleries by staircases enclosed by stairwells.

STAGE DOORS
Doors opening into the Tiring-House

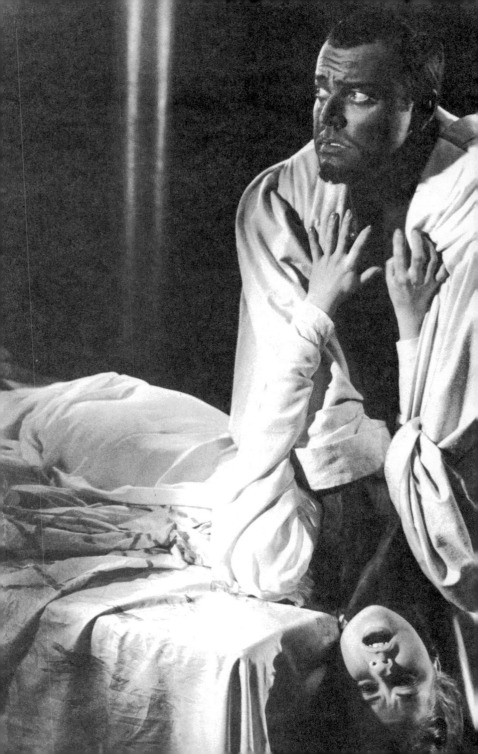

Othello

DRAMATIS PERSONAE

DUKE OF VENICE.
BRABANTIO, *a senator, father to Desdemona.*
Other Senators.
GRATIANO, *brother to Brabantio,* } *two noble*
LODOVICO, *kinsman to Brabantio,* } *Venetians.*
OTHELLO, *the Moor in the military service of Venice.*
CASSIO, *an honourable lieutenant.*
IAGO, *an ensign, a villain.*
RODERIGO, *a gulled gentleman.*
MONTANO, *governor of Cyprus before Othello.*
CLOWN, *servant to Othello.*
DESDEMONA, *daughter to Brabantio and wife to Othello.*
EMILIA, *wife to Iago.*
BIANCA, *a courtezan.*
Gentlemen of Cyprus, Sailors, Officers, Messenger, Herald, Musicians, and Attendants.

SCENE: *Venice; a sea-port in Cyprus.*

Othello

CHARACTERS

DUKE OF VENICE.
BRABANTIO, *A senator, Desdemona's father.*
GRATIANO, *Brabantio's brother.* ⎱ *two noble*
LODOVICO, *a relative of Brabantio.* ⎰ *Venetians.*
OTHELLO, *the Moor, in the military service of Venice.*
CASSIO, *his respected lieutenant.*
IAGO, *Othello's ensign; a villain.*
RODERIGO, *a gullible gentleman.*
MONTANO, *the governor of Cyprus before Othello.*
CLOWN, *Othello's servant.*

DESDEMONA, *Brabantio's daughter and Othello's wife.*
EMILIA, *Iago's wife.*
BIANCA, *a prostitute.*

Gentlemen of Cyprus, sailors, officers, messenger, herald, musicians, attendants, and senators.

SCENE: *Venice; Cyprus.*

Act I, Scene i: [*Venice. A street.*] *Enter* RODERIGO *and*
IAGO.

RODERIGO
    Tush! never tell me! I take it much unkindly
    That thou, Iago, who hast had my purse
    As if the strings were thine, shouldst know of this.

IAGO
    'Sblood, but you'll not hear me.
5   If ever I did dream of such a matter,
    Abhor me.

RODERIGO
    Thou told'st me thou didst hold him in thy hate.

IAGO
    Despise me if I do not. Three great ones of the city,
    In personal suit to make me his lieutenant,
10   Off-capp'd to him; and, by the faith of man,
    I know my price; I am worth no worse a place.
    But he, as loving his own pride and purposes,
    Evades them with a bombast circumstance
    Horribly stuff'd with epithets of war,
15   And, in conclusion,
    Nonsuits my mediators; for, "Certes," says he,
    "I have already chose my officer."
    And what was he?
    Forsooth, a great arithmetician,
20   One Michael Cassio, a Florentine,
    (A fellow almost damn'd in a fair wife)
    That never set a squadron in the field,
    Nor the division of a battle knows
    More than a spinster, unless the bookish theoric,
25   Wherein the toged consuls can propose
    As masterly as he. Mere prattle without practice
    Is all his soldiership. But he, sir, had th' election;
    And I, of whom his eyes had seen the proof
    At Rhodes, at Cyprus, and on other grounds
30   Christen'd and heathen, must be be-lee'd and calm'd

---

4 *'Sblood* an oath meaning "God's blood."   21 *A fellow . . . fair wife* Shakespeare
may have originally intended for Cassio to be married and forgot to correct this reference
when he changed Cassio to a bachelor.

Act I, Scene i: A street in Venice. Enter RODERIGO *and*
IAGO.

RODERIGO
What! Not tell me? I take it very badly
that you, Iago, who have had my money
as if it were your own, would know about this.

IAGO
By God, you just won't listen to me!
5   If I ever dreamed up such a thing,
you can hate me for it.

RODERIGO
You told me you hated him.

IAGO
Despise me if I don't. Three great men in the city
personally asked him to make me his lieutenant
10   and took off their hats to him; and, by God,
I know what I'm worth; I deserve no lower rank.
But he, in love with his own pride and purposes,
evades my friends with roundabout talk,
overblown with lots of epithets of war;
15   and, to sum up,
he denies my mediators. "Certainly," he says,
"I've already picked my officer."
And who is he?
No one but a great tactician,
20   a certain Michael Cassio, a Florentine
(a man whose good-looking wife spells trouble for him)
who never led a squadron on the field,
and doesn't know the first thing about war
no more than a spinster does—unless you mean book learning,
25   in which elderly statesmen are
just as learned as he is. Just talk and no experience:
that's the kind of soldier he is. But he, sir, was chosen;
and I (whose abilities he has seen
at Rhodes, Cyprus, and in other countries
30   both Christian and heathen) must be stopped head-on

By debitor and creditor; this counter-caster,
He, in good time, must his lieutenant be,
And I—God bless the mark!—his Moorship's ancient.

RODERIGO

By heaven, I rather would have been his hangman.

IAGO

35   Why, there's no remedy. 'Tis the curse of service,
Preferment goes by letter and affection,
And not by old gradation, where each second
Stood heir to th' first. Now, sir, be judge yourself
Whether I in any just term am affin'd
40   To love the Moor.

RODERIGO

                    I would not follow him then.

IAGO

O, sir, content you;
I follow him to serve my turn upon him.
We cannot all be masters, nor all masters
45   Cannot be truly follow'd. You shall mark
Many a duteous and knee-crooking knave
That, doting on his own obsequious bondage,
Wears out his time, much like his master's ass,
For nought but provender, and when he's old, cashier'd.
50   Whip me such honest knaves. Others there are
Who, trimm'd in forms and visages of duty,
Keep yet their hearts attending on themselves,
And, throwing but shows of service on their lords,
Do well thrive by them and, when they have lin'd their coats,
55   Do themselves homage. These fellows have some soul;
And such a one do I profess myself. For, sir,
It is as sure as you are Roderigo,
Were I the Moor, I would not be Iago.
In following him, I follow but myself;
60   Heaven is my judge, not I for love and duty,
But seeming so, for my peculiar end;
For when my outward action doth demonstrate
The native act and figure of my heart

by this accountant, this bookkeeper.
He (lucky me!) will be his lieutenant,
and I (God help us all!), the noble Moor's ensign.

RODERIGO
By heaven, I would rather be his hangman.

IAGO
35   Well, there's nothing to be done; this is what comes of good
        service.
        Promotion comes from influence and personal liking
        and not from good old seniority, where a man second in line
        is heir to the one in first place. Now, sir, judge for
            yourself
        if I am bound by any good reason
40   to love the Moor.

RODERIGO
I wouldn't follow him, then.

IAGO
Oh, sir, rest assured.
I'll follow him to get back at him.
We can't all be in charge, and some who are in charge
45   can't be honestly followed. You will notice
        many a dutiful, bowing rascal
        who, delighting in his own subservience,
        uses up his time much like his master's donkey does,
        for nothing except his feed. And when he's old, he's
            dismissed.
50   You can whip those honest rascals for all I care! There are others
        who, putting on a good show of duty,
        are really looking out for their own interests;
        and, giving their lords just a hollow show of duty,
        they get along quite well. When they've stuffed their pockets,
55   they serve themselves and no one else. These fellows have
            some spirit,
        and I consider myself to be one of their sort. Because, sir,
        as sure as your name is Roderigo,
        if I were the Moor, I wouldn't be Iago.
        In following him, I'm really following my own desires.
60   As heaven is my judge, I'll not act with sincere love and duty,
        but I'll seem to, for my own personal ends;
        for when my behavior truly reflects
        the real motives of my heart

In compliment extern, 'tis not long after
65   But I will wear my heart upon my sleeve
For daws to peck at. I am not what I am.

RODERIGO
What a full fortune does the thick-lips owe,
If he can carry 't thus!

IAGO
                              Call up her father,
70   Rouse him. Make after him, poison his delight,
Proclaim him in the streets. Incense her kinsmen,
And, though he in a fertile climate dwell,
Plague him with flies. Though that his joy be joy,
Yet throw such changes of vexation on't,
75   As it may lose some colour.

RODERIGO
Here is her father's house; I'll call aloud.

IAGO
Do, with like timorous accent and dire yell
As when, by night and negligence, the fire
Is spied in populous cities.

RODERIGO
80   What, ho, Brabantio! Signior Brabantio, ho!

IAGO
Awake! what, ho, Brabantio! thieves! thieves!
Look to your house, your daughter, and your bags!
Thieves! thieves!

BRABANTIO *appears above, at a window.*

BRABANTIO
What is the reason of this terrible summons?
85   What is the matter there?

RODERIGO
Signior, is all your family within?

---

66 *daws*   or jackdaws, are birds of the crow family found in Europe.   67 *thick-lips*   a reference to Othello's supposedly Negroid appearance. Scholars have debated whether Shakespeare intended Othello to be seen as a black. Elizabethans, who valued a white complexion, sometimes called a person with a swarthy complexion "black." Moreover, Moors—a

in outward appearance, it won't be long
65   before I wear my heart on my sleeve
for jackdaws to peck at. I'm never what I seem to be.

RODERIGO
What good luck the thick-lips has
if he can get away with this!

IAGO
Wake up her father:
70   get him riled. Chase after Othello and ruin his joy,
mock him in the streets, outrage her relatives,
and though he lives in a pleasant climate,
annoy him with flies. If we can't stop his joy from being joy,
we can at least cause him enough trouble
75   to make it lose some of its flavor.

RODERIGO
Here's her father's house. I'll call out.

IAGO
Do so, and with a terrifying voice and a desperate yell,
as when, because of some carelessness at night, a fire
has been spotted in a populous city.

RODERIGO
80   Hello! Brabantio! Signior Brabantio! Hello!

IAGO
Wake up! Hello, Brabantio! Thieves! Thieves! Thieves!
Check your house, your daughter, and your money!
Thieves! Thieves!

Enter BRABANTIO *at an upstairs window.*

BRABANTIO
What's the reason for this awful racket?
85   What's the matter here?

RODERIGO
Signior, is all your family indoors?

Moslem people living in northwest Africa—are not black. However, Shakespeare quite possibly
did not know or was not discriminating about the racial appearance of Moors. Also, references
such as Roderigo's here, as well as later remarks about Othello's "sooty" and "black"
coloring, seem to indicate that Shakespeare pictured Othello as black. See A.C. Bradley's
discussion of the issue in *Shakespearean Tragedy.*

IAGO
  Are your doors lock'd?

BRABANTIO
                            Why, wherefore ask you this?

IAGO
  'Zounds, sir, you're robb'd! For shame, put on your gown.
90 Your heart is burst, you have lost half your soul;
  Even now, now, very now, an old black ram
  Is tupping your white ewe. Arise, arise!
  Awake the snorting citizens with the bell,
  Or else the devil will make a grandsire of you.
95 Arise, I say!

BRABANTIO
                      What, have you lost your wits?

RODERIGO
  Most reverend signior, do you know my voice?

BRABANTIO
  Not I. What are you?

RODERIGO
  My name is Roderigo.

BRABANTIO
100   The worser welcome;
  I have charg'd thee not to haunt about my doors.
  In honest plainness thou hast heard me say
  My daughter is not for thee; and now, in madness,
  Being full of supper and distemp'ring draughts,
105 Upon malicious bravery dost thou come
  To start my quiet.

RODERIGO
  Sir, sir, sir,—

BRABANTIO
                          But thou must needs be sure
  My spirits and my place have in their power
110 To make this bitter to thee.

---

89 *'Zounds*   a curse meaning "God's wounds."

IAGO
Are your doors locked?

BRABANTIO
Why? What's your reason for asking?

IAGO
Heavens, sir, you've been robbed! For shame, put on your gown!
90   Your heart has been burst, you've lost half your soul.
Even now, now, right now, an old black ram
is mating with your white ewe. Get up, get up!
Wake up your snoring neighbors with the bell,
or else the devil will make you a grandfather.
95   Get up, I tell you!

BRABANTIO
What, are you out of your mind?

RODERIGO
Most honored gentleman, don't you know my voice?

BRABANTIO
No. Who are you?

RODERIGO
My name is Roderigo.

BRABANTIO
100   You're not welcome here!
I've told you not to hang around my door!
You've heard me say quite plainly
that my daughter is not for you. And now, like a crazy man
full of supper and intoxicating drink,
105   you come here with dangerous mischief
to disrupt my peace.

RODERIGO
Sir, sir, sir—

BRABANTIO
But you should be told
that, with my temper and my position, I have it in my power
110   to make you pay for this.

RODERIGO

Patience, good sir.

BRABANTIO

What tell'st thou me of robbing? This is Venice;
My house is not a grange.

RODERIGO

Most grave Brabantio

115   In simple and pure soul I come to you.

IAGO

'Zounds, sir, you are one of those that will not serve God, if the
devil bid you. Because we come to do you service and you think
we are ruffians, you'll have your daughter cover'd with a Barbary
horse; you'll have your nephews neigh to you; you'll have coursers

120   for cousins, and gennets for germans.

BRABANTIO

What profane wretch art thou?

IAGO

I am one, sir, that comes to tell you your daughter and the Moor
are now making the beast with two backs.

BRABANTIO

Thou art a villain.

IAGO

125   You are—a senator.

BRABANTIO

This thou shalt answer; I know thee, Roderigo.

RODERIGO

Sir, I will answer anything. But, I beseech you,
If't be your pleasure and most wise consent,
As partly I find it is, that your fair daughter,

130   At this odd-even and dull watch o' th' night,
Transported, with no worse nor better guard
But with a knave of common hire, a gondolier,
To the gross clasps of a lascivious Moor,—
If this be known to you and your allowance,

135   We then have done you bold and saucy wrongs;

RODERIGO
   Be patient, good sir.

BRABANTIO
   Why do you talk to me of robbing? This is Venice,
   not some out-of-the-way farmhouse.

RODERIGO
   Most reverend Brabantio,
115   I have come here with pure and simple motives.

IAGO
   Heavens, sir, you're one of those who wouldn't serve God if the
   devil told you to. Because we have come to help you, and you think
   we are ruffians, you'll let your daughter be mated with a Moorish
   horse. You'll have your grandsons neigh at you. You'll have
      chargers
120   for relations and Spanish horses for your nearest family.

BRABANTIO
   What kind of foul-mouthed creature are you?

IAGO
   I am a man, sir, who has come to tell you that your daughter
      and the Moor
   are now making the beast with two backs.

BRABANTIO
   You are a villain.

IAGO
125   You are—a senator.

BRABANTIO
   You'll answer for this. I know who you are, Roderigo.

RODERIGO
   Sir, I'll answer everything. But I beg you,
   if it is with your desire and your wise consent
   (as I'm starting to think it is) that your lovely daughter,
130   at this strange hour between night and morning,
   has been carried off with no worse or better a guard
   than a lowly, hired rascal, a gondolier,
   and delivered to the repulsive embraces of a lascivious Moor—
   if you know this already, and you allow it,
135   we then have done you a bold and insolent wrong.

But if you know not this, my manners tell me
We have your wrong rebuke. Do not believe
That, from the sense of all civility,
I thus would play and trifle with your reverence.
140 Your daughter, if you have not given her leave,
I say again, hath made a gross revolt,
Tying her duty, beauty, wit, and fortunes
In an extravagant and wheeling stranger
Of here and everywhere. Straight satisfy yourself.
145 If she be in her chamber or your house,
Let loose on me the justice of the state
For thus deluding you.

BRABANTIO
                    Strike on the tinder, ho!
Give me a taper! Call up all my people!
150 This accident is not unlike my dream;
Belief of it oppresses me already.
Light, I say! light!
          [*Exit above.*]

IAGO
                    Farewell; for I must leave you.
It seems not meet, nor wholesome to my place,
155 To be produc'd—as, if I stay, I shall—
Against the Moor; for, I do know, the state,
However this may gall him with some check,
Cannot with safety cast him, for he's embark'd
With such loud reason to the Cyprus wars,
160 Which even now stand in act, that, for their souls,
Another of his fathom they have none
To lead their business; in which regard,
Though I do hate him as I do hell-pains,
Yet, for necessity of present life,
165 I must show out a flag and sign of love,
Which is indeed but sign. That you shall surely find him,
Lead to the Sagittary the raised search;
And there will I be with him. So, farewell.
          [*Exit.*]

---

167 *Sagittary*   probably the name of an inn.

But if you do not know this, my sense of fair play tells me
that you rebuke us wrongly. Don't believe
that, from a feeling of propriety alone,
I would come like this to tease and play games with a
respectable man like you.
140 Your daughter, if you haven't given her permission,
I tell you again, has rebelled outrageously,
tying her duty, beauty, intelligence, and fortunes
to a wandering and vagrant stranger
who lives here and everywhere. Go see for yourself at once.
145 If she is in her room, or your house,
bring the justice of the state against me
for deceiving you like this.

BRABANTIO
Light the kindling, now!
Give me a candle! Wake up the household!
150 What you've said is not unlike my dream;
I'm already disturbed by my belief in it.
Light, I say! Light!
He exits from above.

IAGO
Goodbye, for I must leave you.
It doesn't seem proper or beneficial to my position
155 to be a witness (as I will be if I stay)
against the Moor. For I know that the state,
though it might give him a slight reprimand,
can't dismiss him safely. For I know he's on his way
with a great to-do to the Cyprus wars,
160 which are going on right now. And to save their souls,
they don't have another man with his abilities
to take charge of their business. Therefore,
though I hate him as much as I hate the pains of hell,
still, the present circumstances make it necessary
165 for me to put on an outward appearance of love—
which is really just a show. To be sure that you'll find him,
bring your search party to the Sagittary,
and I'll be with him there. So, goodbye.
He exits.

Enter below, BRABANTIO *in his night-gown, and Servants with torches.*

BRABANTIO
It is too true an evil; gone she is;
170   And what's to come of my despised time
Is nought but bitterness. Now, Roderigo,
Where didst thou see her? O unhappy girl!
With the Moor, say'st thou? Who would be a father!
How didst thou know 'twas she? O, she deceives me
175   Past thought! What said she to you? Get moe tapers;
Raise all my kindred. Are they married, think you?

RODERIGO
Truly, I think they are.

BRABANTIO
O heaven! How got she out? O treason of the blood!
Fathers, from hence trust not your daughters' minds
180   By what you see them act. Is there not charms
By which the property of youth and maidhood
May be abus'd? Have you not read, Roderigo,
Of some such thing?

RODERIGO
                    Yes, sir, I have indeed.

BRABANTIO
185   Call up my brother.—O, would you had had her!—
Some one way, some another.—Do you know
Where we may apprehend her and the Moor?

RODERIGO
I think I can discover him, if you please
To get good guard and go along with me.

BRABANTIO
190   Pray you, lead on. At every house I'll call;
I may command at most. Get weapons, ho!
And raise some special officers of night.
On, good Roderigo; I'll deserve your pains.
    [*Exeunt.*]

BRABANTIO *enters below in his nightgown, with*
SERVANTS *carrying torches.*

BRABANTIO
This evil thing is all too true. She's gone;
170 and what's left of my wretched life
will be nothing but bitterness. Now, Roderigo,
where did you see her?—Oh, the unfortunate girl!—
With the Moor, you said?—Who would want to be a father?—
How did you know it was her?—Oh, she deceives me
175 beyond imagining!—What did she say to you?—Get more candles!
Wake up my family!—Are they already married, do you think?

RODERIGO
Indeed, I think they are.

BRABANTIO
Oh, heavens! How did she get out? Oh, to have my own flesh and
blood rebel like this!
Fathers, from now on, never trust your daughters' minds
180 on the basis of what you see them do. Aren't there magical spells
by which the nature of youth and virginity
can be deluded? Haven't you read, Roderigo,
about this sort of thing?

RODERIGO
Yes, sir, I certainly have.

BRABANTIO
185 Wake up my brother.—Oh, if only she had been yours!—
(To his servants) Some of you go one way, and some of you go
another. *(To Roderigo)* Do you know
where we may apprehend her and the Moor?

RODERIGO
I think I can find him if you will
get a good escort and come along with me.

BRABANTIO
190 Please lead on. I'll call out at every house;
I'm influential enough to get help from most of them. *(To
his servants)* Get weapons at once,
and wake up the special night guards!
Let's go, good Roderigo. I'll reward your efforts.
They exit.

Scene ii: [*Another street.*] *Enter* OTHELLO, IAGO, *and Attendants with torches.*

IAGO
    Though in the trade of war I have slain men,
    Yet do I hold it very stuff o' th' conscience
    To do no contriv'd murder. I lack iniquity
    Sometimes to do me service. Nine or ten times
5   I'd thought to have yerk'd him here under the ribs.

OTHELLO
    'Tis better as it is.

IAGO
                Nay, but he prated,
    And spoke such scurvy and provoking terms
    Against your honour
10   That, with the little godliness I have,
    I did full hard forbear him. But, I pray you, sir,
    Are you fast married? Be assur'd of this,
    That the magnifico is much belov'd,
    And hath in his effect a voice potential
15   As double as the Duke's. He will divorce you,
    Or put upon you what restraint or grievance
    The law, with all his might to enforce it on,
    Will give him cable.

OTHELLO
                Let him do his spite;
20   My services which I have done the signiory
    Shall out-tongue his complaints. 'Tis yet to know,—
    Which, when I know that boasting is an honour,
    I shall promulgate—I fetch my life and being
    From men of royal siege, and my demerits
25   May speak unbonneted to as proud a fortune
    As this that I have reach'd; for know, Iago,
    But that I love the gentle Desdemona,
    I would not my unhoused free condition
    Put into circumscription and confine
30   For the sea's worth. But, look! what lights come yond?

---

20 *signiory*   the rulers of Venice.

Act I, Scene ii: Another street. Enter OTHELLO, IAGO, ATTENDANTS, *with torches.*

IAGO
  Though in the practice of war I have killed men,
  still, I consider it the very essence of principle
  to not commit premeditated murder. Sometimes I don't have
    enough wickedness
  to serve my own needs. Nine or ten times
5 I considered jabbing him right here, under the ribs.

OTHELLO
  It's better as it is.

IAGO
  No, but he spoke rudely
  and said such insulting and provoking things
  against your honor
10 that, with what little patience I have,
  I could scarcely stop from attacking him. But I ask you, sir,
  are you securely married? You can be sure of this:
  Brabantio is much loved
  and has enough of a voice in things
15 to match the duke. He'll see to it that you're divorced,
  or bring whatever restraints and charges against you
  which the law, with all his power to enforce it,
  will allow him to do.

OTHELLO
  Let him do his worst.
20 The services which I have performed for the state
  will speak louder than his complaints. It's not yet known—
  but when I find out it's honorable to boast,
  I will proclaim it—that I am descended
  from men of royal rank. And for my just deserts,
25 I have the right to claim (without apology) as fine a fortune
  as the one I have gained by marriage. Be sure of this, Iago:
  if I didn't love the gentle Desdemona so much,
  I wouldn't have my unconfined, free condition
  put into boundaries and confines
30 for all the treasure in the sea. But look; some torchbearers
    are coming.

Enter CASSIO, *with lights,* Officers, *and torches.*

IAGO
Those are the raised father and his friends.
You were best go in.

OTHELLO
                    Not I; I must be found.
My parts, my title, and my perfect soul
35   Shall manifest me rightly. Is it they?

IAGO
By Janus, I think no.

OTHELLO
The servants of the Duke, and my lieutenant.
The goodness of the night upon you, friends!
What is the news?

CASSIO
40   The Duke does greet you, general,
And he requires your haste-post-haste appearance,
Even on the instant.

OTHELLO
                    What is the matter, think you?

CASSIO
Something from Cyprus, as I may divine;
45   It is a business of some heat. The galleys
Have sent a dozen sequent messengers
This very night at one another's heels,
And many of the consuls, rais'd and met,
Are at the Duke's already. You have been hotly call'd for;
50   When, being not at your lodging to be found,
The Senate hath sent about three several quests
To search you out.

OTHELLO
                    'Tis well I am found by you.
I will but spend a word here in the house.
55   And go with you.
          [*Exit.*]

---

36 *Janus*   a Roman god with two faces.

Enter CASSIO *and* OFFICERS *with torches.*

IAGO
    They are the awakened father and his friends.
    You'd better get inside.

OTHELLO
    Not I. I must be found.
    My talents, my title, and my clean conscience
35   will speak well of me. Is it them?

IAGO
    By Janus, I don't think so.

OTHELLO
    The duke's servants? And my lieutenant?
    Best wishes of the night to you, friends!
    What's the news?

CASSIO
40   The duke sends his greetings, general;
    and he asks that you immediately appear before him
    this very instant.

OTHELLO
    What do you think is the matter?

CASSIO
    Some news from Cyprus, I imagine.
45   It's urgent business. The officers of the galleys
    have sent a dozen messengers consecutively,
    this very night, at one another's heels.
    And many of the consuls, awake and gathered,
    are already at the duke's. You have been urgently called for.
50   When you were not to be found at your home,
    the senate sent out three separate parties
    to search for you.

OTHELLO
    It's good that you have found me.
    I have just a word to say inside,
55   and then I'll go with you.
          Exit

CASSIO

       Ancient, what makes he here?

IAGO

  Faith, he to-night hath boarded a land carack.
  If it prove lawful prize, he's made for ever.

CASSIO

  I do not understand.

IAGO

60   He's married.

CASSIO

         To who?
    Re-enter OTHELLO.

IAGO

  Marry, to—Come, captain, will you go?

OTHELLO

       Have with you.

CASSIO

  Here comes another troop to seek for you.
    Enter BRABANTIO, RODERIGO, *and* OFFICERS
    with torches and weapons.

IAGO

65 It is Brabantio. General, be advis'd;
  He comes to bad intent.

OTHELLO

       Holla! stand there!

RODERIGO

  Signior, it is the Moor.

BRABANTIO

       Down with him, thief!
    [*They draw on both sides.*]

IAGO

70 You, Roderigo! come, sir, I am for you.

---

62 *Marry* an oath taken from the phrase "by the Virgin Mary" which came to mean
"indeed" or "really."

CASSIO
> Ensign, what's he doing here?

IAGO
> To tell the truth, he has boarded a rich vessel tonight.
> If it proves a lawful prize, he's set for life.

CASSIO
> I don't understand.

IAGO
60 > He's married.

CASSIO
> To whom?
>> *Enter* OTHELLO.

IAGO
> Why, to—Come, captain, are you ready to go?

OTHELLO
> Let's be gone.

CASSIO
> Here comes another group of searchers.
>> *Enter* BRABANTIO, RODERIGO, *and* OFFICERS
>> *with torches and weapons.*

IAGO
65 > It's Brabantio. General, be warned;
> he comes with bad intentions.

OTHELLO
> Hello! Stand right there!

RODERIGO
> Signior, it is the Moor.

BRABANTIO
> Down with him, the thief!
>> *(Both groups of men draw their swords.)*

IAGO
70 > You, Roderigo! Come, sir, I'll fight you.

OTHELLO
Keep up your bright swords, for the dew will rust them.
Good signior, you shall more command with years
Than with your weapons.

BRABANTIO
O thou foul thief, where hast thou stow'd my daughter?
75   Damn'd as thou art, thou hast enchanted her;
For I'll refer me to all things of sense,
If she in chains of magic were not bound,
Whether a maid so tender, fair, and happy,
So opposite to marriage that she shunn'd
80   The wealthy curled darlings of our nation,
Would ever have, t' incur a general mock,
Run from her guardage to the sooty bosom
Of such a thing as thou—to fear, not to delight.
Judge me the world, if 'tis not gross in sense
85   That thou hast practis'd on her with foul charms,
Abus'd her delicate youth with drugs or minerals
That weakens motion. I'll have 't disputed on;
'Tis probable, and palpable to thinking.
I therefore apprehend and do attach thee
90   For an abuser of the world, a practiser
Of arts inhibited and out of warrant.
Lay hold upon him; if he do resist,
Subdue him at his peril.

OTHELLO
                Hold your hands,
95   Both you of my inclining, and the rest.
Were it my cue to fight, I should have known it
Without a prompter. Where will you that I go
To answer this your charge?

BRABANTIO
                To prison, till fit time
100   Of law and course of direct session
Call thee to answer.

OTHELLO

    Put away your shining swords; the dew will rust them.
    Good signior, you'll do better to command on the authority of
      your age
    than with your weapons.

BRABANTIO

    Oh, you foul thief, where have you hidden my daughter?
75   Damned as you are, you've put a spell on her!
    For I ask you in the name of common sense,
    if she weren't bound in the chains of magic,
    would a girl so tender, lovely, and happy,
    so opposed to marriage that she shunned
80   the wealthiest young beaus of our nation,
    would she have ever (at the threat of public shame)
    run from her safety to the sooty bosom
    of such a thing as you—worthy of fear, not delight?
    Let the world judge for me if it isn't grossly obvious
85   that you have practiced foul spells on her,
    deceiving her delicate youth with drugs or minerals
    that weaken the will. I'll have it argued legally.
    It's probable and all too clear to see.
    Therefore, I arrest and charge you
90   as a deceiver of the world, a practitioner
    of forbidden and illegal arts.
    Lay hold of him. If he resists,
    let it be at his own risk.

OTHELLO

    Leave your swords alone—
95   both those of you on my side and the rest.
    If it were my cue to fight, I would have known it
    without a prompter. Where do you want me to go
    to answer this charge of yours?

BRABANTIO

    To prison, till the proper time
100   of law and the regular session of court
    call you to trial.

OTHELLO
What if I do obey?
How may the Duke be therewith satisfi'd,
Whose messengers are here about my side
105   Upon some present business of the state
To bring me to him?

OFFICER
'Tis true, most worthy signior.
The Duke's in council; and your noble self,
I am sure, is sent for.

BRABANTIO
110   How! the Duke in council!
In this time of the night! Bring him away;
Mine's not an idle cause. The Duke himself,
Or any of my brothers of the state,
Cannot but feel this wrong as 'twere their own;
115   For if such actions may have passage free,
Bond-slaves and pagans shall our statesmen be.
[*Exeunt.*]

Scene iii: [*A council-chamber.*] *The* DUKE *and* SENATORS *set at a table, with lights;* OFFICERS *attending.*

DUKE
There is no composition in these news
That gives them credit.

1. SENATOR
Indeed, they are disproportion'd;
My letters say a hundred and seven galleys.

DUKE
5   And mine, a hundred forty.

2. SENATOR
And mine, two hundred!
But though they jump not on a just account,—
As in these cases, where the aim reports,

OTHELLO
What if I obey?
What will I answer to the duke,
whose messengers are here at my side
105   on some pressing business of state,
waiting to bring me to him?

OFFICER
This is true, most worthy signior.
The duke's in council, and you, noble sir,
have been sent for, I'm sure of that.

BRABANTIO
110   What? The duke in council?
At this time of the night? Call him away!
Mine is not a frivolous case. The duke himself,
or any of my fellow senators,
cannot help but feel this wrong as if it were their own;
115   for if such actions are allowed,
our statesmen will all be bondslaves and pagans.
         They exit.

Act I, Scene iii: A council chamber. Enter DUKE *and* SENATORS,
sitting at a table, with lights, and OFFICERS *in attendance.*

DUKE
There is not enough consistency to these reports
to give them credibility.

FIRST SENATOR
Indeed, they are quite different.
My letters say a hundred and seven galleys.

DUKE
5   And mine a hundred and forty.

SECOND SENATOR
And mine two hundred.
But although they don't agree on a certain number
(since in cases where approximation is relied on,

'Tis oft with difference—yet do they all confirm
10   A Turkish fleet, and bearing up to Cyprus.

DUKE
Nay, it is possible enough to judgement.
I do not so secure me in the error
But the main article I do approve
In fearful sense.

SAILOR
15   [*Within.*] What, ho! what, ho! what, ho!
                    Enter a SAILOR.

OFFICER
A messenger from the galleys.

DUKE
                    Now, what's the business?

SAILOR
The Turkish preparation makes for Rhodes;
So was I bid report here to the state
20   By Signior Angelo.

DUKE
How say you by this change?

1. SENATOR
                    This cannot be,
By no assay of reason; 'tis a pageant,
To keep us in false gaze. When we consider
25   Th' importancy of Cyprus to the Turk,
And let ourselves again but understand
That, as it more concerns the Turk than Rhodes,
So may he with more facile question bear it,
For that it stands not in such warlike brace,
30   But altogether lacks th' abilities
That Rhodes is dress'd in; if we make thought of this,
We must not think the Turk is so unskilful
To leave that latest which concerns him first,
Neglecting an attempt of ease and gain
35   To wake and wage a danger profitless.

10   there are often inconsistencies), still, they all confirm
        that a Turkish fleet is approaching Cyprus.

DUKE
     Yes, that seems likely enough upon consideration.
     I'm not so comforted by the fact that these estimates differ
     that I fail to see the news
     as alarming.

SAILOR *(Calling from offstage)*
15   Hello! Hello! Hello!
             Enter a SAILOR.

OFFICER
     It's a messenger from the galleys.

DUKE
     What's happened?

SAILOR
     The Turkish fleet is headed for Rhodes.
     I was sent to report this to the leaders of the state
20   by Signior Angelo.

DUKE
     What do you say about this change?

FIRST SENATOR
     This makes
     no sense at all. It's just a pretense
     to keep us looking the wrong way. If we consider
25   the importance of Cyprus to the Turk
     and remind ourselves again
     that, not only is it of greater concern to the Turk than Rhodes,
     but also that the Turk may take Cyprus more easily
     because it is not militarily prepared
30   and altogether lacks the warlike capabilities
     that Rhodes has—If we think about this,
     we cannot believe that the Turk is inept enough
     to leave for the last the thing which concerns him first,
     neglecting an enterprise which is easy and worthwhile
35   in order to pursue a profitless danger.

DUKE
Nay, in all confidence, he's not for Rhodes.

OFFICER
Here is more news.
Enter a MESSENGER.

MESSENGER
The Ottomites, reverend and gracious,
Steering with due course towards the isle of Rhodes,
40   Have there injointed them with an after fleet.

1. SENATOR
Ay, so I thought. How many, as you guess?

MESSENGER
Of thirty sail; and now they do restem
Their backward course, bearing with frank appearance
Their purposes toward Cyprus. Signior Montano,
45   Your trusty and most valiant servitor,
With his free duty recommends you thus,
And prays you to believe him.

DUKE
'Tis certain, then, for Cyprus.
Marcus Luccicos, is not he in town?

1. SENATOR
50   He's now in Florence.

DUKE
Write from us to him; post-post-haste dispatch.

1. SENATOR
Here comes Brabantio and the valiant Moor.
     Enter BRABANTIO, OTHELLO, CASSIO, IAGO,
     RODERIGO, *and* Officers.

DUKE
Valiant Othello, we must straight employ you
Against the general enemy Ottoman.
55   [*To Brabantio.*] I did not see you; welcome, gentle signior;
We lack'd your counsel and your help to-night.

---

38 *Ottomites*   another name for the Turks.

DUKE
No, we can be sure he's not headed for Rhodes.

OFFICER
Here's more news.
Enter a MESSENGER.

MESSENGER
The Ottomites, you reverend gentlemen,
steering with a due course toward the island of Rhodes,
40   have joined up there with an approaching fleet.

FIRST SENATOR
Yes, just as I thought. How many, do you guess?

MESSENGER
About thirty sails; and now they are sailing
in the opposite direction, very obviously
headed for Cyprus. Signior Montano,
45   your most worthy and most valiant servant,
sends word of this out of his unbounded duty to you
and begs you to believe him.

DUKE
It's certain then it's heading for Cyprus.
Isn't Marcus Luccicos in town?

FIRST SENATOR
50   He's now in Florence.

DUKE
Write to him for me; send the letter off immediately.

FIRST SENATOR
Here come Brabantio and the valiant Moor.
Enter BRABANTIO, OTHELLO, CASSIO, IAGO,
RODERIGO, *and* OFFICERS.

DUKE
Valiant Othello, we must enlist you right away
against our enemy, the Ottoman.
55   *(To Brabantio)* I did not see you. Welcome, gentle signior.
We missed your counsel and help tonight.

BRABANTIO
So did I yours. Good your Grace, pardon me;
Neither my place nor aught I heard of business
Hath rais'd me from my bed, nor doth the general care
60   Take hold on me; for my particular grief
Is of so flood-gate and o'erbearing nature
That it engluts and swallows other sorrows
And it is still itself.

DUKE
                    Why, what's the matter?

BRABANTIO
65   My daughter! O, my daughter!

SENATOR
                    Dead?

BRABANTIO
                              Ay, to me;
She is abus'd, stol'n from me, and corrupted
By spells and medicines bought of mountebanks;
70   For nature so prepost'rously to err,
Being not deficient, blind, or lame of sense,
Sans witchcraft could not.

DUKE
Whoe'er he be that in this foul proceeding
Hath thus beguil'd your daughter of herself
75   And you of her, the bloody book of law
You shall yourself read in the bitter letter
After your own sense, yea, though our proper son
Stood in your action.

BRABANTIO
                    Humbly I thank your Grace.
80   Here is the man,—this Moor, whom now, it seems,
Your special mandate for the state affairs
Hath hither brought.

ALL
                    We are very sorry for 't.

---

69 *mountebanks*   traveling peddlers, often seen at fairs or carnivals.

BRABANTIO
And I missed yours. Your good grace, pardon me.
Neither my position, nor anything I heard of your business,
has raised me from my bed; nor do public concerns
60   disturb me now. My personal grief
is of such an intense and overflowing nature
that it drowns and swallows all other sorrows,
and it still hangs on.

DUKE
Why, what's the matter?

BRABANTIO
65   My daughter! Oh, my daughter!

SENATOR
Dead?

BRABANTIO
Yes, to me!
She has been deceived, stolen from me, and corrupted
by spells and medicines bought from mountebanks.
70   It's not in her nature to behave so outrageously—
when she's not deficient, blind, or half-witted—
without the influence of witchcraft.

DUKE
Whoever he is that, with this foul action,
has tricked your daughter out of her self-possession,
75   and you of her, the severe book of our laws
shall be read to him by you yourself to the strictest letter
according to your own interpretation—yes, even if it were my
    own son
who stood accused by you.

BRABANTIO
I humbly thank you, your grace.
80   Here is the man—this Moor, whom now, it seems,
your special command for state business
has brought here.

ALL
We are very sorry for it.

DUKE
　　[*To Othello.*] What, in your own part, can you say to this?

BRABANTIO
85　　Nothing, but this is so.

OTHELLO
　　Most potent, grave, and reverend signiors,
　　My very noble and approv'd good masters,
　　That I have ta'en away this old man's daughter,
　　It is most true; true, I have married her:
90　　The very head and front of my offending
　　Hath this extent, no more. Rude am I in my speech,
　　And little bless'd with the soft phrase of peace;
　　For since these arms of mine had seven years' pith
　　Till now, some nine moons wasted, they have us'd
95　　Their dearest action in the tented field,
　　And little of this great world can I speak
　　More than pertains to feats of broils and battle,
　　And therefore little shall I grace my cause
　　In speaking for myself. Yet, by your gracious patience,
100　　I will a round unvarnish'd tale deliver
　　Of my whole course of love—what drugs, what charms,
　　What conjuration, and what mighty magic,
　　(For such proceeding I am charg'd withal,)
　　I won his daughter.

BRABANTIO
105　　　　　　　　　A maiden never bold;
　　Of spirit so still and quiet that her motion
　　Blush'd at herself; and she, in spite of nature,
　　Of years, of country, credit, everything,
　　To fall in love with what she fear'd to look on!
110　　It is a judgement maim'd and most imperfect
　　That will confess perfection so could err
　　Against all rules of nature, and most be driven
　　To find out practices of cunning hell,
　　Why this should be. I therefore vouch again
115　　That with some mixtures powerful o'er the blood,

DUKE *(To Othello)*
What can you say for yourself about this?

BRABANTIO
85   Nothing, except that it's true.

OTHELLO
Most powerful, grave, and reverend signiors,
my very noble and proven good masters:
that I have taken away this old man's daughter
is very true; it is true that I have married her.
90   The extent of my offense
amounts to no more than this. I am not articulate
and not very gifted with the soft-spokenness of peace
because between the time my arms had seven years of strength
until about nine months ago, they have done
95   their most important work in the battlefield.
I can speak very little of this great world
that doesn't pertain to deeds of battle and struggle.
For that reason, I won't much help my cause
by speaking for myself. Still, if your gracious patience allows it,
100   I will tell a plain and honest story
of the whole course of my love—what drugs, what charms,
what conjurations, and what mighty magic
(for these are the things I'm charged with)
I used to win his daughter.

BRABANTIO
105   This girl was never bold.
She was of a temper so quiet and modest that she
blushed at every impulse. And she—in spite of her nature,
of her age, of country, reputation, everything—
has fallen in love with what she was afraid to look at!
110   It is a foolish and inaccurate assumption
to suggest perfection could go wrong
against all the rules of nature, and one is driven
to find out what tricks of cunning hell
could have led this to happen. So I insist again
115   that, with some potion that controls the blood,

Or with some dram conjur'd to this effect,
He wrought upon her.

DUKE

To vouch this is no proof,
Without more wider and more overt test
120   Than these thin habits and poor likelihoods
Of modern seeming do prefer against him.

1. SENATOR
But, Othello, speak.
Did you by indirect and forced courses
Subdue and poison this young maid's affections?
125   Or came it by request and such fair question
As soul to soul affordeth?

OTHELLO

I do beseech you,
Send for the lady to the Sagittary,
And let her speak of me before her father.
130   If you do find me foul in her report,
The trust, the office I do hold of you,
Not only take away, but let your sentence
Even fall upon my life.

DUKE

Fetch Desdemona hither.
[*Exeunt two or three.*]

OTHELLO
135   Ancient, conduct them; you best know the place.
[*Exit Iago.*]
And, till she come, as truly as to heaven
I do confess the vices of my blood,
So justly to your grave ears I'll present
How I did thrive in this fair lady's love,
140   And she in mine.

DUKE
Say it, Othello.

or with some drink brewed for this purpose,
he has worked his will on her.

DUKE

To swear this is not proof.
Without more sure and extensive tests
120   than these frail assumptions and slight possibilities
of ordinary appearance, you can hardly speak against him.

FIRST SENATOR

But speak up, Othello.
Did you, by dishonest and deceptive methods,
control and poison this young girl's affection?
125   Or did it come at your request and with the proper kind of discussion
that one person should have with another?

OTHELLO

I ask you
to send to the Sagittary for the lady
and let her speak about me in front of her father.
130   If you find that her report of me is evil,
then let not only the trust and title you have given me
be taken away, but let your sentence
be passed against my life.

DUKE

Bring Desdemona here.
                    Two or three ATTENDANTS *exit.*

OTHELLO

135   Ensign, lead them; you know the place best.
                    IAGO *exits.*
And until she comes, as sincerely as if to heaven
I will confess to you all the wickedness of my blood,
and speak honestly to your serious ears
of how I succeeded in gaining this fair lady's love,
140   and she mine.

DUKE

Tell us, Othello.

OTHELLO
Her father lov'd me; oft invited me;
Still question'd me the story of my life
From year to year, the battles, sieges, fortunes,
145   That I have pass'd.
I ran it through, even from my boyish days
To the very moment that he bade me tell it;
Wherein I spoke of most disastrous chances,
Of moving accidents by flood and field,
150   Of hair-breadth scapes i' th' imminent deadly breach,
Of being taken by the insolent foe
And sold to slavery, of my redemption thence
And portance in my travel's history;
Wherein of antres vast and deserts idle,
155   Rough quarries, rocks, and hills whose heads touch heaven,
It was my hint to speak,—such was my process,—
And of the Cannibals that each other eat,
The Anthropophagi, and men whose heads
Do grow beneath their shoulders. These to hear
160   Would Desdemona seriously incline;
But still the house-affairs would draw her thence,
Which ever as she could with haste dispatch,
She'd come again, and with a greedy ear
Devour up my discourse: which I observing,
165   Took once a pliant hour, and found good means
To draw from her a prayer of earnest heart
That I would all my pilgrimage dilate,
Whereof by parcels she had something heard,
But not intentively. I did consent,
170   And often did beguile her of her tears
When I did speak of some distressful stroke
That my youth suffer'd. My story being done,
She gave me for my pains a world of sighs.
She swore, in faith, 'twas strange, 'twas passing strange,
175   'Twas pitiful, 'twas wondrous pitiful.
She wish'd she had not heard it; yet she wish'd
That Heaven had made her such a man. She thank'd me,
And bade me, if I had a friend that lov'd her,

---

158 *Anthropophagi*   Scythians, who were rumored to be cannibals.

OTHELLO

Her father loved me and often invited me over.
He always asked me for the story of my life
from year to year—the battles, sieges, and fortunes
145   I've experienced.
I told it all, starting with my childhood days and continuing
up to the moment that he asked me to tell it.
I told of very dangerous situations;
of terrible accidents in floods or on the field;
150   of hairbreadth escapes in threatening and deadly battle;
of being taken prisoner by my insolent enemy
and sold into slavery; of my escape from that
and my behavior throughout my travels.
Vast caves and desolate deserts,
155   rough quarries, rocks, and hills whose peaks reach to heaven—
all these were spoken of; that's how it went—
and of cannibals who eat each other,
the Anthropophagi, and men whose heads
grow below their shoulders. To hear all this,
160   Desdemona would lean forward intently;
but still, the business of the house would call her away.
She'd finish her work as quickly as she could
and come back again, and with a greedy ear,
devour my story. I noticed this,
165   found a convenient time, and managed
to elicit from her an earnest request
that, at one sitting, I would tell her all my travels,
which she had heard something of piecemeal
but not without interruptions. I consented
170   and often brought tears from her
when I spoke of some serious danger
I suffered in my youth. When my story was over,
she gave me a world of sighs for my trouble.
She swore, in truth, that it was strange, that it was very strange,
175   that it was sad, that it was terribly sad.
She wished she hadn't heard it; and yet she wished
that heaven had made such a man for her. She thanked me
and told me that if I had a friend who loved her,

I should but teach him how to tell my story,
180   And that would woo her. Upon this hint I spake:
She lov'd me for the dangers I had pass'd,
And I lov'd her that she did pity them.
This only is the witchcraft I have us'd.
Here comes the lady; let her witness it.
                    Enter DESDEMONA, IAGO, *and Attendants.*

DUKE
185   I think this tale would win my daughter too.
Good Brabantio,
Take up this mangled matter at the best;
Men do their broken weapons rather use
Than their bare hands.

BRABANTIO
190   I pray you, hear her speak.
If she confess that she was half the wooer,
Destruction on my head if my bad blame
Light on the man! Come hither, gentle mistress.
Do you perceive in all this noble company
195   Where most you owe obedience?

DESDEMONA
                              My noble father,
I do perceive here a divided duty.
To you I am bound for life and education;
My life and education both do learn me
200   How to respect you; you are the lord of duty;
I am hitherto your daughter. But here's my husband;
And so much duty as my mother show'd
To you, preferring you before her father,
So much I challenge that I may profess
205   Due to the Moor, my lord.

BRABANTIO
                              God be with you! I have done.
Please it your Grace, on to the state-affairs.
I had rather to adopt a child than get it.
Come hither, Moor.

188-89 *Men do their broken . . . hands*   the duke means that like any civilized man, Othello
would have likely used civilized means to accomplish his goals.

I should just teach him how to tell my story,
180   and he could woo her with it. I took this opportunity to speak.
She loved me because of the dangers I had experienced,
and I loved her because she was moved by them.
This is the only witchcraft I have used.
Here comes the lady: let her confirm it.
Enter DESDEMONA, IAGO, *and* ATTENDANTS.

DUKE
185   I think this story would win my daughter, too.
Good Brabantio,
make the best of this difficult situation.
Men prefer to use their broken weapons
rather than their bare hands.

BRABANTIO
190   I ask you to hear her speak.
If she admits that she was half the wooer,
may I be damned for bringing my unjust accusation
against this man! Come here, gentle lady.
Do you know, in all this noble gathering,
195   to whom you owe the most obedience?

DESDEMONA
My noble father,
I see that I have a divided obligation here.
I am indebted to you for my life and education;
my life and education both teach me
200   to respect you: you are the lord of my duty;
before now, I was only your daughter. But here's my husband;
and as much obedience as my mother showed
to you, offering more to you than to her father,
the same, I insist, I now consider
205   due to the Moor, my lord.

BRABANTIO
God be with you! I'm done with it.
If it please you, your grace, let's get on with state business.
I'd rather adopt a child than beget one.
Come here, Moor.

210   I here do give thee that with all my heart
       Which, but thou hast already, with all my heart
       I would keep from thee. For your sake, jewel,
       I am glad at soul I have no other child;
       For thy escape would teach me tyranny,
215   To hang clogs on them. I have done, my lord.

DUKE
       Let me speak like yourself, and lay a sentence,
       Which as a grise or step, may help these lovers
       Into your favour.
       When remedies are past, the griefs are ended
220   By seeing the worst, which late on hopes depended.
       To mourn a mischief that is past and gone
       Is the next way to draw new mischief on.
       What cannot be preserv'd when fortune takes,
       Patience her injury a mock'ry makes.
225   The robb'd that smiles steals something from the thief;
       He robs himself that spends a bootless grief.

BRABANTIO
       So let the Turk of Cyprus us beguile;
       We lose it not, so long as we can smile.
       He bears the sentence well that nothing bears
230   But the free comfort which from thence he hears,
       But he bears both the sentence and the sorrow
       That, to pay grief, must of poor patience borrow.
       These sentences, to sugar or to gall
       Being strong on both sides, are equivocal.
235   But words are words; I never yet did hear
       That the bruis'd heart was pierced through the ear.
       I humbly beseech you, proceed to the affairs of state.

DUKE
       The Turk with a most mighty preparation makes for Cyprus.
       Othello, the fortitude of the place is best known to you; and
240   though we have there a substitute of most allowed sufficiency,
       yet opinion, a sovereign mistress of effects, throws a more safer
       voice on you. You must therefore be content to slubber the gloss
       of your new fortunes with this more stubborn and bois'trous
       expedition.

210   I now give to you with all my heart
that which, if you didn't already have her, with all my heart
I would keep from you. *(To Desdemona)* Because of you, my jewel,
I am glad in my heart that I have no other children,
since your escape would make me tyrannical
215   and lead me to put shackles on them. I am finished, my lord.

DUKE
Let me speak as you should and repeat a proverb
which, one way or another, might help these lovers
find your favor.
When remedies are useless, grief is killed
220   by seeing the worst—a grief which was kept alive by hope.
To complain of a misfortune that is done and over with
is the best way to bring on more misfortunes.
When fortune takes something and one can't get it back,
one makes a mockery of the injury by enduring it patiently.
225   A person who's been robbed and smiles steals something from
the thief.
A person robs himself who persists in grieving pointlessly.

BRABANTIO
So let the Turks trick us out of Cyprus;
we won't lose it, as long as we can smile about it.
He endures the sentence well who doesn't suffer anything
230   except the comfort of freedom when he hears it.
But he endures both the sentence and the suffering
when he has to pay his grief by borrowing from poor patience.
This advice contains sweetness and bitterness,
both very strong, in equal amounts.
235   But words are only words: I haven't yet heard of a
bruised heart being treated through the ear.
I humbly beg you, get on with business of state.

DUKE
The Turks with a very mighty force are heading for Cyprus.
Othello, you best know the strength of the place; and
240   though I have a very capable viceroy in power there,
yet public opinion—the final word on how matters will be
decided—declares you are
the best man for the job. So you'll have to content yourself
to dull the shine
on your new-found luck with this rough and violent
expedition.

OTHELLO
245   The tyrant custom, most grave senators,
         Hath made the flinty and steel couch of war
         My thrice-driven bed of down. I do agnize
         A natural and prompt alacrity
         I find in hardness, and do undertake
250   These present wars against the Ottomites.
         Most humbly therefore bending to your state,
         I crave fit disposition for my wife,
         Due reference of place and exhibition,
         With such accommodation and besort
255   As levels with her breeding.

DUKE
                              If you please,
         Be 't at her father's.

BRABANTIO
                              I'll not have it so.

OTHELLO
         Nor I.

DESDEMONA
260   Nor I; I would not there reside,
         To put my father in impatient thoughts
         By being in his eye. Most gracious Duke,
         To my unfolding lend your prosperous ear;
         And let me find a charter in your voice
265   T' assist my simpleness.

DUKE
         What would you, Desdemona?

DESDEMONA
         That I did love the Moor to live with him,
         My downright violence and storm of fortunes
         May trumpet to the world. My heart's subdu'd
270   Even to the very quality of my lord.
         I saw Othello's visage in his mind,
         And to his honours and his valiant parts
         Did I my soul and fortunes consecrate.

OTHELLO

245   That tyrant, Habit, most serious senators,
has made the flinty and steel couch of war
a carefully prepared feather bed to me. I recognize in myself
a natural and eager willingness
to suffer hardship. I will take part

250   in this current war against the Ottomites.
And so, most humbly bowing before your majesty,
I ask for proper treatment of my wife;
appropriate regard for her rank, and an allowance of money,
with the kind of residence and company

255   that fits with her breeding.

DUKE

If it please you,
let it be at her father's.

BRABANTIO

I won't have that.

OTHELLO

Nor I.

DESDEMONA

260   And I won't stay there
and make my father impatient
by being in his sight. Most gracious duke,
listen to my appeal with favor
and use your voice to give me permission,

265   smoothing out my inept pleading.

DUKE

What do you want, Desdemona?

DESDEMONA

That I have loved the Moor enough to live with him,
my violent behavior and reckless chance-taking
declares to all the world. My heart has been won and converted

270   even to my lord's (soldiering) profession.
I saw Othello's qualities beyond his appearance,
and to his reputation and military abilities,
I have dedicated my fortunes and my soul.

So that, dear lords, if I were left behind,
275   A moth of peace, and he go to the war,
The rites for which I love him are bereft me,
And I a heavy interim shall support
By his dear absence. Let me go with him.

OTHELLO
Let her have your voice.
280   Vouch with me, Heaven, I therefore beg it not
To please the palate of my appetite,
Nor to comply with heat, the young affects
In my defunct and proper satisfaction,
But to be free and bounteous to her mind;
285   And Heaven defend your good souls, that you think
I will your serious and great business scant
When she is with me. No, when light-wing'd toys
Of feather'd Cupid seel with wanton dullness
My speculative and offic'd instruments
290   That my disports corrupt and taint my business,
Let housewives make a skillet of my helm,
And all indign and base adversities
Make head against my estimation!

DUKE
Be it as you shall privately determine,
295   Either for her stay or going. Th' affair cries haste,
And speed must answer it.

1. SENATOR
                    You must away to-night.

DESDEMONA
To-night, my lord?

DUKE
                    This night.

OTHELLO
300   With all my heart.

DUKE
At nine i' th' morning here we'll meet again.

---

288 *Cupid* the Roman god of love, depicted as a winged youth.   288 *seel*   sew up; in falconry, the eyelids of hawks were often sewn shut in order to tame them.

And so, dear lords, if I am left behind,
275 an idle creature of peace, and he goes to the war,
the rights I have as his wife will be taken away from me,
and I will suffer a sad time
during his absence. Let me go with him.

OTHELLO
Let her have your permission.
280 I assure you by heaven, I am not asking this
out of my longing for her
or to suit my lust—this new passion
which has not been consummated—
but to give her freely and generously what she wants.
285 And heaven forbid that you good men should think
I will neglect your great and serious business
if she is with me. No; when light-winged toys
of feathered Cupid close up with lustful blindness
my alert and dutiful eyes,
290 and my pastimes corrupt and interfere with my business,
let housewives make a skillet of my helmet
and all kinds of unworthy and evil adversities
attack my reputation!

DUKE
You may decide for yourselves
295 whether she goes or stays. This business demands haste,
and speed is necessary.

FIRST SENATOR
You must leave tonight.

DESDEMONA
Tonight, my lord?

DUKE
This night.

OTHELLO
300 With all my heart.

DUKE
At nine in the morning we'll meet here again.

Othello, leave some officer behind,
And he shall our commission bring to you,
And such things else of quality and respect
305   As doth import you.

OTHELLO
　　　　So please your Grace, my ancient;
A man he is of honesty and trust.
To his conveyance I assign my wife,
With what else needful your good Grace shall think
310   To be sent after me.

DUKE
　　　　　　Let it be so.
Good-night to every one. [*To Brabantio*] And, noble signior,
If virtue no delighted beauty lack,
Your son-in-law is far more fair than black.

1. SENATOR
315   Adieu, brave Moor; use Desdemona well.

BRABANTIO
Look to her, Moor, if thou hast eyes to see;
She has deceiv'd her father, and may thee.
　　　　[*Exeunt Duke, Senators, Officers, etc.*]

OTHELLO
My life upon her faith! Honest Iago,
My Desdemona must I leave to thee.
320   I prithee, let thy wife attend on her;
And bring them after in the best advantage.
Come, Desdemona; I have but an hour
Of love, of worldly matters and direction,
To spend with thee. We must obey the time.
　　　　[*Exeunt Othello and Desdemona.*]

RODERIGO
325   Iago,—

IAGO
What say'st thou, noble heart?

---

314 *fair*　means here both "white" and "lovely."

Othello, leave some officer behind,
and he will bring our commission to you
and other things which are proper
305   for you to have.

OTHELLO
If it please you, your grace, use my ensign.
He is a trustworthy and honest man.
I give my wife over to his escort
and whatever else you think, your good grace, it is necessary
310   to be sent to me.

DUKE
It's settled, then.
Good night to everyone. *(To Brabantio)* And, noble signior,
if virtue is a sign of beauty,
your son-in-law is far lighter than he is black.

FIRST SENATOR
315   Goodbye, brave Moor. Take care of Desdemona.

BRABANTIO
Watch her, Moor, if you have eyes to see.
She has deceived her father and might deceive you, too.
        BRABANTIO, DUKE, SENATORS, OFFICERS, *etc., exit.*

OTHELLO
I'll stake my life on her fidelity!—Honest Iago,
I must leave my Desdemona to your care.
320   I ask you to please let your wife attend to her
and bring them along when the time is best.
Come along, Desdemona. I have just an hour left
for love, and for practical business and instructions,
to spend with you. We must obey time.
        Exit OTHELLO *and* DESDEMONA.

RODERIGO
325   Iago—

IAGO
What do you say, noble fellow?

RODERIGO
What will I do, think'st thou?

IAGO
Why, go to bed and sleep.

RODERIGO
I will incontinently drown myself.

IAGO
330   If thou dost, I shall never love thee after.
Why, thou silly gentleman!

RODERIGO
It is silliness to live when to live is torment; and then have we
a prescription to die when Death is our physician.

IAGO
O villanous! I have look'd upon the world for four times seven
335   years; and since I could distinguish betwixt a benefit and an injury,
I never found man that knew how to love himself. Ere I would
say I would drown myself for the love of a guinea-hen, I would
change my humanity with a baboon.

RODERIGO
What should I do? I confess it is my shame to be so fond, but
340   it is not in my virtue to amend it.

IAGO
Virtue! a fig! 'tis in ourselves that we are thus or thus. Our bodies
are our gardens, to the which our wills are gardeners; so that if
we will plant nettles or sow lettuce, set hyssop and weed up thyme,
supply it with one gender of herbs or distract it with many, either
345   to have it sterile with idleness or manured with industry, why,
the power and corrigible authority of this lies in our wills. If the
balance of our lives had not one scale of reason to poise another
of sensuality, the blood and baseness of our natures would conduct us to most preposterous conclusions; but we have reason to
350   cool our raging motions, our carnal stings, our unbitted lusts,
whereof I take this that you call love to be a sect or scion.

RODERIGO
It cannot be.

---

341 *fig*   here means "a worthless thing."   343 *hyssop*   a fragrant herb.

RODERIGO
What do you think I should do?

IAGO
Why, go to bed and sleep.

RODERIGO
I'll go drown myself at once.

IAGO
330   If you do, I'll not love you anymore.
Why, what a foolish gentleman you are!

RODERIGO
It is foolish to live when living torments me. And we have
a prescription to die when Death is our doctor.

IAGO
How villainous! I have lived in this world for twenty-eight
335   years; and ever since I could distinguish between a benefit
and an injury,
I've never met a man who knew how to love himself. Before I'd
say I'd drown myself for the love of a guinea hen, I'd
change places with a baboon.

RODERIGO
What should I do? I confess it is to my shame to be so foolish, but I
340   don't have the strength to change it.

IAGO
Strength? A fig! It is in our own natures that we are who we
are. Our bodies
are our gardens, to which our wills are gardeners. So, if
we want to plant nettles or sow lettuce, put in spices and
harvest thyme,
grow one kind of herb or grow many, either
345   have it barren because of laziness or rich through hard work—why,
the power and corrective authority to do so lies in our wills. If the
balance of our lives didn't have one scale of reason to
counterbalance the other scale
of sensuality, the basic savagery of our natures would lead
us into the most outrageous situations. But we have reason to
350   cool our raging appetites, our carnal desires, and our unchecked lusts.
Therefore, I conclude that what you call love is a cutting or offshoot.

RODERIGO
It can't be.

IAGO

It is merely a lust of the blood and a permission of the will. Come, be a man! Drown thyself? drown cats and blind puppies! I have
355   profess'd me thy friend, and I confess me knit to thy deserving with cables of perdurable toughness; I could never better stead thee than now. Put money in thy purse; follow thou the wars; defeat thy favour with an usurp'd beard. I say, put money in thy purse. It cannot be long that Desdemona should continue her love
360   to the Moor,—put money in thy purse,—nor he his to her. It was a violent commencement in her, and thou shalt see an answerable sequestration. Put but money in thy purse. These Moors are changeable in their wills—fill thy purse with money;—the food that to him now is as luscious as locusts, shall be to him shortly
365   as bitter as coloquintida. She must change for youth; when she is sated with his body, she will find the error of her choice; she must have change, she must; therefore put money in thy purse. If thou wilt needs damn thyself, do it a more delicate way than drowning. Make all the money thou canst. If sanctimony and a
370   frail vow betwixt an erring barbarian and a super-subtle Venetian be not too hard for my wits and all the tribe of hell, thou shalt enjoy her; therefore make money. A pox of drowning thyself! it is clean out of the way. Seek thou rather to be hang'd in compassing thy joy than to be drown'd and go without her.

RODERIGO
375   Wilt thou be fast to my hopes, if I depend on the issue?

IAGO

Thou art sure of me. Go, make money. I had told thee often, and I re-tell thee again and again, I hate the Moor. My cause is hearted; thine hath no less reason. Let us be conjunctive in our revenge against him. If thou canst cuckold him, thou dost thyself
380   a pleasure, me a sport. There are many events in the womb of time which will be delivered. Traverse! go, provide thy money. We will have more of this to-morrow. Adieu.

RODERIGO

Where shall we meet i' th' morning?

IAGO

At my lodging.

---

364 *locusts*   probably the sweet fruit of the carob tree.   365 *coloquintida*   a bitter apple that was used to produce a purgative.   379 *cuckold him*   a cuckold is a man whose wife commits adultery.

IAGO
It is just lust of the blood and permission of the will. Come
on, be a man! Drown yourself? Drown cats and blind puppies! I've
355   called myself your friend, and I assure you, I'm bound to you
by cords of enduring toughness. I could never serve
you better than right now. Put money in your purse. Go to the
    wars; disguise
your good looks by wearing a beard. I tell you, put money in your
purse. It isn't possible that Desdemona will continue to love
360   the Moor for long—put money in your purse—nor he her. It had
an explosive beginning for her, and you'll see it end much
the same way. Just put money in your purse. These Moors are
changeable in their lusts. Fill your purse with money. The food
that now seems as sweet as fruit to him will soon seem
365   as bitter as a sour apple. She must grow to prefer someone
    younger. When she
is wearied with his body, she'll see the error of her choice. She'll
need a change, that's certain. So put money in your purse.
If you have to damn yourself, do it in a more delicate way than
drowning. Make all the money you can. If sacred bonds and a
370   frail vow made between a wandering barbarian and a very subtle
    Venetian
is not too much for me and all the devils in hell, she will
be yours. So get money. Forget about drowning yourself!
It's completely ridiculous. Take your chances on being hanged
    for trying to get what
you want instead of drowning and going without her.

RODERIGO
375   Will you steadfastly support my hopes if I rely on the outcome?

IAGO
You can count on me. Go, get money. I've often told you,
and I'll say it again and again, I hate the Moor. I hate him
    from the bottom of my
heart, and you have cause to as well. Let us work together to get
revenge on him. If you can cuckold him, you'll give yourself
380   pleasure and me amusement. There are many things just waiting to
be born which will come to pass soon. Move! Go! Get yourself
    money!
We'll talk more about this tomorrow. Goodbye.

RODERIGO
Where will we meet in the morning?

IAGO
At my lodging.

RODERIGO

385   I'll be with thee betimes.

IAGO

Go to; farewell. Do you hear, Roderigo?

RODERIGO

What say you?

IAGO

No more of drowning, do you hear?

RODERIGO

I am chang'd; I'll sell all my land.
            [*Exit.*]

IAGO

390   Thus do I ever make my fool my purse;
For I mine own gain'd knowledge should profane
If I would time expend with such a snipe
But for my sport and profit. I hate the Moor;
And it is thought abroad that 'twixt my sheets
395   He has done my office. I know not if 't be true;
But I, for mere suspicion in that kind,
Will do as if for surety. He holds me well;
The better shall my purpose work on him.
Cassio's a proper man: let me see now:
400   To get his place and to plume up my will
In double knavery—How, how?—Let's see:—
After some time, to abuse Othello's ear
That he is too familiar with his wife.
He hath a person and a smooth dispose
405   To be suspected, fram'd to make women false.
The Moor is of a free and open nature,
That thinks men honest that but seem to be so,
And will as tenderly be led by th' nose
As asses are.
410   I have't. It is engend'red. Hell and night
Must bring this monstrous birth to the world's light.
            [*Exit.*]

---

392 *snipe*   a bird also known as a woodcock, became a synonym for fool because it was
so easily captured.

RODERIGO

385   I'll meet you early.

IAGO

    Go on, goodbye. Wait, do you hear me, Roderigo?

RODERIGO

    What is it?

IAGO

    No more talk of drowning, do you hear?

RODERIGO

    I've changed my mind. I'll go sell all my land.
        Exit RODERIGO.

IAGO

390   This is how I always make my living off some fool;
    for I would insult my own practical wisdom
    if I spent my time with such a fool
    just for my amusement and profit. I hate the Moor;
    and it is rumored around that, in my own bed,
395   he has taken my place. I don't know if it is true;
    but just out of sheer suspicion, I
    will act as if I were sure of it. He esteems me highly;
    that will make it easier to work my purpose against him.
    Cassio's a handsome man. Let me see now;
400   to get his position and gratify myself
    by double villainy—How, how? Let's see.
    After awhile, I'll deceive Othello by telling him
    that Cassio is too familiar with his wife.
    His good looks and fine manners
405   make it seem possible—he's built to make women turn unfaithful.
    The Moor is free and open-minded
    and thinks men are honest when they only seem to be,
    so he will be as easily led by the nose
    as asses are.
410   I have it! It's planned! Hell and night
    must bring this wicked plot to the light of day.
        Exit.

Act II: Scene i: [*A sea-port in Cyprus. An open place near the quay.*] *Enter* MONTANO *and two* GENTLEMEN.

MONTANO
What from the cape can you discern at sea?

1. GENTLEMAN
Nothing at all; it is a high-wrought flood.
I cannot, 'twixt the heaven and the main,
Descry a sail.

MONTANO
5   Methinks the wind hath spoke aloud at land;
A fuller blast ne'er shook our battlements.
If it hath ruffian'd so upon the sea,
What ribs of oak, when mountains melt on them,
Can hold the mortise? What shall we hear of this?

2. GENTLEMAN
10   A segregation of the Turkish fleet.
For do but stand upon the foaming shore,
The chidden billow seems to pelt the clouds;
The wind-shak'd surge, with high and monstrous mane,
Seems to cast water on the burning Bear
15   And quench the guards of th' ever-fixed Pole.
I never did like molestation view
On the enchafed flood.

MONTANO
                    If that the Turkish fleet
Be not enshelter'd and embay'd, they are drown'd;
20   It is impossible to bear it out.
              Enter a third GENTLEMAN.

3. GENTLEMAN
News, lads! our wars are done.
The desperate tempest hath so bang'd the Turks,
That their designment halts. A noble ship of Venice
Hath seen a grievous wreck and sufferance
25   On most part of their fleet.

---

s.d. *two Gentlemen*   the First Gentleman is generally positioned on a platform above the
other characters to act as lookout.   14 *burning Bear*   the constellation of Ursa Minor.
15 *guards*   stars in the constellation of the Little Bear; companion stars of the Pole Star
(North Star).

Act II, Scene i: A seaport in Cyprus. An open place near the harbor.
Enter MONTANO *and two* GENTLEMEN.

MONTANO
 What can you view of the sea from the cape?

FIRST GENTLEMAN
 Nothing at all; it is a wild and terrible downpour.
 I cannot, between the sky and the water,
 make out a sail.

MONTANO
5 I think the wind has spoken aloud to the land.
 A storm like this has never before shaken our battlements.
 If it has caused as much turbulence upon the sea,
 what oak hulls—when mountains are melted by the rain—
 could hold together? What can we expect to happen?

SECOND GENTLEMAN
10 The Turkish fleet will be scattered.
 If you just stand on the storm-washed shore,
 the beaten waves themselves seem to strike the clouds.
 The wind-shaken tide, with high and huge crests,
 seems to throw water on the shining Bear
15 and drown the guardian stars of the Pole Star.
 I have never seen such turmoil
 on the angry water.

MONTANO
 If the Turkish fleet
 is not protected or at bay, they have been drowned.
20 It's impossible that they could survive this.
   Enter a third GENTLEMAN.

THIRD GENTLEMAN
 News, lads! Our wars are over.
 This terrible tempest has damaged the Turks so much,
 they've been halted in their intentions. A noble Venetian ship
 has seen the terrible wrecks and sufferings
25 of most of their fleet.

MONTANO
How! is this true?

3. GENTLEMAN
                    The ship is here put in.
A Veronese, Michael Cassio,
Lieutenant to the warlike Moor Othello,
30   Is come on shore; the Moor himself at sea,
And is in full commission here for Cyprus.

MONTANO
I am glad on't; 'tis a worthy governor.

3. GENTLEMAN
But this same Cassio, though he speak of comfort
Touching the Turkish loss, yet he looks sadly
35   And prays the Moor be safe, for they were parted
With foul and violent tempest.

MONTANO
                    Pray heavens he be;
For I have serv'd him, and the man commands
Like a full soldier. Let's to the seaside, ho!
40   As well to see the vessel that's come in
As to throw out our eyes for brave Othello,
Even till we make the main and th' aerial blue
An indistinct regard.

3. GENTLEMAN
                    Come, let's do so;
45   For every minute is expectancy
Of more arrivance.
              Enter CASSIO.

CASSIO
Thanks, you the valiant of this warlike isle,
That so approve the Moor! O, let the heavens
Give him defence against the elements,
50   For I have lost him on a dangerous sea.

MONTANO
Is he well shipp'd?

MONTANO
    Really? Is this true?

THIRD GENTLEMAN
    The ship has landed here,
    a ship from Verona. Michael Cassio,
    lieutenant to the warlike Moor, Othello,
30   has come on shore. The Moor himself is still at sea,
    fully commissioned to come to Cyprus.

MONTANO
    I'm glad to hear it. He'll make a worthy governor.

THIRD GENTLEMAN
    But the same Cassio I mentioned, although he tells good news
    about the Turkish loss, is very worried
35   and prays that the Moor is safe, for they were separated
    by a terrible and violent storm.

MONTANO
    Let's pray heaven that he is;
    for I have served under him, and the man commands
    like a real soldier. Let's go to the seaside, come!
40   Not only to meet the vessel that's come in,
    but also to look for the brave Othello,
    and watch until we can't tell the sea and the blue sky
    apart from one another.

THIRD GENTLEMAN
    Come, let's do so;
45   for every minute we are expecting
    more arrivals.
             Enter CASSIO.

CASSIO
    Thanks, you valiant men of this war-torn island,
    who so honor the Moor! Oh, let heaven
    give him defense against the elements,
50   for I have lost him on a dangerous sea!

MONTANO
    Is he in a good ship?

CASSIO
His bark is stoutly timber'd, and his pilot
Of very expert and approv'd allowance;
Therefore my hopes, not surfeited to death,
55   Stand in bold cure. [*Within,* "A sail, a sail, a sail!"]
        Enter a fourth GENTLEMAN.

CASSIO
What noise?

4. GENTLEMAN
The town is empty; on the brow o' th' sea
Stand ranks of people, and they cry, "A sail!"

CASSIO
My hopes do shape him for the governor.
                [*A shot.*]

2. GENTLEMAN
60   They do discharge their shot of courtesy.
Our friends at least.

CASSIO
                I pray you, sir, go forth,
And give us truth who 'tis that is arriv'd.

2. GENTLEMAN
I shall.
        [*Exit.*]

MONTANO
65   But, good Lieutenant, is your General wiv'd?

CASSIO
Most fortunately. He hath achiev'd a maid
That paragons description and wild fame;
One that excels the quirks of blazoning pens,
And in th' essential vesture of creation
70   Does tire the ingener.
                Re-enter second GENTLEMAN.
                        How now! who has put in?

2. GENTLEMAN
'Tis one Iago, ancient to the general.

CASSIO
>His ship has strong timbers, and his pilot
>has very expert and proven abilities.
>And so my hopes, not dead yet,
55 >may well be restored.
>>*(Offstage a voice cries, "A sail, a sail, a sail!")*
>>*Enter a fourth* GENTLEMAN.

CASSIO
>What's this noise?

FOURTH GENTLEMAN
>The town is empty. At the edge of the sea,
>ranks of people are standing, and they cry "A sail!"

CASSIO
>My hopes for the governor grow stronger.
>>*(A shot is heard offstage.)*

SECOND GENTLEMAN
60 >They fire a shot of greeting.
>At least we know they are friends.

CASSIO
>I ask you to go there, sir,
>and truly report back to us who has arrived.

SECOND GENTLEMAN
>I will.
>>*He exits.*

MONTANO
65 >But, good lieutenant, is your general married?

CASSIO
>Well married. He has won a girl
>who surpasses description and exaggerated gossip;
>one who exceeds the fancy descriptions of praising pens.
>In her basic qualities,
70 >she defies the imagination of an ingenuous praiser.
>>*Enter second* GENTLEMAN
>What now? Who has landed?

SECOND GENTLEMAN
>It's a certain Iago, ensign to the general.

CASSIO
    He has had most favourable and happy speed.
    Tempests themselves, high seas, and howling winds,
75   The gutter'd rocks and congregated sands,
    Traitors ensteep'd to enclog the guiltless keel,
    As having sense of beauty, do omit
    Their mortal natures, letting go safely by
    The divine Desdemona.

MONTANO
80   What is she?

CASSIO
    She that I spake of, our great captain's captain,
    Left in the conduct of the bold Iago,
    Whose footing here anticipates our thoughts
    A se'nnight's speed. Great Jove, Othello guard,
85   And swell his sail with thine own powerful breath,
    That he may bless this bay with his tall ship,
    Make love's quick pants in Desdemona's arms,
    Give renew'd fire to our extincted spirits,
    And bring all Cyprus comfort!
        Enter DESDEMONA, EMILIA, IAGO, RODERIGO
        and Attendants.
90   O, behold,
    The riches of the ship is come on shore!
    You men of Cyrpus, let her have your knees.
    Hail to thee, lady! and the grace of heaven,
    Before, behind thee, and on every hand,
95   Enwheel thee round!

DESDEMONA
            I thank you, valiant Cassio.
    What tidings can you tell me of my lord?

CASSIO
    He is not yet arriv'd; nor know I aught
    But that he's well and will be shortly here.

DESDEMONA
100   O, but I fear—How lost you company?

---

84 *Jove*   the head god in the Roman pantheon; he dispensed justice and ruled over the gods and men.

CASSIO
He's had a most favorable and fortunate arrival.
The tempests themselves, the high seas and howling winds,
75   the jagged rocks and gathered sand—
hidden traitors to ensnare the innocent keel—
as if they had a sense of beauty, have forgotten
their deadly natures and let safely pass
the divine Desdemona.

MONTANO
80   Who is she?

CASSIO
She's the one I spoke of, our great captain's captain,
left in the protection of the bold Iago,
whose arrival here comes at least
a week earlier than expected. Great Jove, guard Othello,
85   and fill his sail with your powerful breath
so he might bless this bay with his brave ship,
pant his love in Desdemona's arms,
renew the fire of our exhausted spirits,
and bring all Cyprus comfort!
        Enter DESDEMONA, EMILIA, IAGO, *and* RODERIGO *with*
        ATTENDANTS.
90   Oh, look!
The riches of the ship are now on shore!
You men of Cyprus, bow down before her.
Greetings to you, lady! And may the grace of heaven
be in front of you, behind you, and on both sides of you,
95   and utterly surround you!

DESDEMONA
Thank you, valiant Cassio.
What news can you give me of my husband?

CASSIO
He's not yet arrived; I know nothing
except that he's well and will be here shortly.

DESDEMONA
100   Oh, but I'm afraid! How did you get separated?

CASSIO
    The great contention of sea and skies
    Parted our fellowship.—But, hark! a sail.
                    [*Within,* "A sail, a sail!" *Guns heard.*]

2. GENTLEMAN
    They give their greeting to the citadel.
    This likewise is a friend.

CASSIO
105   See for the news.
                    [*Exit Gentleman.*]
    Good ancient, you are welcome. [*To Emilia.*] Welcome,
        mistress.
    Let it not gall your patience, good Iago,
    That I extend my manners; 'tis my breeding
    That gives me this bold show of courtesy. [*Kissing her.*]

IAGO
110   Sir, would she give you so much of her lips
    As of her tongue she oft bestows on me,
    You'd have enough.

DESDEMONA
                    Alas, she has no speech.

IAGO
    In faith, too much;
115   I find it still, when I have list to sleep.
    Marry, before your ladyship, I grant,
    She puts her tongue a little in her heart,
    And chides with thinking.

EMILIA
    You have little cause to say so.

IAGO
120   Come on, come on; you are pictures out of door,
    Bells in your parlours, wild-cats in your kitchens,
    Saints in your injuries, devils being offended,
    Players in your housewifery, and housewives in your beds.

---

123 *housewives*   also means "hussies."

CASSIO

The great quarrel between the sea and the sky
parted us from one another.—But listen. A sail!
(Offstage a voice cries, "A sail, a sail!"
A shot is also heard.)

SECOND GENTLEMAN

They give their greeting to the fortress.
This is a friend, too.

CASSIO

105   Go see what's the news.
    Exit GENTLEMAN.
Good ensign, you are welcome. *(To Emilia)* Welcome, madam.
I hope it doesn't try your patience, good Iago,
if I stretch my manners. It's my upbringing
that teaches me to make such a bold display of courtesy.
    (He kisses her.)

IAGO

110   Sir, if she gave you as much of her lips
as she often gives me of her tongue,
you'd have plenty.

DESDEMONA

But really, she doesn't chatter at all!

IAGO

I tell you, she talks too much.
115   Even when I want to sleep, she's still talking.
Though, indeed, in front of your ladyship, I'll admit
that she hides her tongue in her heart a little
and scolds me only in her thoughts.

EMILIA

You have little reason to say that.

IAGO

120   Come, come! You women are the picture of virtue away from home,
lilting when playing the hostess, wildcats in your kitchens,
saints when you criticize, devils when you're offended,
slack in your household duties, but really earnest in bed.

DESDEMONA

O, fie upon thee, slanderer!

IAGO

125 Nay, it is true, or else I am a Turk.
You rise to play and go to bed to work.

EMILIA

You shall not write my praise.

IAGO

No, let me not.

DESDEMONA

What wouldst thou write of me, if thou shouldst praise me?

IAGO

130 O gentle lady, do not put me to't;
For I am nothing if not critical.

DESDEMONA

Come on, assay.—There's one gone to the harbour?

IAGO

Ay, madam.

DESDEMONA

I am not merry; but I do beguile
135 The thing I am by seeming otherwise.—
Come, how wouldst thou praise me?

IAGO

I am about it; but indeed my invention
Comes from my pate as birdlime does from frieze;
It plucks out brains and all. But my Muse labours,
140 And thus she is deliver'd:
If she be fair and wise, fairness and wit,
The one's for use, the other useth it.

DESDEMONA

Well prais'd! How if she be black and witty?

IAGO

If she be black, and thereto have a wit,
145 She'll find a white that shall her blackness fit.

---

138 *birdlime* a sticky substance used to trap birds.   139 *Muse* one of the nine goddesses
of classical mythology; patronesses of learning and the arts.   143 *black* here means "unattractive"; light-skinned women were considered more beautiful than dark-skinned women
in Shakespeare's day (see Shakespeare's Sonnet CXXX).   145 *white* puns on the word
"wight" which means "person."

DESDEMONA
Oh, shame on you, slanderer!

IAGO
125 No, it's true, or else I am a Turk.
You get up in the morning to play, and go to bed to work.

EMILIA
I won't let you write my praises.

IAGO
No, I won't.

DESDEMONA
What would you write about me, if you were to praise me?

IAGO
130 Oh, gentle lady, don't ask me to do it,
for I am nothing if not critical.

DESDEMONA
Come on, try it.—Has someone gone to the harbor?

IAGO
Yes, madam.

DESDEMONA *(To herself)*
I am not merry; but I'll forget
135 the way I really feel by seeming to be otherwise.
(To Iago) Come now, how would you praise me?

IAGO
I'm thinking about it, but really, my ideas
are as hard to pull out of my head as birdlime from a heavy cloth—
they pull out my brains and everything. But my Muse is in labor,
140 and here is what she gives birth to:
If she is pretty and clever, beauty and cleverness;
The beauty is to be used, the cleverness is for using it.

DESDEMONA
Well praised! What if she is ugly and clever?

IAGO
If she is ugly but clever too,
145 She'll find a man who will be happy with her.

DESDEMONA
Worse and worse.

EMILIA
How if fair and foolish?

IAGO
She never yet was foolish that was fair;
For even her folly help'd her to an heir.

DESDEMONA
150   These are old fond paradoxes to make fools laugh i' th' alehouse.
What miserable praise hast thou for her that's foul and foolish?

IAGO
There's none so foul and foolish thereunto,
But does foul pranks which fair and wise ones do.

DESDEMONA
O heavy ignorance! thou praisest the worst best. But what praise
155   couldst thou bestow on a deserving woman indeed, one that, in
the authority of her merit, did justly put on the vouch of very
malice itself?

IAGO
She that was ever fair and never proud,
Had tongue at will and yet was never loud,
160   Never lack'd gold and yet went never gay,
Fled from her wish and yet said, "Now I may;"
She that being ang'red, her revenge being nigh,
Bade her wrong stay and her displeasure fly;
She that in wisdom never was so frail
165   To change the cod's head for the salmon's tail;
She that could think and ne'er disclose her mind,
See suitors following and not look behind,
She was a wight, if ever wights were,—

DESDEMONA
To do what?

IAGO
170   To suckle fools and chronicle small beer.

---

170 *To . . . beer*   these are obviously meaningless chores to Iago's mind.

DESDEMONA
Worse and worse.

EMILIA
What if she's pretty and foolish?

IAGO
No woman has ever been foolish who was also pretty,
For even her foolishness helped her to have an heir.

DESDEMONA
150 These are old, silly sayings to make fools laugh in the bar.
What miserable praise do you have for a woman who's ugly and
foolish?

IAGO
There's no one who is so ugly and so foolish as well,
Who doesn't do the same naughty things that pretty and
wise women do.

DESDEMONA
What terrible ignorance! You've praised the worst the most
highly. But what praise
155 would you give to a woman who really deserves it—one who, by
virtue of all her good qualities, can justifiably claim the
praise of even
the most malicious?

IAGO
She who was always pretty, but never boastful;
Could speak well, but never talked too much;
160 Never lacked gold and yet never was extravagantly dressed;
Denied her desires, but yet said, "Now I may have this";
She who being angered and her opportunity for revenge at hand
Made herself hold her temper and forget her anger;
She who in her wisdom never made the mistake
165 Of trading something good for something bad;
She who could think, but never let her thoughts be known;
See suitors following her and not look behind her;
She was a person (if there ever was such a person)—

DESDEMONA
To do what?

IAGO
170 —To coddle fools and keep household accounts.

DESDEMONA
O most lame and impotent conclusion! Do not learn of him,
Emilia, though he be thy husband. How say you, Cassio? Is he
not a most profane and liberal counsellor?

CASSIO
He speaks home, madam. You may relish him more in the soldier
175   than in the scholar.

IAGO
[*Aside.*] He takes her by the palm; ay, well said, whisper. With
as little a web as this will I ensnare as great a fly as Cassio. Ay,
smile upon her, do; I will gyve thee in thine own courtship.—
You say true; 'tis so, indeed.—If such tricks as these strip you
180   out of your lieutenantry, it had been better you had not kiss'd
your three fingers so oft, which now again you are most apt to
play the sir in. Very good; well kiss'd! an excellent curtsy! 'Tis
so, indeed. Yet again your fingers to your lips? Would they were
clyster-pipes for your sake! (*Trumpet within.*)—The Moor! I know
185   his trumpet.

CASSIO
'Tis truly so.

DESDEMONA
Let's meet him and receive him.

CASSIO
Lo, where he comes!
          Enter OTHELLO *and Attendants.*

OTHELLO
O my fair warrior!

DESDEMONA
190   My dear Othello!

OTHELLO
It gives me wonder great as my content
To see you here before me. O my soul's joy!
If after every tempest come such calms,
May the winds blow till they have waken'd death!
195   And let the labouring bark climb hills of seas

---

185 *his trumpet*   men of Othello's standing often had an individual trumpet call.

DESDEMONA
Oh, what a flat and pointless conclusion! Don't believe him,
Emilia, even though he is your husband. What do you think, Cassio?
Isn't he
a most worldly and lewd advisor?

CASSIO
He does talk some common sense, madam. He's easier to appreciate
as a soldier
175 than as a scholar.

IAGO *(To himself)*
He takes her by the hand. Yes, very good, whisper to her! With
this little web, I'll catch a fly as big as Cassio. Yes,
smile at her, go ahead! I'll catch you in your own flirtation.
You agreed with me; and I was right indeed! If this behavior of
yours causes you to
180 lose your lieutenancy, you'll wish you hadn't acted
the gallant so much. And even now you're acting like
the courtly gentleman. Very good! Well kissed! What lovely manners!
I really
mean it! What, are you blowing her another kiss? Better that your
fingers were
an enema tube! *(A trumpet blows offstage.)* It's the Moor! I know
185 his trumpet.

CASSIO
It's really him.

DESDEMONA
Let's go and greet him.

CASSIO
Look, he's coming!
            Enter OTHELLO *and* ATTENDANTS.

OTHELLO
Oh, my pretty warrior!

DESDEMONA
190 My dear Othello!

OTHELLO
I'm as surprised as I am happy
to find you waiting for me. Oh, the joy in my soul!
If every tempest ended with such happiness,
I wish the winds would blow until they'd wakened the dead!
195 And that struggling ships would climb upon waves

Olympus-high, and duck again as low
As hell's from heaven! If it were now to die,
'Twere now to be most happy; for, I fear,
My soul hath her content so absolute
200   That not another comfort like to this
Succeeds in unknown fate.

DESDEMONA
                    The heavens forbid
But that our loves and comforts should increase,
Even as our days do grow!

OTHELLO
205   Amen to that, sweet powers!
I cannot speak enough of this content;
It stops me here; it is too much of joy.
And this, and this, the greatest discords be [*Kissing her.*]
That e'er our hearts shall make!

IAGO
210   [*Aside.*] O, you are well tun'd now!
But I'll set down the pegs that make this music,
As honest as I am.

OTHELLO
                    Come, let us to the castle.
News, friends: our wars are done, the Turks are drown'd.
215   How does my old acquaintance of this isle?
Honey, you shall be well desir'd in Cyprus;
I have found great love amongst them. O my sweet,
I prattle out of fashion, and I dote
In mine own comforts. I prithee, good Iago,
220   Go to the bay and disembark my coffers.
Bring thou the master to the citadel;
He is a good one, and his worthiness
Does challenge much respect. Come, Desdemona,
Once more, well met at Cyprus.
            [*Exeunt Othello, Desdemona and Attendants.*]

IAGO
225   Do thou meet me presently at the harbour.—Come hither. If thou

as tall as Olympus, and fall down as low
as hell is from heaven! If I were to die right now,
I would die perfectly happy; for I'm afraid
I am so splendidly content
200   that I won't have another joy like this one
for the rest of my life.

DESDEMONA
Heaven forbid!
Our love and our happiness should get stronger
with every day!

OTHELLO
205   By heaven, I say amen to that!
I can't speak enough of my delight;
it fills my heart; it is too much joy.
And this, and this, is the greatest discord *(They kiss.)*
that our hearts will ever make!

IAGO *(To himself)*
210   Oh, you are in tune with each other now!
But I'll untune the strings that make this music,
as honest as I am.

OTHELLO
Come, let's go to the castle.
News, friends! Our wars are over; the Turks have been drowned.
215   How are all my old friends here on this island?—
(To Desdemona) My dear, you'll be well beloved in Cyprus;
I've found great love here. Oh, my sweet,
I ramble on unsuitably, and I act foolishly
because of my delight. Good Iago, I ask you
220   to go to the bay and get my money from the ship.
And bring the master to the castle.
He's a good man, and his fine qualities
command much respect. Come, Desdemona.
Oh, it is good to see you here in Cyprus.
                Everyone exits except IAGO *and* RODERIGO.

IAGO
225   Meet me soon at the harbor. Be sure to come. If you

be'st valiant,—as, they say, base men being in love have then a
nobility in their natures more than is native to them,—list me.
The lieutenant to-night watches on the court of guard;—first, I
must tell thee this: Desdemona is directly in love with him.

RODERIGO

230   With him! why, 'tis not possible.

IAGO

Lay thy finger thus, and let thy soul be instructed. Mark me with
what violence she first lov'd the Moor, but for bragging and telling her fantastical lies. To love him still for prating,—let not thy
discreet heart think it. Her eye must be fed; and what delight shall
235   she have to look on the devil? When the blood is made dull with
the act of sport, there should be, again to inflame it and to give
satiety a fresh appetite, loveliness in favour, sympathy in years,
manners, and beauties; all which the Moor is defective in. Now,
for want of these requir'd conveniences, her delicate tenderness
240   will find itself abus'd, begin to heave the gorge, disrelish and abhor
the Moor. Very nature will instruct her in it and compel her to
some second choice. Now, sir, this granted,—as it is a most pregnant and unforc'd position—who stands so eminent in the degree
of this fortune as Cassio does? a knave very voluble; no further
245   conscionable than in putting on the mere form of civil and humane
seeming, for the better compassing of his salt and most hidden
loose affection? Why, none; why, none; a slipper and subtle
knave, a finder of occasion, that has an eye can stamp and
counterfeit advantages, though true advantage never present itself;
250   a devilish knave. Besides, the knave is handsome, young, and hath
all those requisites in him that folly and green minds look after;
a pestilent complete knave, and the woman hath found him
already.

RODERIGO

I cannot believe that in her; she's full of most bless'd condition.

IAGO

255   Bless'd fig's-end! The wine she drinks is made of grapes. If she
had been bless'd, she would never have lov'd the Moor. Bless'd
pudding! Didst thou not see her paddle with the palm of his hand?
Didst not mark that?

---

255 *The wine . . . grapes*   Iago means Desdemona is only human.

are brave (and they say cowardly men who are in love have more
nobility in their natures than usual), listen to me.
The lieutenant keeps watch on the guardhouse tonight. First, I'd
better tell you this: Desdemona is madly in love with him.

RODERIGO
230   With him? Why, it isn't possible.

IAGO
Keep mum, and just listen. Remember how
violently she first loved the Moor, and just because he
    bragged and told
her fantastic lies? Will she keep loving him just because he
    continues to babble? Don't
you believe it. She needs a handsome man; and what joy will
235   she have to look at the devil? When the appetite tires of
love-making, one needs something to spark it again and
renew one's appetite—like good looks, and sameness of age,
manners, and appearances. The Moor has none of these. Now
because she lacks these desirable advantages, her delicate sensibilities
240   will feel abused and reject, hate, and despise
the Moor. Nature itself will teach her to act this way and
    force her to
seek out someone else. Now, sir, if you'll admit this (since
    it's an obvious
and logical conclusion), who possesses these qualities
to a greater degree than Cassio? A very flattering rascal;
    having no more
245   conscience than to put on a mask of civility and politeness,
just to achieve his lecherous and secret
immoral intentions? Why, no one! No one! A slippery and subtle
rascal; a true opportunist; a man who knows how to sniff out an
advantage, even if a real advantage never turns up;
250   a devilish rascal! Besides, this rascal is handsome, young, and has
all those qualities about him that foolish and young minds
    are always looking for.
A completely rotten rascal! And the woman has fallen for him
already.

RODERIGO
I can't believe that about her. She's blessed with a most
    admirable character.

IAGO
255   Blessed, my eye! The wine she drinks is made of grapes. If she
were so blessed, she wouldn't have fallen in love with the
    Moor. Blessed,
my foot! Didn't you see her holding his hand?
Didn't you see that?

RODERIGO
Yes, that I did; but that was but courtesy.

IAGO
260   Lechery, by this hand; an index and obscure prologue to the history of lust and foul thoughts. They met so near with their lips that their breaths embrac'd together. Villanous thoughts, Roderigo! When these mutualities so marshal the way, hard at hand comes the master and main exercise, th' incorporate con-
265   clusion. Pish! But, sir, be you rul'd by me; I have brought you from Venice. Watch you to-night; for the command, I'll lay 't upon you. Cassio knows you not. I'll not be far from you. Do you find some occasion to anger Cassio, either by speaking too loud, or tainting his discipline; or from what other course you
270   please, which the time shall more favourably minister.

RODERIGO
Well?

IAGO
Sir, he's rash and very sudden in choler, and haply may strike at you. Provoke him, that he may; for even out of that will I cause these of Cyprus to mutiny, whose qualification shall come into
275   no true taste again but by the displanting of Cassio. So shall you have a shorter journey to your desires by the means I shall then have to prefer them; and the impediment most profitably removed, without the which there were no expectation of our prosperity.

RODERIGO
280   I will do this, if you can bring it to any opportunity.

IAGO
I warrant thee. Meet me by and by at the citadel; I must fetch his necessaries ashore. Farewell.

RODERIGO
Adieu.
        [*Exit.*]

RODERIGO
Yes, I did; but that was just politeness.

IAGO
260 It was lechery, I tell you! Just the indication and secret
prologue to a
history of lust and filthy thoughts. Their lips were so close
that their breaths embraced. Wicked thoughts,
Roderigo! When these mutual courtesies show the way, hard by
comes the lead and main event, the carnal conclusion.
265 Bah! But, sir, you do exactly as I say. I've brought you here
from Venice. Take good care tonight; as to your orders, I'll
give them
to you. Cassio doesn't know you. I'll be close by. Figure
out some way to make Cassio angry, either by talking too
loud or slandering his conduct or whatever way you
270 can think of when the time is most favorable.

RODERIGO
Well?

IAGO
Sir, he is hotheaded and very short-tempered, and perhaps he'll try
to hit you with his baton. Provoke him to that. That's all I
need to start
a mutiny among those of Cyprus, who won't be happy until
275 Cassio is thrown out. So you will
have a quicker route to what you desire by the means I'll then
suggest. And we'll have removed most profitably the one obstacle
which might have made it impossible for either of us to achieve our
hopes.

RODERIGO
280 I'll do this if it will bring me any advantage.

IAGO
I guarantee it. Meet me at the castle soon. I have to bring
his belongings ashore. Goodbye.

RODERIGO
Goodbye.
        Exit RODERIGO.

IAGO
    That Cassio loves her, I do well believe 't;
285   That she loves him, 'tis apt and of great credit;
    The Moor, howbeit that I endure him not,
    Is of a constant, loving, noble nature,
    And I dare think he'll prove to Desdemona
    A most dear husband. Now, I do love her too;
290   Not out of absolute lust, though peradventure
    I stand accountant for as great a sin,
    But partly led to diet my revenge,
    For that I do suspect the lusty Moor
    Hath leap'd into my seat; the thought whereof
295   Doth, like a poisonous mineral, gnaw my inwards;
    And nothing can or shall content my soul
    Till I am even'd with him, wife for wife;
    Or failing so, yet that I put the Moor
    At least into a jealousy so strong
300   That judgement cannot cure. Which thing to do,
    If this poor trash of Venice, whom I trash
    For his quick hunting, stand the putting on,
    I'll have our Michael Cassio on the hip,
    Abuse him to the Moor in the rank garb—
305   For I fear Cassio with my night-cap too—
    Make the Moor thank me, love me, and reward me
    For making him egregiously an ass
    And practising upon his peace and quiet
    Even to madness. 'Tis here, but yet confus'd;
310   Knavery's plain face is never seen till us'd.
        [*Exit.*]

Scene ii: [A street.] Enter Othello's HERALD, *with a proclamation.* [People *following.*]

HERALD
    It is Othello's pleasure, our noble and valiant general, that, upon certain tidings now arriv'd importing the mere perdition of the Turkish fleet, every man put himself into triumph; some to dance, some to make bonfires, each man to what sport and revels his

IAGO
That Cassio loves her, I really do believe;
285   that she loves him too is natural and likely.
The Moor (as much as I may hate him)
is of a dedicated, loving, and noble nature,
and I'm sure he'll prove to Desdemona
a very costly husband. I love her too;
290   not completely out of lust (although it's likely
that I'm guilty of a sin just as great),
but partly because she'll help me get revenge,
since I suspect the lusty Moor
has taken my place. The thought of that
295   gnaws at me like a poisonous mineral,
and nothing can or will satisfy me
till we are even, wife for wife.
Or if I fall short of that, I'll still put the Moor
in a state of jealousy so extreme
300   that good sense won't cure it. In order to do this,
if this worthless Venetian, whom I'm hounding
to keep him on the track, will only do as I've urged him,
I'll have Michael Cassio in my pocket,
slander him to the Moor in the proper fashion
305   (because I'm afraid Cassio has been in my bed too),
make the Moor thank me, love me, and reward me
for making a complete fool of him
and scheming against his peace and quiet—
even to the point of madness. That's the plan, though the
    details must be flushed out.
310   Villainous work is never recognized until the villainy's been done.
     Exit IAGO.

Act II, Scene ii: A street. Enter Othello's HERALD, *with a
proclamation; people are following him.*

HERALD
It is the wish of Othello, our noble and brave general, that,
    because of the
news we've just heard, telling of the total destruction of the
Turkish fleet, everyone should rejoice. Some should dance,
some should make bonfires, and everyone should engage in
    whatever amusement and celebration

5   addiction leads him; for, beside these beneficial news, it is the celebration of his nuptial. So much was his pleasure should be proclaimed. All offices are open, and there is full liberty of feasting from this present hour of five till the bell have told eleven. Heaven bless the isle of Cyprus and our noble general Othello!
[*Exeunt.*]

Scene iii: [*A hall in the castle.*] *Enter* OTHELLO, DESDEMONA, CASSIO, *and Attendants.*

OTHELLO
Good Michael, look you to the guard to-night.
Let's teach ourselves that honourable stop,
Not to outsport discretion.

CASSIO
Iago hath direction what to do;
5   But, notwithstanding, with my personal eye
Will I look to't.

OTHELLO
                                Iago is most honest.
Michael, good-night; to-morrow with your earliest
Let me have speech with you. [*To Desdemona.*] Come, my
        dear love,
10   The purchase made, the fruits are to ensue;
That profit's yet to come 'tween me and you.
Good-night.
        [*Exeunt Othello, Desdemona, and Attendants.*]
        Enter IAGO.

CASSIO
Welcome, Iago; we must to the watch.

IAGO
Not this hour, Lieutenant; 'tis not yet ten o' th' clock. Our general
15   cast us thus early for the love of his Desdemona; who let us not
therefore blame. He hath not yet made wanton the night with her;
and she is sport for Jove.

5 that is to their taste. Because, besides this welcome news, it's also
his wedding celebration. His joy is so great, he wants it
proclaimed. All kitchens are open, and there's free
feasting from the present hour of five until the bell rings eleven.
Heaven bless the island of Cyprus and our noble general Othello!
  Exit.

Act II, Scene iii: A hall in the castle. Enter OTHELLO,
DESDEMONA, CASSIO, *and* ATTENDANTS.

OTHELLO
  Good Michael, you are in charge of the guard tonight.
  Let's make sure things don't get out of hand
  and no one celebrates indiscreetly.

CASSIO
  Iago already has instructions to do so.
5 Nevertheless, I'll see to it
  myself.

OTHELLO
  Iago is very honest.
  Good night, Michael. The first thing tomorrow morning,
  come and talk to me. *(To Desdemona)* Come, my dear love.
10 Once the purchase has been made, the fruits will follow;
  the two of us have not yet enjoyed our profits.
  Good night.
      Exit OTHELLO, DESDEMONA *and* ATTENDANTS.
      Enter IAGO.

CASSIO
  Welcome, Iago. We'd better go on watch.

IAGO
  Not at this hour, lieutenant; it's not ten o'clock yet. Our general
15 dismissed us early because of his love for Desdemona; but let's not
  blame her for that. He hasn't yet enjoyed the night with her,
  and she's a lover worthy of Jove.

CASSIO
She's a most exquisite lady.

IAGO
And, I'll warrant her, full of game.

CASSIO
20   Indeed, she's a most fresh and delicate creature.

IAGO
What an eye she has! Methinks it sounds a parley to provocation.

CASSIO
An inviting eye; and yet methinks right modest.

IAGO
And when she speaks, is it not an alarum to love?

CASSIO
She is indeed perfection.

IAGO
25   Well, happiness to their sheets! Come, lieutenant, I have a stoup
of wine; and here without are a brace of Cyprus gallants that
would fain have a measure to the health of black Othello.

CASSIO
Not to-night, good Iago. I have very poor and unhappy brains
for drinking; I could well wish courtesy would invent some other
30   custom of entertainment.

IAGO
O, they are our friends. But one cup; I'll drink for you.

CASSIO
I have drunk but one cup to-night, and that was craftily qualified
too, and, behold, what innovation it makes here. I am unfortunate
in the infirmity, and dare not task my weakness with any more.

IAGO
35   What, man! 'tis a night of revels. The gallants desire it.

CASSIO
Where are they?

IAGO
Here at the door; I pray you, call them in.

CASSIO
She's a very beautiful lady.

IAGO
And I'll bet she's full of fire.

20 CASSIO
Certainly, she's a very young and refined creature.

IAGO
What an eye she has! I think it's downright provocative.

CASSIO
An inviting eye; but a modest one, I think.

IAGO
And when she speaks, isn't it a temptation to love?

CASSIO
She is certainly perfect.

25 IAGO
Well, happiness to their sheets! Come, lieutenant, I have a cup
of wine, and just outside are a few fellows of Cyprus who
would like to drink to the health of black Othello.

CASSIO
Not tonight, good Iago. Wine goes straight to
my head. I really wish there was some other
30 means of courteous entertainment.

IAGO
But they are our friends. Just one cup! I'll drink when you
make a toast.

CASSIO
I've had just one cup tonight and that was quite diluted.
But look how flushed I am just from that. I really can't
handle wine and must not overdo it with any more.

35 IAGO
What! This is a night of celebration. The fellows wish it.

CASSIO
Where are they?

IAGO
Right here at the door. Please, call them in.

CASSIO
> I'll do't; but it dislikes me.
> > [*Exit.*]

IAGO
> If I can fasten but one cup upon him,
> With that which he hath drunk to-night already,
> He'll be as full of quarrel and offence
> As my young mistress' dog. Now, my sick fool Roderigo,
> Whom love hath turn'd almost the wrong side out,
> To Desdemona hath to-night carous'd
> Potations pottle-deep; and he's to watch.
> Three lads of Cyprus, noble swelling spirits
> That hold their honours in a wary distance,
> The very elements of this warlike isle,
> Have I to-night fluster'd with flowing cups,
> And they watch too. Now, 'mongst this flock of drunkards
> Am I to put our Cassio in some action
> That may offend the isle. But here they come.
> > *Re-enter* CASSIO; *with him* MONTANO *and*
> > GENTLEMEN. [*Servants follow with wine.*]
> If consequence do but approve my dream,
> My boat sails freely, both with wind and stream.

CASSIO
> 'Fore God, they have given me a rouse already.

MONTANO
> Good faith, a little one; not past a pint, as I am a soldier.

IAGO
> Some wine, ho!
> [*Sings.*] "And let me the canakin clink, clink;
> > And let me the canakin clink.
> > > A soldier's a man;
> > > O, man's life's but a span;
> > > Why, then, let a soldier drink."
> Some wine, boys!

CASSIO
> 'Fore God, an excellent song.

40

45

50

55

60

CASSIO
>I'll do it, but I don't like the idea.
>>*Exit* CASSIO.

IAGO
>If I can get him to drink just one more cup
40 on top of what he's had to drink tonight already,
>he'll be as quarrelsome and disagreeable
>as my young lady's dog. Now my sick fool Roderigo,
>who has been turned almost inside out by love,
>has been toasting Desdemona tonight
45 and draining many cups to the bottom; and he's supposed to be
>>on guard.
>Three boys of Cyprus—fine and noble fellows,
>who are very quick to respond to an insult,
>and of a very suitable temperament to this warlike island—
>I've made tipsy tonight with overflowing cups,
50 and they're on guard, too. Now, amid this flock of drunkards,
>I'll provoke Cassio to some action
>that's bound to cause offense on this island. But here they come.
>>*Enter* CASSIO, MONTANO, *and several*
>>GENTLEMEN. SERVANTS *follow with some wine.*
>If things only go the way I hope,
>my boat will sail freely, with both the wind and the stream.

CASSIO
55 By God, they've given me a huge cup already.

MONTANO
>Really now, it's just a little one; no more than a pint, or
>I'm not a soldier.

IAGO
>Some wine over here!
>>*(He sings.)*
>>And let me clink the cup, clink;
>>And let me clink the cup.
60   A soldier's a man;
>> A life is short,
>>So then let a soldier drink.
>Some wine, boys!

CASSIO
>By God, that's an excellent song!

IAGO

65   I learn'd it in England, where, indeed, they are most potent in
potting; your Dane, your German, and your swag-belli'd
Hollander—Drink, ho!—are nothing to your English.

CASSIO

Is your Englishman so exquisite in his drinking?

IAGO

Why, he drinks you, with facility, your Dane dead drunk; he
70   sweats not to overthrow your Almain; he gives your Hollander
a vomit ere the next pottle can be fill'd.

CASSIO

To the health of our general!

MONTANO

I am for it, Lieutenant; and I'll do you justice.

IAGO

O Sweet England!
75   "King Stephen was and-a worthy peer,
His breeches cost him but a crown;
He held them sixpence all too dear,
With that he call'd the tailor lown.

"He was a wight of high renown,
80   And thou art but of low degree.
'Tis pride that pulls the country down;
And take thy auld cloak about thee."
Some wine, ho!

CASSIO

Why, this is a more exquisite song than the other.

IAGO

85   Will you hear 't again?

CASSIO

No; for I hold him to be unworthy of his place that does those
things. Well, God's above all; and there be souls must be saved,
and there be souls must not be saved.

IAGO

65   I learned it in England, where they really know how to
drink. Your Danes, your Germans, and your pot-bellied
Hollanders—Drink up!—are nothing compared to your English.

CASSIO

Is your Englishman such an expert drinker?

IAGO

Why, he'll drink your Dane dead drunk with no trouble; it's no
70   sweat for him to outdo your German; he'll have your Hollander
vomiting before the next cup gets filled.

CASSIO

To the health of our general!

MONTANO

I'll drink to that, lieutenant, and I'll match your toast.

IAGO

Oh, sweet England!
(He sings.)
75   King Stephen was a worthy gentleman;
His pants only cost him a crown;
He thought they were a sixpence too expensive,
So he called the tailor a lout.
He was a man of great renown,
80   And you are but of low birth.
It's pride that's ruining this country;
So keep wearing your old coat.
Some wine, over here!

CASSIO

By God, this is an even better song than the other one.

IAGO

85   Do you want to hear it again?

CASSIO

No, because I don't think a man who does those things is
worthy of his
rank. Well, God's above us all; and there are souls that will
be saved,
and there are souls that will not be saved.

IAGO
  It's true, good Lieutenant.

CASSIO
90 For mine own part—no offence to the general, nor any man of
  quality—I hope to be saved.

IAGO
  And so do I too, Lieutenant.

CASSIO
  Ay, but, by your leave, not before me; the lieutenant is to be saved
  before the ancient. Let's have no more of this; let's to our
95 affairs.—God forgive us our sins!—Gentlemen, let's look to our
  business. Do not think, gentlemen, I am drunk. This is my ancient;
  this is my right hand, and this is my left. I am not drunk now;
  I can stand well enough, and I speak well enough.

GENTLEMEN
  Excellent well.

CASSIO
100 Why, very well then; you must not think then that I am drunk.
      [*Exit.*]

MONTANO
  To the platform, masters; come, let's set the watch.

IAGO
  You see this fellow that is gone before:
  He is a soldier fit to stand by Caesar
  And give direction; and do but see his vice.
105 'Tis to his virtue a just equinox,
  The one as long as th' other; 'tis pity of him.
  I fear the trust Othello puts him in,
  On some odd time of his infirmity,
  Will shake this island.

IAGO
That's the truth, good lieutenant.

CASSIO
90 For my own part—I mean no offense to the general, nor to any
other man of
high rank—I hope to be saved.

IAGO
And so do I, lieutenant.

CASSIO
Yes, but if you don't mind, not before me. The lieutenant has
to be saved
before the ensign. Let's not talk about this anymore; let's
get down to
95 business. God forgive us for our sins! Gentlemen, let's see to our
business. Gentlemen, don't think I'm drunk. This is my ensign.
This is my right hand, and this is my left. I'm not drunk now.
I can stand well enough and speak well enough.

ALL
Extremely well.

CASSIO
100 Well, very good then. As long as you don't think I'm drunk.
Exit CASSIO.

MONTANO
Let's go on guard, gentlemen. Come, let's begin the watch.

IAGO
Take a look at this fellow who has gone ahead.
He is a soldier fit to stand beside Caesar
and give orders; and take a look at this vice of his.
105 It's the exact counterpart of his virtue—
the one's the equal of the other. It's a pity about him.
I'm afraid that the trust Othello puts in him,
due to his infirmity, will one of these days
cause trouble on this island.

MONTANO

110   But is he often thus?

IAGO

'Tis evermore his prologue to his sleep.
He'll watch the horologe a double set
If drink rock not his cradle.

MONTANO

                         It were well

115   The general were put in mind of it.
Perhaps he sees it not; or his good nature
Prizes the virtue that appears in Cassio,
And looks not on his evils. Is not this true?
                    Enter RODERIGO.

IAGO

[*Aside to him.*] How now, Roderigo!

120   I pray you, after the lieutenant; go.
                    [*Exit Roderigo.*]

MONTANO

And 'tis great pity that the noble Moor
Should hazard such a place as his own second
With one of an ingraft infirmity.
It were an honest action to say

125   So to the Moor.

IAGO

                    Not I, for this fair island.
I do love Cassio well; and would do much
To cure him of this evil.—But, hark! what noise?
    [*Cry within:* "Help! help!"]
            Re-enter CASSIO, *pursuing* RODERIGO.

CASSIO

'Zounds, you rogue! you rascal!

MONTANO

130   What's the matter, Lieutenant?

MONTANO
110   But is he like this very often?

IAGO
    All the time, before he goes to bed.
    He'd watch the clock for twenty-four hours
    if his drinking didn't put him to sleep.

MONTANO
    It would be a good idea
115   to let the general know about this.
    Maybe he doesn't know about this, or his good nature
    values Cassio's good qualities
    and overlooks his evils. Isn't this true?
        Enter RODERIGO.

IAGO *(Aside to Roderigo)*
    What is this, Roderigo?
120   I'm telling you, go after the lieutenant!
        Exit RODERIGO.

MONTANO
    It's a terrible pity that the noble Moor
    should risk the position of his own second in command
    to a man with such an ingrained infirmity.
    It would be an honest deed to say
125   so to the Moor.

IAGO
    I wouldn't do it for this entire lovely island!
    I love Cassio very much, and will do what I can
    to cure him of this problem.—But listen! What's that noise?
        (A voice from offstage cries "Help! Help!")
        Enter CASSIO, *chasing* RODERIGO.

CASSIO
    Damn, you villain! You rascal!

MONTANO
130   What's the matter, lieutenant?

CASSIO

A knave teach me my duty!
I'll beat the knave into a twiggen bottle.

RODERIGO

Beat me!

CASSIO

Dost thou prate, rogue?
[*Striking Roderigo.*]

MONTANO

135   Nay, good Lieutenant;
[*Staying him.*]
I pray you, sir, hold your hand.

CASSIO

Let me go, sir,
Or I'll knock you o'er the mazzard.

MONTANO

Come, come, you're drunk.

CASSIO

140   Drunk!   [*They fight.*]

IAGO

[*Aside to Roderigo.*] Away, I say; go out, and cry a mutiny.
[*Exit Roderigo.*]
Nay, good Lieutenant,—God's will, gentlemen;—
Help, ho!—Lieutenant,—sir,—Montano,—sir;—
Help, masters!—Here's a goodly watch indeed!
[*Bell rings.*]
145   Who's that which rings the bell?—Diablo, ho!
The town will rise. Fie, fie, Lieutenant, hold!
You will be sham'd for ever.
Re-enter OTHELLO *and Attendants.*

OTHELLO

What is the matter here?

CASSIO
  Do I need some villain to teach me my duty?
  I'll beat this villain until he's ready to crawl inside a
    wicker-covered bottle.

RODERIGO
  Beat me?

CASSIO
  Still rattling on, rascal?
      (He strikes Roderigo.)

MONTANO
135 No, good lieutenant!
      (Grabs Cassio by the arm.)
  Please, sir, stop fighting.

CASSIO
  Let go of me, sir,
  or I'll beat you over the head.

MONTANO
  Come, come, you're drunk!

CASSIO
140 Drunk?
      (MONTANO and CASSIO fight.)

IAGO *(Aside to Roderigo)*
  Get going, I tell you! Go and warn everybody of a mutiny!
      Exit RODERIGO.
  Stop, good lieutenant. For God's sake, gentlemen!
  Help, please!—lieutenant—sir—Montano—sir—
  Help, gentlemen!—This is certainly a fine watch!
      (A bell rings.)
145 Who's that ringing the bell? Oh, the devil!
  The whole town will be awakened. For God's sake, lieutenant, stop!
  You'll be humiliated forever.
      Enter OTHELLO and ATTENDANTS.

OTHELLO
  What's the matter here?

MONTANO
    'Zounds, I bleed still; I am hurt to the death. He dies!

OTHELLO
150   Hold, for your lives!

IAGO
    Hold, ho! Lieutenant,—sir,—Montano,—gentlemen,—
    Have you forgot all sense of place and duty?
    Hold! the general speaks to you; hold, for shame!

OTHELLO
    Why, how now, ho! from whence ariseth this?
155   Are we turn'd Turks, and to ourselves do that
    Which Heaven hath forbid the Ottomites?
    For Christian shame, put by this barbarous brawl.
    He that stirs next to carve for his own rage
    Holds his soul light; he dies upon his motion.
160   Silence that dreadful bell; it frights the isle
    From her propriety. What is the matter, masters?
    Honest Iago, that looks dead with grieving,
    Speak, who began this? On thy love, I charge thee.

IAGO
    I do not know. Friends all but now, even now,
165   In quarter, and in terms like bride and groom
    Devesting them for bed; and then, but now—
    As if some planet had unwitted men—
    Swords out, and tilting one at other's breast,
    In opposition bloody. I cannot speak
170   Any beginning to this peevish odds;
    And would in action glorious I had lost
    Those legs that brought me to a part of it!

OTHELLO
    How comes it, Michael, you are thus forgot?

CASSIO
    I pray you, pardon me; I cannot speak.

OTHELLO
175   Worthy Montano, you were wont to be civil;

MONTANO
Damn, I'm bleeding! I'm fatally wounded! He'll die for it!

OTHELLO
150   Stop, if you want to live!

IAGO
Stop, stop! lieutenant—sir—Montano—gentlemen!
Have you lost all sense of your positions and duty?
Stop! The general is talking to you. Stop, stop, shame on you!

OTHELLO
Why, what is this? How did this get started?
155   Have we turned into Turks, and are we doing to ourselves
what heaven has stopped the Ottomites from doing?
Out of Christian dignity, stop this barbarous fighting!
The man who next makes a move to vent his anger
values his life lightly; he'll be killed at once.
160   Silence that awful bell! It scares the island
out of its peace and quiet. What's the matter, gentlemen?
Honest Iago, you look like you're sick with grief.
Speak up. Who started this? If you love me, I command you to
     speak.

IAGO
I don't know. They were friends just a moment ago,
165   at peace, just like a bride and groom
getting ready for bed; and then, the next moment,
(as if the influence of some planet had made them crazy)
their swords were out and pointed at each other's chests
in a bloody fight. I can't tell you
170   how this silly quarrel started,
but I wish I had lost in glorious battle
these legs that brought me here to take part in it.

OTHELLO
Michael, why have you forgotten yourself like this?

CASSIO
Please, pardon me; I cannot speak.

OTHELLO
175   Worthy Montano, you've always been well-behaved.

The gravity and stillness of your youth
The world hath noted, and your name is great
In mouths of wisest censure. What's the matter
That you unlace your reputation thus,
180   And spend your rich opinion for the name
Of a night-brawler? Give me answer to it.

MONTANO
    Worthy Othello, I am hurt to danger.
Your officer, Iago, can inform you—
While I spare speech, which something now offends me—
185   Of all that I do know; nor know I aught
By me that's said or done amiss this night,
Unless self-charity be sometimes a vice,
And to defend ourselves it be a sin
When violence assails us.

OTHELLO
190   Now, by heaven,
My blood begins my safer guides to rule;
And passion, having my best judgement collied,
Assays to lead the way. If I once stir
Or do but lift this arm, the best of you
195   Shall sink in my rebuke. Give me to know
How this foul rout began, who set it on;
And he that is approv'd in this offence,
Though he had twinn'd with me, both at a birth,
Shall lose me. What! in a town of war,
200   Yet wild, the people's hearts brimful of fear,
To manage private and domestic quarrel,
In night, and on the court and guard of safety!
'Tis monstrous. Iago, who began 't?

MONTANO
    If partially affin'd, or leagu'd in office,
205   Thou dost deliver more or less than truth,
Thou art no soldier.

The seriousness and earnestness of your younger days
was noted by the world, and your name is always mentioned
by people with the best judgment. What happened
to cause you to ruin your reputation this way
180   and waste the value of your good name to become known as
a night-brawler? Give me an answer.

MONTANO
Worthy Othello, I am seriously hurt.
Your officer, Iago, can tell you,
while I spare myself from talking—which is painful to me—
185   of everything I know. And I don't know anything
I've said or done that's wrong tonight,
unless it's not right to look out for one's safety
and if it's a sin to defend oneself
when one is violently attacked.

OTHELLO
190   Now, by God,
my anger is starting to overcome my prudence,
and passion, blotting out my better judgment,
is taking charge. If I just make a move
or only lift this arm, the best of you
195   will be cut down by my sword. I want to know
how this disgusting fight began and who started it.
And the one who is proved at fault,
even if he were my twin, born from the same mother,
will lose my friendship. I can't believe that in a garrison town,
200   still on edge and filled with frightened people,
you'd start a private, personal fight like this.
At night, and while you're on guard and at headquarters?
This is outrageous. Iago, who started it?

MONTANO
If you're biased because of friendship or comradeship
205   and tell more or less than the truth,
you're no real soldier.

IAGO
                    Touch me not so near.
I had rather have this tongue cut from my mouth
Than it should do offence to Michael Cassio;
210 Yet, I persuade myself, to speak the truth
Shall nothing wrong him. Thus it is, General:
Montano and myself being in speech,
There comes a fellow crying out for help;
And Cassio following him with determin'd sword
215 ⸱ To execute upon him. Sir, this gentleman
Steps in to Cassio and entreats his pause;
Myself the crying fellow did pursue,
Lest by his clamour—as it so fell out—
The town might fall in fright. He, swift of foot,
220 Outran my purpose; and I return'd the rather
For that I heard the clink and fall of swords,
And Cassio high in oath; which till to-night
I ne'er might say before. When I came back—
For this was brief—I found them close together,
225 At blow and thrust; even as again they were
When you yourself did part them.
More of this matter cannot I report.
But men are men; the best sometimes forget.
Though Cassio did some little wrong to him,
230 As men in rage strike those that wish them best,
Yet surely Cassio, I believe, receiv'd
From him that fled some strange indignity
Which patience could not pass.

OTHELLO
                    I know, Iago,
235 Thy honesty and love doth mince this matter,
Making it light to Cassio. Cassio, I love thee;
But never more be officer of mine.
          Re-enter DESDEMONA, *attended.*
Look, if my gentle love be not rais'd up!
I'll make thee an example.

IAGO
>Please, that comes too close to the truth.
>I'd rather have this tongue cut out of my mouth
>than say anything to hurt Michael Cassio.
>210 Still, I've convinced myself that speaking the truth
>will do no harm to him. So here it is, general.
>As Montano and I were talking,
>a young fellow, crying for help, came upon us,
>with Cassio following him with a drawn sword
>215 trying to kill him. Sir, this gentleman
>stepped up to Cassio and begged him to stop.
>I chased down the fellow who'd been crying out,
>to see that the terrible racket he was making (but it did anyway)
>wouldn't frighten the whole town. He, being fast-footed,
>220 got away from me, and I returned quickly
>because I heard the clanking and rattling of swords
>and Cassio swearing loudly—which until this night,
>I could never have said about him. When I came back
>(and I was fast about it), I found them close together
>225 thrusting and striking at each other, just as they were
>when you yourself parted them.
>I have nothing more to report about this matter;
>but men are like that—even the best sometimes slip.
>While Cassio did Montano a small injustice,
>230 as enraged men will strike those who only wish them the best,
>I still believe that Cassio received
>an insult of some sort from the man that ran away,
>which was beyond his patience to tolerate.

OTHELLO
>I know, Iago,
>235 that, in your honesty and love, you make light of this matter,
>making it easier on Cassio. Cassio, I love you,
>but you will never again serve as my officer.
>>*Enter* DESDEMONA, *with* ATTENDANTS.
>Look; my gentle love has been awakened!
>I'll make an example of you.

DESDEMONA
240   What's the matter, dear?

OTHELLO
All's well now, sweeting; come away to bed.
Sir, for your hurts, myself will be your surgeon.—
Lead him off.   [*To Montano, who is led off.*]
Iago, look with care about the town,
245   And silence those whom this vile brawl distracted.
Come, Desdemona; 'tis the soldiers' life
To have their balmy slumbers wak'd with strife.
          [*Exeunt all but Iago and Cassio.*]

IAGO
What, are you hurt, Lieutenant?

CASSIO
Ay, past all surgery.

IAGO
250   Marry, God forbid!

CASSIO
Reputation, reputation, reputation! O, I have lost my reputation!
I have lost the immortal part of myself, and what remains is
bestial. My reputation, Iago, my reputation!

IAGO
As I am an honest man, I thought you had received some bodily
255   wound; there is more sense in that than in reputation. Reputation is an idle and most false imposition; oft got without merit,
and lost without deserving. You have lost no reputation at all,
unless you repute yourself such a loser. What, man! there are more
ways to recover the general again. You are but now cast in his
260   mood, a punishment more in policy than in malice; even so as
one would beat his offenceless dog to affright an imperious lion.
Sue to him again, and he's yours.

CASSIO
I will rather sue to be despis'd than to deceive so good a
commander with so slight, so drunken, and so indiscreet an
265   officer. Drunk? and speak parrot? and squabble? swagger? swear?

DESADEMONA
240   What's the matter, dear?

OTHELLO
       Everything's all right now, sweetheart; let's go to bed.
       (To Montano) Sir, I'll personally see to your injuries.
       Help him away.
             Exit MONTANO, *attended.*
       Iago, look carefully around the town
245   and calm down those who have been disturbed by this terrible fight.
       Come, Desdemona. It's the story of a soldier's life
       to have a quiet sleep disturbed with fighting.
             Everyone exits except Iago and Cassio.

IAGO
       Why, have you been hurt, lieutenant?

CASSIO
       Yes, beyond any hope of recovery.

IAGO
250   Oh, God forbid!

CASSIO
       Reputation, reputation, reputation! Oh, I have lost my reputation!
       I've lost the one immortal part of myself, and everything
             that remains is
       bestial. My reputation, Iago, my reputation!

IAGO
       As sure as I'm honest, I thought you'd been physically
255   wounded; that's more serious than your reputation. Reputation
       is a foolish thing, falsely imposed by others; it's often
             gained without merit
       and lost undeservedly. You haven't lost your reputation at all
       unless you really believe you have lost it. Come on, man! There are
       ways to get back in the general's favor again. You were only
             dismissed because of his
260   anger—more as a disciplinary example than because of real
             resentment, just as
       one might beat an innocent dog to scare off a threatening lion.
       Appeal to him, again, and he'll listen.

CASSIO
       I'd rather appeal to him to hate me than deceive such a good
       commander with a weak, drunken, and indiscreet officer like
265   me. Drunk? And babbling? And quarreling? Swaggering? Swearing?

and discourse fustian with one's own shadow? O thou invisible
spirit of wine, if thou hast no name to be known by, let us call
thee devil!

IAGO

What was he that you follow'd with your sword? What had he
270   done to you?

CASSIO

I know not.

IAGO

Is't possible?

CASSIO

I remember a mass of things, but nothing distinctly; a quarrel,
but nothing wherefore. O God, that men should put an enemy
275   in their mouths to steal away their brains! That we should, with
joy, pleasance, revel, and applause, transform ourselves into
beasts!

IAGO

Why, but you are now well enough. How came you thus
recovered?

CASSIO

280   It hath pleas'd the devil drunkenness to give place to the devil
wrath. One unperfectness shows me another, to make me frankly
despise myself.

IAGO

Come, you are too severe a moraler. As the time, the place, and
the condition of this country stands, I could heartily wish this
285   had not befallen; but since it is as it is, mend it for your own good.

CASSIO

I will ask him for my place again; he shall tell me I am a drunkard!
Had I as many mouths as Hydra, such an answer would stop them
all. To be now a sensible man, by and by a fool, and presently
a beast! O strange! Every inordinate cup is unbless'd and the
290   ingredient is a devil.

IAGO

Come, come, good wine is a good familiar creature, if it be well

---

287 *Hydra* a mythical monster with many heads. 291 *familiar* means both "friendly"
as well as "a spirit summoned by an enchanter." (This latter meaning plays on Cassio's
remark about the devil in wine.)

And talking nonsense with my own shadow? Oh, you unseen
spirit of wine, if you have no name to be known by, let us call
you the devil!

IAGO
Who was the man you were chasing with your sword? What had he
270 done to you?

CASSIO
I don't know.

IAGO
Is that possible?

CASSIO
I remember a lot of things, but nothing clearly; a quarrel,
but I don't know why. Oh, God, why do men drink an enemy
275 to steal their brains! To think that we should, with
joy, merriment, celebration, and applause, turn ourselves into
beasts!

IAGO
Well, you seem a lot better now. How did you recover so
quickly?

CASSIO
280 That devil of drunkenness has been so kind as to make way for
the devil
of anger. One flaw in myself leads me to another, and I'm
starting to really
hate myself.

IAGO
Come, you're being too moralistic. As far as the time, place,
and the way things stand in this country, I certainly wish
285 this hadn't happened. But since it has, make the best of it.

CASSIO
I'll ask him for my position again. He'll tell me I'm a drunkard!
If I had as many mouths as Hydra, I'd have nothing to say to
that. To be a sensible man one minute, a fool the next, and soon
after
a beast! How strange! Every excess cup of wine is wicked
290 and contains the devil.

IAGO
Come, come, good wine is a very friendly thing if it's wisely

us'd; exclaim no more against it. And, good Lieutenant, I think
you think I love you.

CASSIO

I have well approved it, sir. I drunk!

IAGO

295 You or any man living may be drunk at a time, man. I'll tell you
what you shall do. Our general's wife is now the general;—I may
say so in this respect, for that he hath devoted and given up himself
to the contemplation, mark, and denotement of her parts and
graces;—confess yourself freely to her; importune her help to put
300 you in your place again. She is of so free, so kind, so apt, so
blessed a disposition, she holds it a vice in her goodness not to
do more than she is requested. This broken joint between you
and her husband entreat her to splinter; and, my fortunes against
any lay worth naming, this crack of your love shall grow stronger
305 than it was before.

CASSIO

You advise me well.

IAGO

I protest, in the sincerity of love and honest kindness.

CASSIO

I think it freely; and betimes in the morning I will beseech the
virtuous Desdemona to undertake for me. I am desperate of my
310 fortunes if they check me here.

IAGO

You are in the right. Good-night, lieutenant; I must to the watch.

CASSIO

Good-night, honest Iago.
[*Exit.*]

IAGO

And what's he then that says I play the villain?
When this advice is free I give and honest,
315 Probal to thinking and indeed the course
To win the Moor again? For 'tis most easy
Th' inclining Desdemona to subdue

taken. Don't say anything else against it. And, good lieutenant, I'm sure
you realize that I love you.

CASSIO
I can testify to that, sir. But even when I'm drunk?

IAGO
295 You or any other man alive may be drunk on occasion, man. I'll tell you
what to do. The general's wife is practically in charge. The reason I say
this is he has completely given himself over
to contemplating, observing, and cataloging her wonderful
qualities. Tell her everything freely. Ask for her help to get
300 your position back. She is of such a generous, kind, sympathetic,
and blessed temper that she considers it wrong not to
do more than people ask her to do. Ask her to put a splint on this break
between you and her husband; and I'll bet all my fortune against
any wager you want to make, this break in your love will grow back stronger
305 than it was before.

CASSIO
You give me good advice.

IAGO
I assure you, it is out of the sincerest love and honest kindness.

CASSIO
I'm convinced of that; and first thing in the morning, I'll beg the
virtuous Desdemona to speak on my behalf. I'll be in a very bad way
310 if I'm stopped by this.

IAGO
You're making the right choice. Good night, lieutenant; I
must go on guard duty.

CASSIO
Good night, honest Iago.
Exit CASSIO.

IAGO
And why would anyone say I'm playing the villain
when I give away such free and honest advice,
315 so sensible when you think about it, and obviously the way
to get back in the Moor's good favor? Because it's very easy
to win over the agreeable Desdemona

In any honest suit; she's fram'd as fruitful
As the free elements. And then for her
320   To win the Moor, were't to renounce his baptism,
All seals and symbols of redeemed sin,
His soul is so enfetter'd to her love,
That she may make, unmake, do what she list,
Even as her appetite shall play the god
325   With his weak function. How am I then a villain
To counsel Cassio to this parallel course,
Directly to his good? Divinity of hell!
When devils will the blackest sins put on,
They do suggest at first with heavenly shows,
330   As I do now; for whiles this honest fool
Plies Desdemona to repair his fortune
And she for him pleads strongly to the Moor,
I'll pour this pestilence into his ear,
That she repeals him for her body's lust;
335   And by how much she strives to do him good,
She shall undo her credit with the Moor.
So will I turn her virtue into pitch,
And out of her own goodness make the net
That shall enmesh them all.
              Re-enter RODERIGO.
340   How now, Roderigo!

RODERIGO
I do follow here in the chase, not like a hound that hunts, but
one that fills up the cry. My money is almost spent; I have been
to-night exceedingly well cudgell'd; and I think the issue will be,
I shall have so much experience for my pains; and so, with no
345   money at all and a little more wit, return again to Venice.

IAGO
How poor are they that have not patience!
What wound did ever heal but by degrees?
Thou know'st we work by wit, and not by witchcraft;
And wit depends on dilatory time.
350   Does't not go well? Cassio hath beaten thee,
And thou, by that small hurt, hast cashier'd Cassio.

341-42 *not like a hound . . . cry*   in hunting, dogs were sometimes used only for the sound
of their barking and not for actual tracking. Roderigo is saying that he has felt useless during
the preceding events.

to any honest cause. She is as generous
as nature itself. And then it's easy for her
320   to persuade the Moor—even to renounce his baptism,
or his entire religious faith—
because his soul is so infatuated with her
that she can help him, ruin him, or do whatever she pleases;
her wishes completely control
325   his weak reason. Why, then, should I be called a villain
for advising Cassio to take this same way
that is directly in his best interests? Why, that's hell's own preaching!
When devils urge you to do the most wicked things,
they tempt you by making everything seem heavenly—
330   the same as I'm doing now. Because while this honest fool
is appealing to Desdemona to make things better for him,
and she pleads strongly to the Moor on his behalf,
I'll tell him this poisonous thing about Cassio—
that she asks for him to be reinstated only out of lust for him.
335   And the more good she tries to do for him,
the worse she'll look in the eyes of the Moor.
This is how I'll turn her virtue into wickedness,
and, out of her own goodness, make a net
to catch everyone in.
        Enter RODERIGO.
340   What is it, Roderigo?

RODERIGO
I've come here after the chase, not like a real tracker, but like
one which does nothing but bark. My money is almost gone, I've
    been
thoroughly beaten tonight, and I think the result will be that
I'll have nothing to show for my trouble except my pains. And
    so, with no
345   money at all and just a little more wit, I'll end up going
        back to Venice.

IAGO
How pathetic are people who don't have any patience!
What wound doesn't take some time to heal?
You know we accomplish things by scheming and not by witchcraft,
and our schemes need time to unfold.
350   Didn't things go well? Cassio has beaten you,
and because of that small hurt, you've ruined Cassio.

Though other things grow fair against the sun,
Yet fruits that blossom first will first be ripe.
Content thyself a while. In troth, 'tis morning;
355   Pleasure and action make the hours seem short.
Retire thee; go where thou are billeted.
Away, I say; thou shalt know more hereafter.
Nay, get thee gone. [*Exit Roderigo.*] Two things are to
be done:
My wife must move for Cassio to her mistress;
360   I'll set her on;
Myself a while to draw the Moor apart,
And bring him jump when he may Cassio find
Soliciting his wife. Ay, that's the way;
Dull not device by coldness and delay.
[*Exit.*]

Act III, Scene i: [*Cyprus before the castle.*] *Enter* CASSIO,
with MUSICIANS.

CASSIO
Masters, play here; I will content your pains;
Something that's brief; and bid "Good morrow, general."
[*They play.*]
Enter CLOWN.

CLOWN
Why, masters, have your instruments been in Naples, that they
speak i' th' nose thus?

1. MUSICIAN
5   How, sir, how?

CLOWN
Are these, I pray you, wind-instruments?

1. MUSICIAN
Ay, marry, are they, sir.

CLOWN
O, thereby hangs a tail.

---

s.d. *Clown* means "fool," and does not refer to a harlequin.   3-4 *have your
instruments . . . thus* - a reference not only to the Neapolitans' nasal voices but to an out-
break of syphilis in Naples. Syphilis can cause decomposition in the nose.

No matter how things seem to be going,
things will come to pass in their own sweet time.
Be patient awhile. Good Lord, it's morning!
355   Pleasure and action make the time pass quickly.
Get to bed; go to where you've been put up.
Go on, I say! You'll know more later on.
Go on, get going! *(Exit* RODERIGO.*)* Two things have to be done;
my wife must intercede on Cassio's behalf to her mistress;
360   I'll put her up to it.
In the meantime, I'll work on the Moor separately
and bring him in at the very moment when he'll find Cassio
appealing to his wife. Yes, that's how to do it!
I won't spoil this plan by hesitation or delay.
       Exit IAGO.

Act III, Scene i: Cyprus, in front of the castle. Enter CASSIO,
with several MUSICIANS.

CASSIO
    Gentlemen, play here, I'll reward your efforts.
    Play something short, and say good day to the general.
       (They play.)
       Enter the CLOWN.

CLOWN
    Well, gentlemen, is it because your instruments have been to
      Naples that they
    have that nasal sound?

FIRST MUSICIAN
5   What do you mean, sir?

CLOWN
    I ask you, aren't these called wind instruments?

FIRST MUSICIAN
    They certainly are, sir.

CLOWN
    Well, there's a tail hanging from that.

1. MUSICIAN
Whereby hangs a tale, sir?

CLOWN

10   Marry, sir, by many a wind-instrument that I know. But, masters,
here's money for you; and the General so likes your music, that
he desires you, for love's sake, to make no more noise with it.

1. MUSICIAN
Well, sir, we will not.

CLOWN

If you have any music that may not be heard, to't again; but,
15   as they say, to hear music the General does not greatly care.

1. MUSICIAN
We have none such, sir.

CLOWN

Then put up your pipes in your bag, for I'll away. Go, vanish
into air, away!
[*Exeunt Musicians.*]

CASSIO
Dost thou hear mine honest friend?

CLOWN

20   No, I hear not your honest friend; I hear you.

CASSIO
Prithee, keep up thy quillets. There's a poor piece of gold for thee.
If the gentlewoman that attends the General's wife be stirring,
tell her there's one Cassio entreats her a little favour of speech.
Wilt thou do this?

CLOWN

25   She is stirring, sir. If she will stir hither, I shall seem to notify
unto her.

CASSIO
Do, good my friend.
[*Exit Clown.*]

25-26 *If . . . her*   the clown is mimicking Cassio's overblown courtesy.

FIRST MUSICIAN
Where does a tale hang, sir?

CLOWN
10   Why, sir, from many wind instruments I know about. But
here's some money for you, gentlemen. The general likes your
    music so much that
he asks, for the respect you bear for him, that you not play
anymore.

FIRST MUSICIAN
Well, sir, we won't.

CLOWN
If you know any music that can't be heard, go right ahead. But,
15   as they say, the general doesn't much care for music.

FIRST MUSICIAN
We don't know any music like that, sir.

CLOWN
Then put your instruments back in your bags, because I must
    leave. Go, vanish
into thin air, go on!
              The MUSICIANS *exit.*

CASSIO
Can you hear (me), my honest friend?

CLOWN
20   No, I don't hear your honest friend. I hear you.

CASSIO
Please, keep your puns to yourself. Here's a little gold
    piece for you.
If the lady that waits on the general's wife is awake,
tell her a certain Cassio begs to talk to her for a bit.
Will you do that?

CLOWN
25   She's awake, sir. If she comes this way, I'll agree to notify her.

CASSIO
Do so, good friend.
          Exit CLOWN.

Enter IAGO.

In happy time, Iago.

IAGO
You have not been a-bed, then?

CASSIO
30   Why, no; the day had broke
Before we parted. I have made bold, Iago,
To send in to your wife. My suit to her
Is that she will to virtuous Desdemona
Procure me some access.

IAGO
35   I'll send her to you presently;
And I'll devise a mean to draw the Moor
Out of the way, that your converse and business
May be more free.

CASSIO
I humbly thank you for't. [*Exit Iago.*] I never knew
40   A Florentine more kind and honest.
             Enter EMILIA.

EMILIA
Good morrow, good Lieutenant. I am sorry
For your displeasure; but all will sure be well.
The General and his wife are talking of it,
And she speaks for you stoutly. The Moor replies
45   That he you hurt is of great fame in Cyprus
And great affinity, and that in wholesome wisdom
He might not but refuse you; but he protests he loves you,
And needs no other suitor but his likings
To take the safest occasion by the front
50   To bring you in again.

CASSIO
                    Yet, I beseech you,
If you think fit, or that it may be done,
Give me advantage of some brief discourse
With Desdemon alone.

---

40 *Florentine*   Cassio is from Florence; he means that not even his fellow citizens are as
kind and honest as Iago.

Enter IAGO.
What luck meeting with you, Iago.

IAGO
You haven't been to bed, then?

CASSIO
30   Why, no. Day had come
before we left each other. Iago, I have been so bold
as to ask to see your wife. What I wish to ask from her
is that she will arrange for me
to talk to the virtuous Desdemona.

IAGO
35   I'll have her come to you right away,
and I'll figure out some means to get the Moor
out of the way so that your business and your conversation
won't be interrupted.

CASSIO
I humbly thank you. *(Exit* IAGO.*)* I never knew
40   any Florentine who was as kind and honest.
Enter EMILIA.

EMILIA
Good day, good lieutenant. I'm sorry
that you've been disgraced; but everything will be better soon.
The general and his wife are talking about it,
and she's strongly defending you. The Moor has replied
45   that the man you hurt is very famous in Cyprus,
with a good family, and for the sake of discretion,
his only choice is to refuse you. But he still says he loves you,
and he needs no other suitor than his own feelings
to find the best possible moment
50   to reinstate you.

CASSIO
Still, I beg you,
if you think it appropriate or possible,
give me a chance to talk a little
alone to Desdemona.

EMILIA

55   Pray you, come in.
I will bestow you where you shall have time
To speak your bosom freely.

CASSIO

              I am much bound to you.
        [*Exeunt.*]

Scene ii: [*A room in the castle.*] *Enter* OTHELLO, IAGO, *and*
GENTLEMEN.

OTHELLO

These letters give, Iago, to the pilot;
And by him do my duties to the Senate.
That done, I will be walking on the works;
Repair there to me.

IAGO

5   Well, my good lord, I'll do't.

OTHELLO

This fortification, gentlemen, shall we see't?

GENTLEMEN

We'll wait upon your lordship.
        [*Exeunt.*]

Scene iii: [*The garden of the castle.*] *Enter* DESDEMONA,
CASSIO, *and* EMILIA.

DESDEMONA

Be thou assur'd, good Cassio, I will do
All my abilities in thy behalf.

EMILIA

Good madam, do. I warrant it grieves my husband
As if the cause were his.

DESDEMONA

5 O, that's an honest fellow. Do not doubt, Cassio,
But I will have my lord and you again
As friendly as you were.

EMILIA
55   Please come in, then.
     I'll take you to where you'll have the time
     to freely speak your mind to her.

CASSIO
     I'm very indebted to you.
          They exit.

Act III, Scene ii: Inside the castle. Enter OTHELLO, IAGO, *and* GENTLEMEN.

OTHELLO
     Iago, give these letters to the pilot
     so that my duties in the senate will be taken care of.
     When you've finished, I'll be walking on the castle walls.
     Come and see me there.

IAGO
5   Certainly, my good lord; I'll see to everything.

OTHELLO
     Shall we examine the fortifications, gentlemen?

GENTLEMEN
     Whatever you wish, your lordship.
          They exit.

Act III, Scene iii: The castle garden. Enter DESDEMONA, CASSIO, *and* EMILIA.

DESDEMONA
     Good Cassio, rest assured that I'll do
     everything in my power that I can for you.

EMILIA
     Please do, dear lady. I tell you, it makes my husband so unhappy,
     you'd think it was his own cause.

DESDEMONA
5   Oh, there's an honest fellow. You can be certain, Cassio,
     that I'll make sure that you and my lord
     will be as friendly as ever.

CASSIO
                    Bounteous madam,
Whatever shall become of Michael Cassio,
10   He's never anything but your true servant.

DESDEMONA
I know 't; I thank you. You do love my lord;
You have known him long; and be you well assur'd
He shall in strangeness stand no farther off
Than in a politic distance.

CASSIO
15   Ay, but, lady,
That policy may either last so long,
Or feed upon such nice and waterish diet,
Or breed itself so out of circumstances,
That, I being absent and my place supplied,
20   My general will forget my love and service.

DESDEMONA
Do not doubt that; before Emilia here
I give thee warrant of thy place. Assure thee,
If I do vow a friendship, I'll perform it
To the last article. My lord shall never rest;
25   I'll watch him tame, and talk him out of patience;
His bed shall seem a school, his board a shrift;
I'll intermingle everything he does
With Cassio's suit. Therefore be merry, Cassio;
For thy solicitor shall rather die
30   Than give thy cause away.
                Enter OTHELLO *and* IAGO.

EMILIA
Madam, here comes my lord.

CASSIO
Madam, I'll take my leave.

DESDEMONA
Why, stay, and hear me speak.

---

25 *watch him tame*   hawks were sometimes tamed by being kept awake.

CASSIO
    Generous lady,
    whatever else might happen to Michael Cassio,
10 he'll never be anything but your faithful servant.

DESDEMONA
    I know that and thank you. You love my lord;
    you've known him for a long time; so be assured
    that he'll only be cold to you
    for the sake of appearance.

CASSIO
15 Yes, but lady,
    that attitude might exist for a long time,
    or be fed by small and trifling considerations,
    or grow out of all proportion due to some new circumstances,
    so that, while I'm gone and my position is filled by another,
20 my general will forget my love and good service.

DESDEMONA
    Don't worry about that. As Emilia here is my witness,
    I guarantee you your position. Rest easy;
    when I promise something out of friendship, I'll see it through
    to the last detail. My lord won't get any rest;
25 I'll keep him awake and talk enough to him to wear out his
        patience;
    his bed will seem like a school and his table like a confessional.
    With everything he does, I'll mix in talk
    of Cassio's suit. So cheer up, Cassio,
    for your intercessor would rather die
30 than fail in your cause.
                Enter OTHELLO *and* IAGO.

EMILIA
    Madam, here comes my lord.

CASSIO
    Madam, I'll leave now.

DESDEMONA
    Why, stay here and listen to me speak.

CASSIO
Madam, not now; I am very ill at ease,
35   Unfit for mine own purposes.

DESDEMONA
Well, do your discretion.
    [*Exit Cassio.*]

IAGO
Ha! I like not that.

OTHELLO
                What dost thou say?

IAGO
Nothing, my lord; or if—I know not what.

OTHELLO
40   Was not that Cassio parted from my wife?

IAGO
Cassio, my lord! No, sure, I cannot think it,
That he would steal away so guilty-like,
Seeing your coming.

OTHELLO
             I do believe 'twas he.

DESDEMONA
45   How now, my lord!
I have been talking with a suitor here,
A man that languishes in your displeasure.

OTHELLO
Who is't you mean?

DESDEMONA
Why, your lieutenant, Cassio. Good my lord,
50   If I have any grace or power to move you,
His present reconciliation take;
For if he be not one that truly loves you,
That errs in ignorance and not in cunning,
I have no judgement in an honest face.
55   I prithee, call him back.

CASSIO
    Not now, madam. I'm very ill at ease,
35   which won't help my situation at all.

DESDEMONA
    Well, do as you think best.
        Exit CASSIO.

IAGO
    Ha! I don't like the looks of that.

OTHELLO
    What did you say?

IAGO
    Nothing, my lord; or maybe—I just don't know.

OTHELLO
40   Wasn't that Cassio who just left my wife?

IAGO
    Cassio, my lord? No, surely not, I can't believe
    he'd sneak away so guilty-looking
    when he saw you coming.

OTHELLO
    I really think it was him.

DESDEMONA
45   How are you doing, my lord?
    I have been talking to a man who has a problem here,
    someone who suffers from your disapproval.

OTHELLO
    Who do you mean?

DESDEMONA
    Why, your lieutenant, Cassio. My good lord,
50   if I have any ability or power to persuade you,
    take his apology at once.
    Because if he doesn't love you very sincerely,
    and if he hasn't erred out of ignorance and not deliberately,
    then I can't tell an honest face when I see one.
55   Please, call him back.

OTHELLO

Went he hence now?

DESDEMONA

Yes, faith; so humbled
That he hath left part of his grief with me
To suffer with him. Good love, call him back.

OTHELLO

60   Not now, sweet Desdemon; some other time.

DESDEMONA

But shall't be shortly?

OTHELLO

The sooner, sweet, for you.

DESDEMONA

Shall't be to-night at supper?

OTHELLO

No, not to-night.

DESDEMONA

65   To-morrow dinner, then?

OTHELLO

I shall not dine at home;
I meet the captains at the citadel.

DESDEMONA

Why, then, to-morrow night; on Tuesday morn;
On Tuesday noon, or night; on Wednesday morn.
70   I prithee, name the time, but let it not
Exceed three days. In faith, he's penitent;
And yet his trespass, in our common reason—
Save that, they say, the wars must make example
Out of their best—is not almost a fault
75   T' incur a private check. When shall he come?
Tell me, Othello. I wonder in my soul
What you would ask me that I should deny,
Or stand so mamm'ring on. What! Michael Cassio,
That came a-wooing with you, and so many a time,
80   When I have spoke of you dispraisingly,

OTHELLO
Was that him who left just now?

DESDEMONA
Yes, it was; and he was so humbled
that he made me feel his grief
and suffer with him. My love, call him back.

OTHELLO
60 Not now, sweet Desdemona; some other time.

DESDEMONA
But will it be shortly?

OTHELLO
As soon as possible, sweetheart, on your account.

DESDEMONA
Will it be tonight at suppertime?

OTHELLO
No, not tonight.

DESDEMONA
65 Before dinner tomorrow, then?

OTHELLO
I will not dine at home.
I'm meeting the captains at the castle.

DESDEMONA
Well then, make it tomorrow night, or Tuesday morning,
or Tuesday noon or night, or Wednesday morning.
70 Please name the time, but don't let it
be more than three days. Really, he's very sorry;
and his crime, by everyday standards
(except that, as they say, military order demands that
the best men serve as examples), isn't even enough of a fault
75 to merit a private scolding. When will he come?
Tell me, Othello. In my heart, I wonder
what kind of thing you might ask of me that I would deny
or hesitate so much about as you do. What? Michael Cassio,
who came wooing with you, and so many times
80 when I've said disagreeable things about you,

Hath ta'en your part,—to have so much to do
To bring him in! Trust me, I could do much,—

OTHELLO
Prithee, no more; let him come when he will,
I will deny thee nothing.

DESDEMONA

85   Why, this is not a boon.
'Tis as I should entreat you wear your gloves,
Or feed on nourishing dishes, or keep you warm,
Or sue to you to do a peculiar profit
To your own person. Nay, when I have a suit

90   Wherein I mean to touch your love indeed,
It shall be full of poise and difficult weight
And fearful to be granted.

OTHELLO
                        I will deny thee nothing;
Whereon, I do beseech thee, grant me this,

95   To leave me but a little to myself.

DESDEMONA
Shall I deny you? No. Farewell, my lord.

OTHELLO
Farewell, my Desdemona; I'll come to thee straight.

DESDEMONA
Emilia, come.—Be as your fancies teach you;
Whate'er you be, I am obedient.
        [*Exeunt Desdemona and Emilia.*]

OTHELLO

100   Excellent wretch! Perdition catch my soul,
But I do love thee! and when I love thee not,
Chaos is come again.

IAGO
My noble lord,—

OTHELLO
                        What dost thou say, Iago?

took your part—why is it so much trouble
to make up with him? Trust me, I could do much—

OTHELLO
Please, say no more. He can come when he wants to!
I won't deny you anything.

DESDEMONA
85   Why, I'm not asking for some favor.
It's as if I were telling you to wear your gloves,
or eat nourishing food, or stay warm,
or ask you to do something helpful
for yourself. No, when I want to ask something
90   and appeal to you out of your love,
it will be a weighty and serious thing
and difficult to grant.

OTHELLO
I won't deny you anything!
And so I ask you to do this for me;
95   just leave me alone for a little while.

DESDEMONA
Would I refuse you? No. Goodbye, my lord.

OTHELLO
Goodbye, Desdemona. I'll join you at once.

DESDEMONA
Emilia, come along. *(To Othello)* Do whatever you like.
Whatever you want, I'll obey you.
        Exit DESDEMONA *and* EMILIA.

OTHELLO
100   You sweet thing! Hell take me,
but I really love you! And when I don't love you,
chaos will have come again.

IAGO
My noble lord—

OTHELLO
What is it, Iago?

IAGO

105   Did Michael Cassio, when you woo'd my lady,
    Know of your love?

OTHELLO
    He did, from first to last. Why dost thou ask?

IAGO
    But for a satisfaction of my thought;
    No further harm.

OTHELLO

110   Why of thy thought, Iago?

IAGO
    I did not think he had been acquainted with her.

OTHELLO
    O, yes; and went between us very oft.

IAGO
    Indeed!

OTHELLO
    Indeed! ay, indeed. Discern'st thou aught in that?

115   Is he not honest?

IAGO
                   Honest, my lord?

OTHELLO
                   Honest! ay, honest.

IAGO
    My lord, for aught I know.

OTHELLO
    What dost thou think?

IAGO

120   Think, my lord?

OTHELLO
               Think, my lord!
    By heaven, he echoes me,
    As if there were some monster in his thought

IAGO

105   When you wooed my lady, did Michael Cassio
know about your love for her?

OTHELLO

Yes, from beginning to end. Why do you ask?

IAGO

I just wanted to satisfy my curiosity about something;
nothing important.

OTHELLO

110   What were you curious about, Iago?

IAGO

I didn't realize that he had known her.

OTHELLO

Oh, yes, and he often served as our go-between.

IAGO

Really?

OTHELLO

Really? Yes, really! Do you see anything wrong with that?
115   Isn't he honest?

IAGO

Honest, my lord?

OTHELLO

Honest? Yes, honest.

IAGO

For all I know, my lord.

OTHELLO

What are you thinking?

IAGO

120   Thinking, my lord?

OTHELLO

Thinking, my lord?
By God, he's echoing me
as if he had something so awful on his mind

Too hideous to be shown.—Thou dost mean something.
125 I heard thee say even now, thou lik'st not that,
When Cassio left my wife. What didst not like?
And when I told thee he was of my counsel
In my whole course of wooing, thou criedst, "Indeed!"
And didst contract and purse thy brow together,
130 As if thou then hadst shut up in thy brain
Some horrible conceit. If thou dost love me,
Show me thy thought.

IAGO
My lord, you know I love you.

OTHELLO
                  I think thou dost;
135 And, for I know thou'rt full of love and honesty,
And weigh'st thy words before thou giv'st them breath,
Therefore these stops of thine fright me the more;
For such things in a false disloyal knave
Are tricks of custom; but in a man that's just
140 They're close dilations, working from the heart
That passion cannot rule.

IAGO
               For Michael Cassio,
I dare be sworn I think that he is honest.

OTHELLO
I think so too.

IAGO
145   Men should be what they seem;
Or those that be not, would they might seem none!

OTHELLO
Certain, men should be what they seem.

IAGO
Why, then, I think Cassio's an honest man.

OTHELLO
Nay, yet there's more in this.
150 I prithee, speak to me as to thy thinkings,

that he was afraid to tell me. You have something on your
mind.
125 I heard you say just a moment ago that you didn't like it
when you saw Cassio leaving my wife. What didn't you like?
And when I told you that he was in my confidence
during my whole courtship, you cried, "Really?"
And you wrinkled your forehead
130 as if you had shut up inside your brain
some terrible thought. If you love me,
tell me what you're thinking.

IAGO
My lord, you know I love you.

OTHELLO
I believe you do;
135 and, because I know you are full of love and honesty
and weigh your words carefully before you say them,
I'm all the more frightened by your hesitation.
This kind of behavior in a dishonest, disloyal rascal
is a customary trick; but in a good man,
140 it is a true sign of secret concern, coming from the heart
in spite of one's intentions.

IAGO
As for Michael Cassio,
I'd venture to swear that I think he is honest.

OTHELLO
I think so too.

IAGO
145 Men should be what they seem to be;
and men who aren't men shouldn't seem like men.

OTHELLO
Certainly, men should be what they seem to be.

IAGO
Well then, I think Cassio's an honest man.

OTHELLO
No, you're still not telling me something.
150 Please, tell me what you're thinking,

As thou dost ruminate, and give thy worst of thoughts
The worst of words.

IAGO

                    Good my lord, pardon me.
Though I am bound to every act of duty,
155   I am not bound to that all slaves are free to.
Utter my thoughts? Why, say they are vile and false;
As where's that palace whereinto foul things
Sometimes intrude not? Who has that breast so pure
But some uncleanly apprehensions
160   Keep leets and law-days and in sessions sit
With meditations lawful?

OTHELLO

Thou dost conspire against thy friend, Iago,
If thou but think'st him wrong'd and mak'st his ear
A stranger to thy thoughts.

IAGO

165   I do beseech you—
Though I perchance am vicious in my guess,
As, I confess, it is my nature's plague
To spy into abuses, and oft my jealousy
Shapes faults that are not—that your wisdom yet,
170   From one that so imperfectly conceits,
Would take no notice, nor build yourself a trouble
Out of his scattering and unsure observance.
It were not for your quiet nor your good,
Nor for my manhood, honesty, and wisdom,
175   To let you know my thoughts.

OTHELLO

                  What dost thou mean?

IAGO

Good name in man and woman, dear my lord,
Is the immediate jewel of their souls.
Who steals my purse steals trash; 'tis something, nothing;
180   'Twas mine, 'tis his, and has been slave to thousands;
But he that filches from me my good name

---

160 *leets and law-days*   days when the local courts held sessions.

what's on your mind, and give me your worst thoughts
as bluntly as you can.

IAGO
My good lord, pardon me.
Though I am obliged to perform all sorts of duties to you,
155   I am not obliged to do something even slaves are free not to do.
Tell my thoughts? Why, suppose they are rotten and untrue?
And what palace is so secure that bad things
don't sometimes get in? Who has such a pure heart
that unclean ideas
160   don't keep regular session, sitting side by side
with better thoughts?

OTHELLO
You are doing an injustice to a friend, Iago,
if you believe he's been wronged and you won't tell him
what you're thinking.

IAGO
165   I beg you—
since I may be wrong in my suspicion
(and I admit it is a flaw in my nature
to seek out wrongs, and often my suspicious mind
finds faults that aren't real)—that, in your wisdom,
170   you keep in mind that I often imagine things,
and take no notice, and don't get worked up
about my random and doubtful observations.
It's not good for your peace of mind or your best interests,
or for my manhood, honesty, or wisdom,
175   to tell you what I'm thinking.

OTHELLO
What do you mean?

IAGO
A man or a woman's good name, my dear lord,
is the most important thing they have.
Someone who steals my money steals trash; it was something,
    now it's nothing;
180   it was mine, now it's his—and has belonged to thousands of others.
But someone who takes my good name away from me

Robs me of that which not enriches him,
And makes me poor indeed.

OTHELLO
By heaven, I'll know thy thoughts.

IAGO
185 You cannot, if my heart were in your hand;
Nor shall not, whilst 'tis in my custody.

OTHELLO
Ha!

IAGO
         O, beware, my lord, of jealousy!
It is the green-ey'd monster which doth mock
190 The meat it feeds on. That cuckold lives in bliss
Who, certain of his fate, loves not his wronger;
But, O, what damned minutes tells he o'er
Who dotes, yet doubts, suspects, yet soundly loves!

OTHELLO
O misery!

IAGO
195 Poor and content is rich, and rich enough;
But riches fineless is as poor as winter
To him that ever fears he shall be poor.
Good heaven, the souls of all my tribe defend
From jealousy!

OTHELLO
200   Why, why is this?
Think'st thou I'd make a life of jealousy,
To follow still the changes of the moon
With fresh suspicions? No! to be once in doubt
Is once to be resolv'd. Exchange me for a goat
205 When I shall turn the business of my soul
To such exsufflicate and blown surmises,
Matching thy inference. 'Tis not to make me jealous
To say my wife is fair, feeds well, loves company,
Is free of speech, sings, plays, and dances well;

robs me of something which does him no good
and leaves me very poor indeed.

OTHELLO
By God, I want to know what you're thinking!

IAGO
185   You couldn't, even if you were holding my heart in your hand;
and you won't as long as it's in my custody.

OTHELLO
Ha!

IAGO
Oh, watch out for jealousy, my lord!
It is a green-eyed monster, and it laughs at
190   the meat it eats. A cuckold can be happy
who, sure of his situation, hates the man who wrongs him.
But, oh, how time drags on for the man
who adores, but doubts; suspects, but loves strongly!

OTHELLO
Oh, misery!

IAGO
195   To be poor and happy is to be rich, and plenty rich;
but limitless wealth is just so much poverty
to a man who is frightened he'll wind up poor.
May heaven protect the souls of everyone I know
from jealousy!

OTHELLO
200   Why, why do you say this?
Do you think I'd choose to live for jealousy,
to constantly change like the moon,
feeling new suspicions? No! To be in doubt once
is to be satisfied as to the truth. Exchange me for a goat
205   when I would become obsessed
with such inflated and far-fetched thoughts
as you suggest. You won't make me jealous
by saying that my wife is lovely, dines elegantly, likes company,
speaks freely, sings, plays, and dances well.

210 Where virtue is, these are more virtuous.
    Nor from mine own weak merits will I draw
    The smallest fear or doubt of her revolt;
    For she had eyes, and chose me. No, Iago;
    I'll see before I doubt; when I doubt, prove;
215 And on the proof, there is no more but this,—
    Away at once with love or jealousy!

IAGO
    I am glad of this, for now I shall have reason
    To show the love and duty that I bear you
    With franker spirit; therefore, as I am bound,
220 Receive it from me. I speak not yet of proof.
    Look to your wife; observe her well with Cassio;
    Wear your eyes thus, not jealous nor secure.
    I would not have your free and noble nature,
    Out of self-bounty, be abus'd; look to't.
225 I know our country disposition well;
    In Venice they do let Heaven see the pranks
    They dare not show their husbands. Their best conscience
    Is not to leave 't undone, but keep 't unknown.

OTHELLO
    Dost thou say so?

IAGO
230 She did deceive her father, marrying you;
    And when she seem'd to shake and fear your looks,
    She lov'd them most.

OTHELLO
                        And so she did.

IAGO
                        Why, go to then.
235 She that, so young, could give out such a seeming,
    To seel her father's eyes up close as oak—
    He thought 'twas witchcraft—but I am much to blame.
    I humbly do beseech you of your pardon
    For too much loving you.

---

236 *close as oak*   Iago means Brabantio's eyes were closed up as tightly as the close woodgrain
of the oak.

210 These good qualities make a virtuous person all the more virtuous.
And though I might not be the best-looking man alive,
I won't fear rejection on that account
because she had eyes and chose me. No, Iago;
I must see evidence before I doubt, and when I doubt, I must
have proof;
215 and when there's proof, that's the end of it—
and that's the end of love or jealousy!

IAGO
I'm glad to hear that; now I have cause
to show the love and duty that I owe you
more openly. Therefore, since I'm obliged,
220 listen to me. I've no proof yet.
Watch your wife; observe her carefully when she's with Cassio;
just keep your eyes open, neither suspicious nor careless.
I don't want your generous and noble nature
to be abused because of your natural kindness.
225 Keep your eyes open.
In Venice, women let heaven see them do wicked things
that their husbands never see. The height of their morality
is not to do no wrong, but to not get caught.

OTHELLO
Do you really mean it?

IAGO
230 She deceived her father by marrying you;
and when she seemed most frightened by your looks,
she really loved them most.

OTHELLO
And so she did.

IAGO
Well, there you have it!
235 Here's a girl who is so young but could still put on an appearance
to completely hoodwink her father;
he thought it was witchcraft—but I shouldn't be saying this.
I humbly beg your pardon
for being too concerned about you.

OTHELLO

240   I am bound to thee for ever.

IAGO
I see this hath a little dash'd your spirits.

OTHELLO
Not a jot, not a jot.

IAGO
                        Trust me! I fear it has.
I hope you will consider what is spoke
245   Comes from my love. But I do see you're mov'd.
I am to pray you not to strain my speech
To grosser issues nor to larger reach
Than to suspicion.

OTHELLO
I will not.

IAGO
250   Should you do so, my lord,
My speech should fall into such vile success
Which my thoughts aim'd not at. Cassio's my worthy
        friend,—
My lord, I see you're mov'd.

OTHELLO
                        No, not much mov'd.
255   I do not think but Desdemona's honest.

IAGO
Long live she so! and long live you to think so!

OTHELLO
And yet, how nature erring from itself,—

IAGO
Ay, there's the point; as—to be bold with you—
Not to affect many proposed matches
260   Of her own clime, complexion, and degree,
Whereto we see in all things nature tends—
Foh! one may smell in such, a will most rank,
Foul disproportions, thoughts unnatural.

OTHELLO

240   I'm forever indebted to you.

IAGO

I see this has dampened your good spirits a little.

OTHELLO

Not a bit, not a bit.

IAGO

Really, I'm afraid it has.
I hope you'll remember that what I've said
245   was spoken simply out of love. But I see you're disturbed.
I really beg you not to apply what I've said
to larger issues or to go further
than my suspicions.

OTHELLO

I will not.

IAGO

250   If you should do that, my lord,
my words would have evil consequences
that I really didn't intend. Cassio's my very good friend—
My lord, I see you're disturbed.

OTHELLO

No, not terribly disturbed.
255   I can't think that Desdemona's anything but honest.

IAGO

And long may she live so! And long may you live to think so!

OTHELLO

But still, one can sometimes forget oneself—

IAGO

Yes, that's the point! Since (to be quite blunt)
she hasn't shown an inclination toward another match
260   of her own temperament, nature, and social status,
which is simply the tendency of all things in nature—
Really! One might smell in that kind of desire rotten
and foul abnormalities, unnatural thoughts—

But pardon me; I do not in position
265   Distinctly speak of her; though I may fear
Her will, recoiling to her better judgement,
May fall to match you with her country forms,
And happily repent.

OTHELLO
                    Farewell, farewell!
270   If more thou dost perceive, let me know more;
Set on thy wife to observe. Leave me, Iago.

IAGO
[*Going.*] My lord, I take my leave.

OTHELLO
Why did I marry? This honest creature doubtless
Sees and knows more, much more, than he unfolds.

IAGO
275   [*Returning.*] My lord, I would I might entreat your honor
To scan this thing no farther; leave it to time.
Although 'tis fit that Cassio have his place,
For, sure, he fills it up with great ability,
Yet, if you please to hold him off a while,
280   You shall by that perceive him and his means.
Note if your lady strain his entertainment
With any strong or vehement importunity;
Much will be seen in that. In the mean time,
Let me be thought too busy in my fears—
285   As worthy cause I have to fear I am—
And hold her free, I do beseech your honour.

OTHELLO
Fear not my government.

IAGO
I once more take my leave.
       [*Exit.*]

OTHELLO
This fellow 's of exceeding honesty,
290   And knows all qualities, with a learn'd spirit,

But pardon me—in delivering this argument, I don't
265   specifically speak about her; although I'm afraid
that her desires, overwhelming her better judgment,
might bring her to compare you to men of her own race
and perhaps lead her to reject you.

OTHELLO
Goodbye, goodbye!
270   If you see anything else, let me know.
Tell your wife to keep her eyes open too. Leave me alone, Iago.

IAGO *(Walking away from him)*
My lord, I'll take my leave.

OTHELLO
Why did I get married? This honest man doubtless
has seen and knows more, much more, than he's told me.

IAGO *(Returning)*
275   My lord, I would really like to beg your honor
to think no more about this business. Give it time.
Though it's right that Cassio should have his position back,
for he certainly does his job well,
still, if you'll only make him wait awhile,
280   you'll get a chance to watch him and see how he goes about
      appealing to you.
Watch if your lady pushes for his reappointment
too strongly or too vehemently.
You'll be able to tell much by that. In the meantime,
just assume that my fears are groundless
285   (as I have good cause to think they are)
and consider her innocent, I beg you, your honor.

OTHELLO
Don't worry about my self-control.

IAGO
Once again, I'll take my leave.
      Exit IAGO.

OTHELLO
This fellow's exceptionally honest
290   and knows all types of people, as well as having a keen eye

Of human dealings. If I do prove her haggard,
Though that her jesses were my dear heartstrings,
I'd whistle her off and let her down the wind
To prey at fortune. Haply, for I am black
295 And have not those soft parts of conversation
That chamberers have, or for I am declin'd
Into the vale of years,—yet that's not much—
She's gone. I am abus'd; and my relief
Must be to loathe her. O curse of marriage,
300 That we can call these delicate creatures ours.
And not their appetites! I had rather be a toad
And live upon the vapour of a dungeon
Than keep a corner in the thing I love
For others' uses. Yet, 'tis the plague of great ones;
305 Prerogativ'd are they less than the base.
'Tis destiny unshunnable, like death.
Even then this forked plague is fated to us
When we do quicken. Look where she comes,
          Re-enter DESDEMONA *and* EMILIA.
If she be false, O, then heaven mocks itself!
310 I'll not believe 't.

DESDEMONA
                    How now, my dear Othello!
Your dinner, and the generous islanders
By you invited, do attend your presence.

OTHELLO
I am to blame.

DESDEMONA
315   Why do you speak so faintly?
Are you not well?

OTHELLO
I have a pain upon my forehead here.

DESDEMONA
Why, that's with watching; 'twill away again.
Let me but bind it hard, within this hour
320 It will be well.

---

291 *haggard* Othello uses falconry terminology in this speech. A haggard is an untamed hawk. The word also means "unchaste."   292 *jesses* straps of leather which held a falcon to a leash.   293 *whistle her off* send her away; a whistle was a falconer's signal for a bird to take wing.   293 *down the wind* a hawk was usually flown against the wind.

for human behavior. If I find out she's unfaithful,
even if she was tethered to me by my own dear heartstrings,
I'd pack her off and let her fend her own way
against fortune. Possibly because I'm black
295   and don't have that gentle way of behaving
which gallants have, or because I'm getting along
in years (though still not very old),
she's betrayed me. I've been wronged, and my only comfort
will be to hate her. Oh, what a curse of marriage
300   that we can call these delicate creatures our own
and not control their longings! I'd rather be a toad
and live in some damp dungeon
than let a part of something I loved
be used by others. Yet this is the curse of those in high positions;
305   they're less likely to be free of it than the low born.
It's an inescapable destiny, like death:
we're doomed to wear the horns of the cuckold
from the moment we're born. Desdemona is coming.
        Enter DESDEMONA *and* EMILIA.
If she's unfaithful, oh, then heaven has given itself an insult!
310   I won't believe it.

DESDEMONA
    How are you, my dear Othello?
    Your dinner and the noble islanders
    you've invited are waiting for you to come.

OTHELLO
    I am to blame.

DESDEMONA
315   Why are you speaking so softly?
    Aren't you well?

OTHELLO
    I have a pain in my forehead, here.

DESDEMONA
    Well, that's from staying up too long; it will go away.
    I'll bind it up, and in less than an hour,
320   it will be just fine.

To fly down the wind was a phrase that indicated someone was facing formidable odds.
307 *forked plague*   a reference to the tradition that cuckolds supposedly had horns.
317 *I have a pain . . . here*   Othello is pointing to the place on his head where his cuckold's "horns" would be.

OTHELLO
Your napkin is too little; [*He puts the handkerchief from him; and it drops.*]
Let it alone. Come, I'll go in with you.

DESDEMONA
I am very sorry that you are not well.
[*Exeunt Othello and Desdemona.*]

EMILIA
I am glad I have found this napkin;
325   This was her first remembrance from the Moor.
My wayward husband hath a hundred times
Woo'd me to steal it; but she so loves the token,
For he conjur'd her she should ever keep it,
That she reserves it evermore about her
330   To kiss and talk to. I'll have the work ta'en out
And give 't Iago. What he will do with it
Heaven knows, not I;
I nothing but to please his fantasy.
Re-enter IAGO.

IAGO
How now! what do you here alone?

EMILIA
335   Do not you chide; I have a thing for you.

IAGO
A thing for me? It is a common thing—

EMILIA
Ha!

IAGO
To have a foolish wife.

EMILIA
O, is that all? What will you give me now
340   For that same handkerchief?

IAGO
                    What handkerchief?

OTHELLO
>Your handkerchief isn't large enough.
>*(He pushes it away and it falls to the ground.)*
>Don't bother with it. Come along, I'll go with you.

DESDEMONA
>I'm very sorry you're not feeling well.
>>*Exit* OTHELLO *and* DESDEMONA.

EMILIA *(Picking up the handkerchief)*
>I'm glad I've found this handkerchief.
325   This was her first gift from the Moor.
>My willful husband has asked me a hundred times
>to steal it. But she loves it so much
>(since Othello made her promise she would always keep it)
>that she keeps it with her all the time
330   to kiss and talk to. I'll have the embroidery copied
>and give it to Iago.
>What he'll do with it, heaven knows; I don't.
>I want nothing but to please his whims.
>>*Enter* IAGO.

IAGO
>What is this? What are you doing here alone?

EMILIA
335   Don't scold me; I've got something for you.

IAGO
>Something for me? It's an ordinary something—

EMILIA
>What?

IAGO
>To have a foolish wife.

EMILIA
>Oh, is that all? What would you give me
340   for that handkerchief?

IAGO
>What handkerchief?

EMILIA

What handkerchief!

Why, that the Moor first gave to Desdemona;

That which so often you did bid me steal.

IAGO

345   Hast stol'n it from her?

EMILIA

No, faith; she let it drop by negligence,

And, to th' advantage, I, being here, took 't up.

Look, here it is.

IAGO

A good wench; give it me.

EMILIA

350   What will you do with 't, that you have been so earnest

To have me filch it?

IAGO

[*Snatching it.*] Why, what is that to you?

EMILIA

If it be not for some purpose of import,

Give 't me again. Poor lady, she'll run mad

355   When she shall lack it.

IAGO

Be not acknown on't; I have use for it.

Go, leave me.

[*Exit Emilia.*]

I will in Cassio's lodging lose this napkin,

And let him find it. Trifles light as air

360   Are to the jealous confirmations strong

As proofs of holy writ; this may do something.

The Moor already changes with my poison.

Dangerous conceits are, in their natures poisons,

Which at the first are scarce found to distaste,

365   But with a little act upon the blood

Burn like the mines of sulphur. I did say so.

Re-enter OTHELLO.

EMILIA
>What handkerchief?
>Why, the one the Moor gave to Desdemona;
>the one you've asked me to steal so often.

IAGO
345   Have you stolen it from her?

EMILIA
>Certainly not; she dropped it by accident,
>and I was lucky enough to be on hand to pick it up.
>Look, here it is.

IAGO
>Good girl! Give it to me.

EMILIA
350   What do you want to do with it after insisting all this time
>that I steal it?

IAGO *(Snatching it away from her)*
>Why, what's it to you?

EMILIA
>If it's not for anything important,
>give it back to me. The poor lady; she'll go crazy
355   when she finds out she's lost it.

IAGO
>Don't let on that you know anything; I have use for it.
>Go on, leave me alone.
>>*Exit* EMILIA.
>I'll put this handkerchief in Cassio's lodging
>and let him find it. Little things like this
360   are as convincing to those of a jealous nature
>as the Holy Scriptures themselves. This might have an effect.
>The Moor already shows some change, due to my poisonous
>>influence.
>Dangerous ideas are poisonous by nature;
>at first they do not even taste bad,
365   but in a short time, they get into the blood
>and burn like sulfur mines. I said as much.
>>*Enter* OTHELLO.

Look, where he comes! Not poppy, nor mandragora,
Nor all the drowsy syrups of the world
Shall ever medicine thee to that sweet sleep
370   Which thou ow'dst yesterday.

OTHELLO

Ha! ha! false to me?

IAGO

Why, how now, General! no more of that.

OTHELLO

Avaunt! be gone! thou hast set me on the rack.
I swear 'tis better to be much abus'd
375   Than but to know 't a little.

IAGO

How now, my lord!

OTHELLO

What sense had I of her stol'n hours of lust?
I saw 't not, thought it not, it harm'd not me.
I slept the next night well, fed well, was free and merry;
380   I found not Cassio's kisses on her lips.
He that is robb'd, not wanting what is stolen,
Let him not know 't, and he's not robb'd at all.

IAGO

I am sorry to hear this.

OTHELLO

I had been happy, if the general camp,
385   Pioners and all, had tasted her sweet body,
So I had nothing known. O, now, for ever
Farewell the tranquil mind! farewell content!
Farewell the plumed troops and the big wars
That make ambition virtue! O, farewell!
390   Farewell the neighing steed and the shrill trump,
The spirit-stirring drum, th' ear-piercing fife,
The royal banner, and all quality,
Pride, pomp, and circumstance of glorious war!
And, O you mortal engines, whose rude throats

---

367 *poppy nor mandragora* extracts from these plants were used to induce sleep.
373 *rack* a torture device that painfully stretched a victim's body.   385 *Pioners* the lowest
rank of soldiers; they dug trenches and laid mines.

Look at him coming! Neither poppies nor herbs
nor all the sleeping potions in the world
will ever restore you to that sweet sleep
370   which you knew only yesterday.

OTHELLO
What! What! Unfaithful to me!

IAGO
Why, what is it, general? No more of that kind of talk!

OTHELLO
Away! Be gone! You have put me on the rack.
I swear, it's better to be greatly wronged
375   than to know anything about it.

IAGO
What do you mean, my lord?

OTHELLO
What did I know about her secret hours of lust?
I didn't see it, didn't suspect it, and wasn't hurt by it.
I slept well that night and was free and happy;
380   I didn't know that Cassio had been kissing her.
If a man's been robbed and has no need of what's been stolen,
he shouldn't be told; then he's not really robbed at all.

IAGO
I'm sorry to hear this.

OTHELLO
I'd have been happy if the whole army,
385   foot soldiers and everyone, had made love to her,
as long as I didn't know. Oh, now I must say
farewell to peace of mind forever! Farewell to contentment!
Farewell to the glorious troops and the great wars
that make ambition into a virtue! Oh, farewell!
390   Farewell to the neighing horse and the shrill trumpet,
to the spirit-stirring drum, and the ear-shattering fife,
the royal banner, and all the good men,
pride, pomp, and pageantry of glorious war!
And, oh, you deadly cannons whose horrible voices

395 Th' immortal Jove's dread clamours counterfeit,
Farewell! Othello's occupation 's gone!

IAGO
Is 't possible, my lord?

OTHELLO
Villain, be sure thou prove my love a whore;
Be sure of it. Give me the ocular proof;
400 Or, by the worth of mine eternal soul,
Thou hadst been better have been born a dog
Than answer my wak'd wrath!

IAGO
                    Is 't come to this?

OTHELLO
Make me to see 't; or, at the least, so prove it
405 That the probation bear no hinge nor loop
To hang a doubt on; or woe upon thy life!

IAGO
My noble lord,—

OTHELLO
If thou dost slander her and torture me,
Never pray more; abandon all remorse;
410 On horror's head horrors accumulate;
Do deeds to make heaven weep, all earth amaz'd;
For nothing canst thou to damnation add
Greater than that.

IAGO
                    O grace! O Heaven forgive me!
415 Are you a man? Have you a soul or sense?
God buy you; take mine office. O wretched fool,
That lov'st to make thine honesty a vice!
O monstrous world! Take note, take note, O world,
To be direct and honest is not safe.
420 I thank you for this profit; and from hence
I'll love no friend, sith love breeds such offence.

395   imitate the thunderclaps of the god Jove,
             farewell! Othello's occupation is gone!

IAGO
    Can this be possible, my lord?

OTHELLO
    Villain, you'd better be sure you prove my love's a whore!
    Be sure of it; give me visible proof;
400   or, by the value of a man's eternal soul,
    you would have been better off to have been born a dog
    than to face my roused wrath!

IAGO
    Has it come to this?

OTHELLO
    Make me see it; or at least prove it so well
405   that there's no hinge or loop in the proof
    to hang a doubt on—or woe upon your life!

IAGO
    My noble lord—

OTHELLO
    If you're slandering her and torturing me,
    never pray again; stop feeling remorse;
410   heap new horrors on top of horrors;
    do deeds that will make heaven weep, and shock the world into
        speechlessness;
    for you can't add anything to your own damnation
    greater than that.

IAGO
    Oh, God! Oh, heaven forgive me!
415   Are you a man? Have you a soul or reason?
    May God be with you! You do my duty. What a fool I am,
    who has lived to see his honesty become a vice!
    Oh, monstrous world! Take note, take note, world:
    to be truthful and honest is not safe.
420   I thank you for teaching me this lesson; and from now on,
    I'll love no friend, since love causes such offense.

OTHELLO

Nay, stay. Thou shouldst be honest.

IAGO

I should be wise, for honesty 's a fool
And loses that it works for.

OTHELLO

425   By the world,
I think my wife be honest and think she is not;
I think that thou art just and think thou art not.
I'll have some proof. Her name, that was as fresh
As Dian's visage, is now begrim'd and black
430 As mine own face. If there be cords, or knives,
Poison, or fire, or suffocating streams,
I'll not endure it. Would I were satisfied!

IAGO

I see, sir, you are eaten up with passion;
I do repent me that I put it to you.
435 You would be satisfied?

OTHELLO

      Would! nay, I will.

IAGO

And may; but, how? How satisfied, my lord?
Would you, the supervisor, grossly gape on—
Behold her topp'd?

OTHELLO

440   Death and damnation! O!

IAGO

It were a tedious difficulty, I think,
To bring them to that prospect; damn them then,
If ever mortal eyes do see them bolster
More than their own! What then? How then?
445 What shall I say? Where's satisfaction?
It is impossible you should see this,
Were they as prime as goats, as hot as monkeys,
As salt as wolves in pride, and fools as gross

---

424 *loses that it works for* Iago means honesty does not gain the trust it deserves.
429 *Dian's visage* refers to the Greek goddess of chastity and hunting.

OTHELLO
No, stay. You should be honest.

IAGO
I should be wise; honest men are fools
and lose what they try to gain.

OTHELLO
425   By all the world,
I believe my wife to be honest, and I believe that she is not;
I believe that you are truthful, and believe that you are not.
I must have some proof. Her name used to be as clean
as Diana's face, but is now as grimy and black
430   as my own face. As long as there are ropes, knives,
poison, fires, or rivers where I can drown myself,
I won't suffer this. I wish I were certain!

IAGO
I see, sir, that you are eaten up by your emotions.
I'm very sorry that I brought this on.
435   Do you really want to be certain?

OTHELLO
Want to be? No, I will be.

IAGO
And you might be. But how? How will you be certain, my lord?
Do you want to be an onlooker, grossly staring at it all?
Do you want to see her in the act?

OTHELLO
440   Death and damnation! Oh!

IAGO
I think it would be very difficult
to get them to do it where they can be seen. Damn them, then,
if mortal eyes ever do see them go to bed
other than their own! So how? How then?
445   What's there to say? How will you be satisfied?
It's impossible that you would see it happen,
even if they were as ready as goats, as hot as monkeys,
as lustful as wolves in heat, and as stupidly foolish

As ignorance made drunk. But yet, I say,
450 If imputation and strong circumstances
Which lead directly to the door of truth
Will give you satisfaction, you might have't.

OTHELLO
Give me a living reason she's disloyal.

IAGO
I do not like the office;
455 But, sith I am ent'red in this cause so far,
Prick'd to't by foolish honesty and love,
I will go on. I lay with Cassio lately;
And, being troubled with a raging tooth,
I could not sleep.
460 There are a kind of men so loose of soul,
That in their sleeps will mutter their affairs;
One of this kind is Cassio.
In sleep I heard him say, "Sweet Desdemona,
Let us be wary, let us hide our loves;"
465 And then, sir, would he gripe and wring my hand,
Cry, "O sweet creature!" then kiss me hard,
As if he pluck'd up kisses by the roots
That grew upon my lips; then lay his leg
Over my thigh, and sigh, and kiss; and then
470 Cry, "Cursed fate that gave thee to the Moor!"

OTHELLO
O monstrous! monstrous!

IAGO
Nay, this was but his dream.

OTHELLO
But this denoted a foregone conclusion.
'Tis a shrewd doubt, though it be but a dream.

IAGO
475 And this may help to thicken other proofs
That do demonstrate thinly.

450

as if they were drunk. But still, let me tell you,
if accusation and the strongest circumstantial evidence
which point straight to the truth of the matter
will satisfy you, you may have that.

OTHELLO
Give me absolute proof that she's unfaithful.

IAGO

455

460

465

470

I don't like being put in this position.
But since I'm so deep into this business already,
driven on by my foolish honesty and love,
I'll continue. I was lying next to Cassio recently,
and since I had a terrible toothache,
I couldn't sleep.
There's a certain kind of man of so loose a soul
that he'll talk about his private business in his sleep.
Cassio is this kind of man.
In his sleep, I heard him say, "Sweet Desdemona,
let's be careful, let's hide our love!"
And then, sir, he'd grip and wring my hand,
cry "Oh, sweet creature!" and then kiss me hard,
as if he were pulling up kisses by the roots
which grew on my lips. Then he laid his leg
over my thigh and sighed and kissed me, and then
cried "Curse the fate that gave you to the Moor!"

OTHELLO
Oh, monstrous! Monstrous!

IAGO
Still, this only happened in his dream.

OTHELLO
But it told of something which had already actually occurred.
It's very suspicious, even though it was only a dream.

IAGO

475

And we might use this to strengthen other evidence
of a flimsier nature.

OTHELLO

                    I'll tear her all to pieces.

IAGO

Nay, but be wise; yet we see nothing done.
She may be honest yet. Tell me but this,
480   Have you not sometimes seen a handkerchief
Spotted with strawberries in your wife's hand?

OTHELLO

I gave her such a one; 'twas my first gift.

IAGO

I know not that; but such a handkerchief—
I am sure it was your wife's—did I to-day
485   See Cassio wipe his beard with.

OTHELLO

                   If it be that,—

IAGO

If it be that, or any that was hers,
It speaks against her with the other proofs.

OTHELLO

O, that the slave had forty thousand lives!
490   One is too poor, too weak for my revenge.
Now do I see 'tis true. Look here, Iago;
All my fond love thus do I blow to heaven.
'Tis gone.
Arise, black vengeance, from the hollow hell!
495   Yield up, O love, thy crown and hearted throne
To tyrannous hate! Swell, bosom, with thy fraught,
For 'tis of aspics' tongues!

IAGO

                 Yet be content.

OTHELLO

O, blood, blood, blood!

IAGO

500   Patience, I say; your mind perhaps may change.

OTHELLO
> I'll tear her all to pieces!

IAGO
> No, be sensible. We haven't seen anything done;
> she still might be faithful. Just tell me this—
480 > haven't you sometimes seen a handkerchief
> decorated with strawberries in your wife's hand?

OTHELLO
> I gave her one like that; it was my first gift to her.

IAGO
> I didn't know that; but I saw a handkerchief like that
> (and I'm sure it was your wife's) just today;
485 > Cassio wiped his beard with it.

OTHELLO
> If it's the same one—

IAGO
> If it's the same one, or any one that belongs to her,
> it speaks against her, along with the other evidence.

OTHELLO
> Oh, I wish the wretch had forty thousand lives!
490 > One is too little, too small to satisfy my revenge.
> Now I see that it's true. Look here, Iago:
> all my dear love for her I send straight to heaven.
> It's gone.
> Black vengeance, arise out of the depths of hell!
495 > Oh, love, give up your crown and your throne in my heart
> to tyrannous hatred! Breast, swell up with your burden;
> it's filled with the poison of vipers.

IAGO
> Still, calm yourself.

OTHELLO
> Oh, blood, blood, blood!

IAGO
500 > Be patient, I tell you. You might change your mind.

OTHELLO
    Never, Iago. Like to the Pontic Sea,
    Whose icy current and compulsive course
    Ne'er feels retiring ebb, but keeps due on
    To the Propontic and the Hellespont,
505   Even so my bloody thoughts, with violent pace,
    Shall ne'er look back, ne'er ebb to humble love,
    Till that a capable and wide revenge
    Swallow them up. Now, by yond marble heaven,
    In the due reverence of a sacred vow [*Kneels.*]
510   I here engage my words.

IAGO
               Do not rise yet.
    Witness, you ever-burning lights above,
    You elements that clip us round about, [*Kneels.*]
    Witness that here Iago doth give up
515   The execution of his wit, hands, heart,
    To wrong'd Othello's service! Let him command,
    And to obey shall be in me remorse,
    What bloody business ever. [*They rise.*]

OTHELLO
               I greet thy love,
520   Not with vain thanks, but with acceptance bounteous,
    And will upon the instant put thee to't:
    Within these three days let me hear thee say
    That Cassio's not alive.

IAGO
    My friend is dead; 'tis done at your request.
525   But let her live.

OTHELLO
    Damn her, lewd minx! O, damn her! damn her!
    Come, go with me apart; I will withdraw
    To furnish me with some swift means of death
    For the fair devil. Now art thou my lieutenant.

IAGO
530   I am your own for ever.
        [*Exeunt.*]

OTHELLO
     Never, Iago. Just like the Black Sea's
     icy current and relentless course,
     which never ebbs but keeps moving on
     toward the Sea of Marmora and the Bosporus,
505 that's what my bloody thoughts are, moving violently
     and never looking back, never ebbing to love's gentleness
     until complete and far-reaching revenge
     swallows them up. Now, by the cloud-streaked heavens,
     I sacredly and reverently promise *(He kneels.)*
510 to make good my words.

IAGO
     Do not rise yet.
     Be witness, you ever-burning stars in the sky,
     and you elements that embrace us, *(He kneels.)*
     be witness that Iago is now dedicating
515 the use of his intelligence, hands, and heart
     to the wronged Othello's service! Let him command me,
     and I'll obey out of pity,
     no matter how bloody the deed may be.
          (They rise.)

OTHELLO
     I'll match your love,
520 not with useless thanks, but with complete acceptance,
     and I'll put you to work at it immediately.
     Before three days are up, come to me and say
     that Cassio's no longer alive.

IAGO
     My friend is as good as dead; it's done at your request.
525 But let her live.

OTHELLO
     Damn her, the lewd minx! Oh, damn her!
     Come, step aside with me. I will leave
     so I can think up some quick means to kill
     that lovely devil. You are my lieutenant now.

IAGO
530 I'm your servant forever.
          They exit.

Scene iv: [*Before the castle.*] *Enter* DESDEMONA, EMILIA, *and* CLOWN.

DESDEMONA
Do you know, sirrah, where Lieutenant Cassio lies?

CLOWN
I dare not say he lies anywhere.

DESDEMONA
Why, man?

CLOWN
He's a soldier, and for me to say a soldier lies, 'tis stabbing.

DESDEMONA
5   Go to! Where lodges he?

CLOWN
To tell you where he lodges, is to tell you where I lie.

DESDEMONA
Can anything be made of this?

CLOWN
I know not where he lodges, and for me to devise a lodging and say he lies here or he lies there, were to lie in mine own throat.

DESDEMONA
10   Can you inquire him out, and be edified by report?

CLOWN
I will catechize the world for him; that is, make questions, and by them answer.

DESDEMONA
Seek him, bid him come hither. Tell him I have mov'd my lord on his behalf, and hope all will be well.

CLOWN
15   To do this is within the compass of man's wit; and therefore I will attempt the doing it.
        [*Exit.*]

DESDEMONA
Where should I lose the handkerchief, Emilia?

---

1 *lies* lodges.   10 *can . . . report?* Desdemona is mimicking the clown's overly formal language.

Act III, Scene iv: In front of the castle. Enter DESDEMONA,
EMILIA, *and* CLOWN.

DESDEMONA
Do you know, fellow, where Lieutenant Cassio lies?

CLOWN
I don't dare say he lies anywhere.

DESDEMONA
Why, man?

CLOWN
He's a soldier; and to say a soldier lies could get me stabbed.

DESDEMONA
5   Don't talk nonsense! Where is he staying?

CLOWN
To tell you where he's staying would be to tell you where I lie.

DESDEMONA
What's that supposed to mean?

CLOWN
I don't know where he's staying; and for me to make up an address
and say he lies here or lies there, I'd be lying for sure.

DESDEMONA
10   Can you enquire around for him, and be instructed by report?

CLOWN
I'll interrogate the world to find him; that is, I'll make up
questions and
come back with answers.

DESDEMONA
Find him, and tell him to come here. Tell him I've persuaded
my lord
on his behalf and have reason to hope that all will be well.

CLOWN
15   It's within the range of human intelligence to do that, so I'll
give it a try.
      Exit CLOWN.

DESDEMONA
Where could I have lost that handkerchief, Emilia?

EMILIA
I know not, madam.

DESDEMONA
Believe me, I had rather have lost my purse
20   Full of crusadoes; and, but my noble Moor
Is true of mind and made of no such baseness
As jealous creatures are, it were enough
To put him to ill thinking.

EMILIA
                    Is he not jealous?

DESDEMONA
25   Who, he? I think the sun where he was born
Drew all such humours from him.

EMILIA
                    Look, where he comes.
        Enter OTHELLO.

DESDEMONA
I will not leave him now till Cassio
Be call'd to him.—How is't with you, my lord?

OTHELLO
30   Well, my good lady. [*Aside.*] O, hardness to dissemble!—
How do you, Desdemona?

DESDEMONA
                    Well, my good lord.

OTHELLO
Give me your hand. This hand is moist, my lady.

DESDEMONA
It yet hath felt no age nor known no sorrow.

OTHELLO
35   This argues fruitfulness and liberal heart;
Hot, hot, and moist. This hand of yours requires
A sequester from liberty, fasting and prayer,
Much castigation, exercise devout;
For here's a young and sweating devil here

---

20 *crusadoes*   are Portuguese gold coins.   **33** *moist*   a moist, warm hand was supposed to indicate lustfulness.

EMILIA
    I don't know, madam.

DESDEMONA
    Believe me, I'd rather have lost my purse
20   full of gold coins. If my noble Moor
    were not sensible and were made of the same bad stuff
    as jealous creatures are, this would be enough
    to put evil thoughts in his head.

EMILIA
    Isn't he jealous?

DESDEMONA
25   Who? Him? I think the sun where he was born
    dried all such tendencies out of him.

EMILIA
    Look, he's coming.
          Enter OTHELLO.

DESDEMONA
    I won't leave him until Cassio
    is summoned. *(To Othello)* How are you, my lord?

OTHELLO
30   Well, my good lady. *(To himself)* Oh, how hard it is to pretend!—
    How are you doing, Desdemona?

DESDEMONA
    Well, my good lord.

OTHELLO
    Give me your hand. Your hand is moist, my lady.

DESDEMONA
    It hasn't yet felt age or known sorrow.

OTHELLO
35   This suggests fruitfulness and a generous heart.
    Hot; hot and moist. This hand of yours requires
    a separation from the world, fasting and praying,
    mortification of spirit and devout duties;
    because I see a young, sweating devil here

40   That commonly rebels. 'Tis a good hand,
           A frank one.

DESDEMONA
                   You may, indeed, say so;
           For 'twas that hand that gave away my heart.

OTHELLO
           A liberal hand. The hearts of old gave hands;
45   But our new heraldry is hands, not hearts.

DESDEMONA
           I cannot speak of this. Come now, your promise.

OTHELLO
           What promise, chuck?

DESDEMONA
           I have sent to bid Cassio come speak with you.

OTHELLO
           I have a salt and sorry rheum offends me;
50   Lend me thy handkerchief.

DESDEMONA
                           Here, my lord.

OTHELLO
           That which I gave you.

DESDEMONA
                           I have it not about me.

OTHELLO
           Not?

DESDEMONA
55   No, indeed, my lord.

OTHELLO
           That's a fault. That handkerchief
           Did an Egyptian to my mother give;
           She was a charmer, and could almost read
           The thoughts of people. She told her, while she kept it
60   'Twould make her amiable and subdue my father
           Entirely to her love, but if she lost it,

---

44 *liberal*   on the surface, Othello means Desdemona is generous. However, he also is suggesting that Desdemona is too free with her favors; i.e., immoral. Othello uses double meanings throughout the speech to hint at Desdemona's infidelity, though she is unaware of his insinuations.

40   who often rebels. This is a good hand,
      a frank one.

DESDEMONA
      You have good reason to say so;
      this was the hand that gave away my heart.

OTHELLO
      A generous hand! In the past, hearts gave away hands.
45   But the new custom is to give the hands, not necessarily the hearts.

DESDEMONA
      I don't know anything about this. Come, now, your promise!

OTHELLO
      What promise do you mean, dear?

DESDEMONA
      I have sent for Cassio to come and speak to you.

OTHELLO
      I have a terrible head cold bothering me.
50   Lend me your handkerchief.

DESDEMONA
      Here it is, my lord.

OTHELLO
      I mean the one I gave you.

DESDEMONA
      I don't have it with me.

OTHELLO
      You don't?

DESDEMONA
55   I really don't, my lord.

OTHELLO
      That's wrong of you. That handkerchief
      was given to my mother by a gypsy.
      She was a magician and could almost
      read people's thoughts. She told her that, as long as she kept it,
60   it would make her desirable and cause my father
      to love her completely. But if she lost it

Or made a gift of it, my father's eye
Should hold her loathed and his spirits should hunt
After new fancies. She, dying, gave it me
65   And bid me, when my fate would have me wiv'd,
To give it her. I did so; and take heed on't;
Make it a darling like your precious eye.
To lose't or give't away were such perdition
As nothing else could match.

DESDEMONA
70   Is't possible?

OTHELLO
'Tis true; there's magic in the web of it.
A sibyl, that had numb'red in the world
The sun to course two hundred compasses,
In her prophetic fury sew'd the work;
75   The worms were hallowed that did breed the silk;
And it was dy'd in mummy which the skilful
Conserv'd of maidens' hearts.

DESDEMONA
                    Indeed! is't true?

OTHELLO
Most veritable; therefore look to't well.

DESDEMONA
80   Then would to God that I had never seen 't!

OTHELLO
Ha! wherefore?

DESDEMONA
Why do you speak so startingly and rash?

OTHELLO
Is't lost? Is't gone? Speak, is't out o' th' way?

DESDEMONA
Heaven bless us!

OTHELLO
85   Say you?

---

76 *mummy*   or fluids from embalmed corpses, which were supposed to have magical powers.

or gave it as a gift, my father's eyes
would find her loathsome, and he'd begin
to seek out other women. She gave it to me when she was dying,
65   and asked me, when it came time for me to marry,
to give it to my wife. I did so; so remember what I said—
consider it as precious to you as your own eye.
If you were to lose it or give it away, that would be a loss
that you could never make up.

DESDEMONA
70   Is it possible?

OTHELLO
It's true. There's magic in the weaving of it.
A prophetess who had lived
two hundred years
sewed this handkerchief while she was possessed and able to
    prophesy.
75   The silk came from sacred worms,
and it was dyed in a liquid skillfully drained
and preserved from maidens' hearts.

DESDEMONA
Really? Is that true?

OTHELLO
Very true. So take good care of it.

DESDEMONA
80   Then I wish to God I'd never seen it!

OTHELLO
What? Why is that?

DESDEMONA
Why are you speaking so angrily and abruptly?

OTHELLO
Have you lost it? Is it gone? Tell me, have you left it somewhere?

DESDEMONA
Heaven help us!

OTHELLO
85   What did you say?

DESDEMONA
It is not lost; but what an if it were?

OTHELLO
How?

DESDEMONA
I say, it is not lost.

OTHELLO
                    Fetch 't, let me see 't.

DESDEMONA
90   Why, so I can, sir, but I will not now.
      This is a trick to put me from my suit.
      Pray you, let Cassio be receiv'd again.

OTHELLO
Fetch me the handkerchief; my mind misgives.

DESDEMONA
Come, come;
95   You'll never meet a more sufficient man.

OTHELLO
The handkerchief!

DESDEMONA
                    I pray, talk me of Cassio.

OTHELLO
The handkerchief!

DESDEMONA
                    A man that all his time
100   Hath founded his good fortunes on your love,
      Shar'd dangers with you,—

OTHELLO
The handkerchief!

DESDEMONA
In sooth, you are to blame.

OTHELLO
'Zounds!
      [*Exit.*]

DESDEMONA
It hasn't been lost. But what if it had been?

OTHELLO
What?

DESDEMONA
I tell you, it's not lost.

OTHELLO
Go get it; let me see it!

DESDEMONA
90 Well, I can do that, sir, but I won't right now.
This is just a trick to distract me from my appeal.
Please, reinstate Cassio.

OTHELLO
Get me the handkerchief! I'm very mistrustful.

DESDEMONA
Come, come!
95 You'll never meet a more capable man.

OTHELLO
The handkerchief!

DESDEMONA
Please, let's talk about Cassio.

OTHELLO
The handkerchief!

DESDEMONA
A man who, all his life,
100 has depended on your love for everything he has,
shared dangers with you—

OTHELLO
The handkerchief!

DESDEMONA
Really, you have no reason to act like this.

OTHELLO
Get away from me!
        Exit OTHELLO.

EMILIA

105   Is not this man jealous?

DESDEMONA

I ne'er saw this before.
Sure, there's some wonder in this handkerchief;
I am most unhappy in the loss of it.

EMILIA

'Tis not a year or two shows us a man.
110   They are all but stomachs, and we all but food;
They eat us hungerly, and when they are full
They belch us.
Enter CASSIO *and* IAGO.
Look you, Cassio and my husband!

IAGO

There is no other way, 'tis she must do't;
115   And, lo, the happiness! Go, and importune her.

DESDEMONA

How now, good Cassio! What's the news with you?

CASSIO

Madam, my former suit. I do beseech you
That by your virtuous means I may again
Exist, and be a member of his love
120   Whom I with all the office of my heart
Entirely honour. I would not be delay'd.
If my offence be of such mortal kind
That nor my service past, nor present sorrows,
Nor purpos'd merit in futurity
125   Can ransom me into his love again,
But to know so must be my benefit;
So shall I clothe me in a forc'd content,
And shut myself up in some other course,
To fortune's alms.

DESDEMONA

130   Alas, thrice-gentle Cassio!
My advocation is not now in tune.
My lord is not my lord; nor should I know him

EMILIA
105   And this man isn't jealous?

DESDEMONA
     I've never seen this side of him.
     There must be something magical about this handkerchief.
     I'm very unlucky to have lost it.

EMILIA
     It doesn't take a year or two to find out what a man's like.
110   They are only stomachs, and we are only food.
     They eat us hungrily, and when they are full,
     they belch us.
          Enter IAGO *and* CASSIO.
     Look, Cassio and my husband!

IAGO
     There is no other way; she must be the one to do it.
115   And then you'll be happy! Go to her and ask her.

DESDEMONA
     How are you, good Cassio? What's new with you?

CASSIO
     Madam, the same appeal as before. I beg you
     that, with your good help, I might
     exist again and be one of those loved
120   by a man whom, with all my heart,
     I deeply honor. I don't want to wait.
     If my offense is of such a serious nature
     that neither my past service nor my present sorrow
     nor my promises of worthy behavior in the future
125   can restore me to his love again,
     it would at least help me to know it.
     Then I can resign myself to the situation
     and accept whatever kind of life
     fortune has in mind for me.

DESDEMONA
130   Oh, gentle Cassio!
     My pleading won't help at the moment.
     My lord is not himself; and I wouldn't recognize him

Were he in favour as in humour alter'd.
So help me every spirit sanctified
135   As I have spoken for you all my best
And stood within the blank of his displeasure
For my free speech! You must a while be patient.
What I can do I will; and more I will
Than for myself I dare. Let that suffice you.

IAGO
140   Is my lord angry?

EMILIA
                              He went hence but now,
And certainly in strange unquietness.

IAGO
Can he be angry? I have seen the cannon
When it hath blown his ranks into the air,
145   And, like the devil, from his very arm
Puff'd his own brother:—and is he angry?
Something of moment then. I will go meet him.
There's matter in't indeed, if he be angry.
                    [*Exit Iago.*]

DESDEMONA
I pritheee, do so. Something, sure, of state,
150   Either from Venice, or some unhatch'd practice
Made demonstrable here in Cyprus to him,
Hath puddled his clear spirit; and in such cases
Men's natures wrangle with inferior things,
Though great ones are their object. 'Tis even so;
155   For let our finger ache, and it indues
Our other, healthful members even to a sense
Of pain. Nay, we must think men are not gods,
Nor of them look for such observancy
As fits the bridal. Beshrew me much, Emilia,
160   I was, unhandsome warrior as I am,
Arraigning his unkindness with my soul;
But now I find I had suborn'd the witness,
And he's indicted falsely.

---

136 *blank*   the white bull's-eye of a target.

if he were as altered in looks as he is in mood.
I swear by every sacred spirit
135   that I've said everything I can for you
and found myself to be the target of his anger
because of what I frankly said! You must be patient awhile.
I'll do what I can; and I'll do more
than I'd dare to do for myself. Please be content with that.

IAGO
140   Is my lord angry?

EMILIA
He left just now,
certainly very strangely agitated.

IAGO
How can he be angry? I've seen him at times when cannons
have blown his troops sky high
145   and, like some devil, blasted his own brother
standing at his arm—so can he really be angry?
There's something seriously wrong, then. I'll go meet him.
There's something very urgent, indeed, if he is angry.
     Exit IAGO.

DESDEMONA
(Calling after him) Please, do so. Surely some business of state,
150   either in Venice, or some unexecuted plot
just now revealed here in Cyprus to him,
has muddied his clear mind. In such cases,
it's man's nature to become obsessed with little things,
though important things are really the problem. This is the truth.
155   If one of your fingers hurts, it causes
your other healthier fingers to feel
that pain as well. No, we mustn't think that men are gods,
nor expect the same kind of consideration from them
that one expects from a bride. Be the first to scold me, Emilia,
160   since I (unsportsmanlike warrior that I am!)
thought his judgment against me was unkind of him.
Now I realize that I misunderstood him,
and accused him unfairly.

EMILIA
Pray Heaven it be state-matters, as you think,
165　And no conception nor no jealous toy
Concerning you.

DESDEMONA
Alas the day! I never gave him cause.

EMILIA
But jealous souls will not be answer'd so;
They are not ever jealous for the cause,
170　But jealous for they're jealous. It is a monster
Begot upon itself, born on itself.

DESDEMONA
Heaven keep the monster from Othello's mind!

EMILIA
Lady, amen.

DESDEMONA
I will go seek him. Cassio, walk hereabout;
175　If I do find him fit, I'll move your suit
And seek to effect it to my uttermost.

CASSIO
I humbly thank your ladyship.
[*Exeunt Desdemona and Emilia.*]
Enter BIANCA.

BIANCA
Save you, friend Cassio!

CASSIO
What make you from home?
180　How is it with you, my most fair Bianca?
Indeed, sweet love, I was coming to your house.

BIANCA
And I was going to your lodging, Cassio.
What, keep a week away? seven days and nights?
Eightscore eight hours? and lovers' absent hours,
185　More tedious than the dial eightscore times?
O weary reck'ning!

EMILIA

165   Pray to heaven that it really is state business, as you think,
and no ideas or jealous whims
concerning you.

DESDEMONA

Heaven forbid! I never gave him cause.

EMILIA

But jealous minds won't take that for an answer.
They are never jealous for the apparent reason,
170   but they are really jealous because they are jealous. It's a
monster that creates more of itself and was born of itself.

DESDEMONA

May heaven keep that monster away from Othello's mind!

EMILIA

Amen to that, lady.

DESDEMONA

I'll go look for him. Cassio, stay near here.
175   If I find him receptive, I'll bring up your appeal
and try my best to win it for you.

CASSIO

I thank your ladyship very humbly.
        Exit DESDEMONA *and* EMILIA.
        Enter BIANCA.

BIANCA

God save you, my friend Cassio!

CASSIO

Why are you away from home?
180   How are things with you, my most lovely Bianca?
As a matter of fact, sweet love, I was just coming to your house.

BIANCA

And I was going to your lodging, Cassio.
Why have you been away for a week? For seven days and nights?
One hundred sixty-eight hours? When an hour in the absence of
    a lover
185   is more tedious than a hundred sixty days?
Oh, what tiring addition!

CASSIO
                    Pardon me, Bianca.
I have this while with leaden thoughts been press'd;
But I shall, in a more continuate time,
190   Strike off this score of absence. Sweet Bianca, [*Giving her
          Desdemona's handkerchief.*]
Take me this work out.

BIANCA
                    O Cassio, whence came this?
This is some token from a newer friend;
To the felt absence now I feel a cause.
195   Is't come to this? Well, well.

CASSIO
                    Go to, woman!
Throw your vile guesses in the devils' teeth,
From whence you have them. You are jealous now
That this is from some mistress, some remembrance.
200   No, in good troth, Bianca.

BIANCA
                    Why, whose is it?

CASSIO
I know not, sweet; I found it in my chamber.
I like the work well; ere it be demanded—
As like enough it will—I'd have it copied.
205   Take it, and do't; and leave me for this time.

BIANCA
Leave you! Wherefore?

CASSIO
I do attend here on the General;
And think it no addition, nor my wish,
To have him see me woman'd.

BIANCA
210   Why, I pray you?

CASSIO
Not that I love you not.

CASSIO
   Pardon me, Bianca.
   During this time, I've been weighed down by heavy thoughts;
   but, when things are better,
190   I'll make up for this period of absence. Sweet Bianca,
   (Gives her Desdemona's handkerchief.)
   copy this embroidery for me.

BIANCA
   Oh, Cassio, where did you get this?
   This is a gift from some new friend.
   Now I know the cause of your absence.
195   Has it come to this? Well, well.

CASSIO
   Go on, woman!
   Throw your wicked ideas back into the devil's teeth,
   where you got them in the first place. Now you're jealous
   that this is from some mistress of mine, that it's a remembrance.
200   No, honestly, Bianca.

BIANCA
   Well, whose is it?

CASSIO
   I don't know, sweetheart. I found it in my bedroom.
   I like the embroidery very much. Before it is reclaimed,
   which it probably will be, I'd like to have it copied.
205   Take it and do it, and leave me alone awhile.

BIANCA
   Leave you alone? Why?

CASSIO
   I'm waiting here for the general
   and don't think it would be to my credit, nor is it my wish,
   that he should see me with a woman.

BIANCA
210   Why, please tell me?

CASSIO
   It's not that I don't love you.

BIANCA
                        But that you do not love me.
    I pray you, bring me on the way a little,
    And say if I shall see you soon at night.

CASSIO
215 'Tis but a little way that I can bring you,
    For I attend here; but I'll see you soon.

BIANCA
    'Tis very good; I must be circumstanc'd.
            [*Exeunt.*]

Act IV, Scene i: [*Cyprus. Before the castle.*] *Enter* OTHELLO
and IAGO.

IAGO
    Will you think so?

OTHELLO
                        Think so, Iago!

IAGO
                                    What,
    To kiss in private?

OTHELLO
5   An unauthoriz'd kiss.

IAGO
    Or to be naked with her friend in bed
    An hour or more, not meaning any harm?

OTHELLO
    Naked in bed, Iago, and not mean harm!
    It is hypocrisy against the devil.
10 They that mean virtuously, and yet do so,
    The devil their virtue tempts, and they tempt heaven.

IAGO
    If they do nothing, 'tis a venial slip;
    But if I give my wife a handkerchief,—

BIANCA
>You seem not to love me!
>Please walk with me a little way,
>and tell me if I will see you soon at night.

CASSIO
215   I can only walk a little way
>since I'm waiting here; but I'll see you soon.

BIANCA
>That's very good. I must accept things as they are.
>>*They exit.*

Act IV, Scene i: In front of the castle. Enter OTHELLO
and IAGO.

IAGO
>Do you think so?

OTHELLO
>Do I think so, Iago?

IAGO
>Well,
>just a kiss in private?

OTHELLO
5   An improper kiss.

IAGO
>Or maybe to be naked with her friend in bed
>for an hour or so, but not really meaning any harm?

OTHELLO
>Naked in bed, Iago, and not really meaning any harm?
>They'd be putting on a show of wickedness without meaning it.
10   People who have virtuous intentions but act that way
>will be tempted by the devil, and they will tempt heaven.

IAGO
>Yet suppose they don't do anything; that's a forgivable sin.
>But if I've given my wife a handkerchief—

OTHELLO
What then?

IAGO
15   Why, then, 'tis hers, my lord; and, being hers,
She may, I think, bestow 't on any man.

OTHELLO
She is protectress of her honour too;
May she give that?

IAGO
Her honour is an essence that's not seen;
20   They have it very oft that have it not:
But, for the handkerchief,—

OTHELLO
By heaven, I would most gladly have forgot it.
Thou said'st—O, it comes o'er my memory,
As doth the raven o'er the infectious house,
25   Boding to all—he had my handkerchief.

IAGO
Ay, what of that?

OTHELLO
That's not so good now.

IAGO
What
If I had said I had seen him do you wrong?
30   Or heard him say,—as knaves be such abroad,
Who having, by their own importunate suit,
Or voluntary dotage of some mistress,
Convinced or suppli'd them, cannot choose
But they must blab—

OTHELLO
35   Hath he said anything?

IAGO
He hath, my lord; but be you well assur'd,
No more than he'll unswear.

---

24 *raven*   an omen of death.

OTHELLO
What then?

IAGO
15   Well, then it's hers, my lord; and as long as it's hers,
she has the right, I think, to give it to any man.

OTHELLO
Her honor belongs to her as well.
Does she have the right to give that away?

IAGO
Her honor is a quality you cannot see.
20   Some seem to have it when they really don't.
But as for the handkerchief—

OTHELLO
By heaven, I'd gladly have forgotten all about it!
You told me (Oh, it comes over my memory
like a raven over a house of death,
25   boding ill to all!) that he had my handkerchief.

IAGO
Yes, what of it?

OTHELLO
That's not so good now.

IAGO
What
if I were to tell you that I had seen him do you wrong?
30   Or heard him say—since there are such rascals around
who once they have succeeded, by means of their persistence
or by the weakness of will of some lady,
in seducing and satisfying them, can't help it
but they have to blab—

OTHELLO
35   Has he said anything?

IAGO
He has, my lord; but you can be very sure
that he'll unsay everything.

OTHELLO

What hath he said?

IAGO

Why, that he did—I know not what he did.

OTHELLO

40   What? what?

IAGO

Lie—

OTHELLO

With her?

IAGO

With her, on her; what you will.

OTHELLO

Lie with her! lie on her! We say lie on her, when they belie her.
45   Lie with her! 'Zounds, that's fulsome! —Handkerchief—
confessions—handkerchief!— To confess, and be hang'd for his
labour;—first to be hang'd, and then to confess.— I tremble at
it. Nature would not invest herself in such shadowing passion
without some instruction. It is not words that shakes me thus.
50   Pish! Noses, ears, and lips.—Is't possible?—Confess—handkerchief—O devil! [*Falls in a trance.*]

IAGO

Work on,
My medicine, work! Thus credulous fools are caught;
And many worthy and chaste dames even thus,
55   All guiltless, meet reproach.—What, ho! my lord!
My lord, I say! Othello!
        Enter CASSIO.
                How now, Cassio!

CASSIO

What's the matter?

IAGO

My lord is fall'n into an epilepsy.
60   This is his second fit; he had one yesterday.

OTHELLO
What has he said?

IAGO
To tell the truth, that he did—I don't know what he did.

OTHELLO
40   What? What?

IAGO
Lie—

OTHELLO
With her?

IAGO
With her, on her; what you will.

OTHELLO
Lie with her? Lie on her? We say this while she continues to
    seem innocent.
45   Lie with her! By God, that's repulsive.—Handkerchief—
confessions—handkerchief!—He should confess and be hanged
    for this
deed—hanged first, and confess later! It makes me tremble.
I wouldn't be so angered by this if there
weren't some truth in it. It isn't just the words themselves
    that make me shake like this.
50   What! Noses, ears, and lips? Is it possible?—Confess?—
Handkerchief?—Oh, devil!
        (He falls into a trance.)

IAGO
Keep working,
my medicine, keep working! This is how gullible fools are caught
and how many worthy and chaste women,
55   all guiltless, wind up accused.—What is it? My lord!
My lord, listen! Othello!
        Enter CASSIO.
What is it, Cassio?

CASSIO
What's the matter?

IAGO
My lord has fallen into an epileptic seizure.
60   This is his second one; he had one yesterday.

CASSIO
Rub him about the temples.

IAGO
                              No, forbear;
The lethargy must have his quiet course;
If not, he foams at mouth and by and by
65   Breaks out to savage madness. Look, he stirs.
Do you withdraw yourself a little while;
He will recover straight. When he is gone,
I would on great occasion speak with you.
        [*Exit Cassio.*]
How is it, General? Have you not hurt your head?

OTHELLO
70   Dost thou mock me?

IAGO
                        I mock you not, by heaven.
Would you would bear your fortune like a man!

OTHELLO
A horned man's a monster and a beast.

IAGO
There's many a beast then in a populous city,
75   And many a civil monster.

OTHELLO
Did he confess it?

IAGO
                        Good sir, be a man,
Think every bearded fellow that's but yok'd
May draw with you. There's millions now alive
80   That nightly lie in those unproper beds
Which they dare swear peculiar; your case is better.
O, 'tis the spite of hell, the fiend's arch-mock,
To lip a wanton in a secure couch,
And to suppose her chaste! No, let me know;
85   And knowing what I am, I know what she shall be.

---

70 *Dost thou mock me?*   Othello believes that Iago mocks him by referring to the
proverbial cuckold's horns.

CASSIO
    Rub his temples.

IAGO
    No, don't do that.
    This coma must run its course quietly.
    If it doesn't, he'll foam at the mouth, and soon
65   he'll explode into savage madness. Look, he's stirring.
    Step out of the way for a little while.
    He'll recover soon. When he's gone,
    I need to talk to you about something very important.
            Exit CASSIO.
    How are you, general? Have you hurt your head?

OTHELLO
70   Are you mocking me?

IAGO
    I, mock you? No, by heaven.
    I wish you would bear your fortune like a man!

OTHELLO
    A man with cuckold's horns is a monster and a beast.

IAGO
    Then there are many beasts in any populous city
75   and many civilized monsters.

OTHELLO
    Did he confess it?

IAGO
    Good sir, take it like a man.
    Remember, take any mature man, and if he's married,
    he's probably in the same position. There are millions of men alive
80   who go to beds every night that are not solely their own,
    which they'll insist are theirs alone. Your case is better.
    Oh, it's a curse of hell, the supreme mockery of fiends,
    to kiss a wanton woman in a carefree bed
    and imagine her to be chaste! No, I'd rather know the truth;
85   and as long as I know what I am, I'll know what she is, too.

OTHELLO
O, thou art wise; 'tis certain.

IAGO
                    Stand you a while apart;
Confine yourself but in a patient list.
Whilst you were here o'erwhelmed with your grief—
90   A passion most unsuiting such a man—
Cassio came hither. I shifted him away,
And laid good 'scuse upon your ecstasy;
Bade him anon return and here speak with me,
The which he promis'd. Do but encave yourself,
95   And mark the fleers, the gibes, and notable scorns
That dwell in every region of his face;
For I will make him tell the tale anew,
Where, how, how oft, how long ago, and when
He hath, and is again to cope your wife.
100 I say, but mark his gesture. Marry, patience;
Or I shall say you're all in all in spleen,
And nothing of a man.

OTHELLO
                    Dost thou hear, Iago?
I will be found most cunning in my patience;
105 But—dost thou hear?—most bloody.

IAGO
                    That's not amiss;
But yet keep time in all. Will you withdraw?
     [*Othello retires.*]
Now will I question Cassio of Bianca,
A housewife that by selling her desires
110 Buys herself bread and clothes. It is a creature
That dotes on Cassio, as 'tis the strumpet's plague
To beguile many and be beguil'd by one.
He, when he hears of her, cannot refrain
From the excess of laughter. Here he comes.
     Re-enter CASSIO.
115 As he shall smile, Othello shall go mad;
And his unbookish jealousy must conster

OTHELLO
>Oh, you are wise! That's certain.

IAGO
>Step aside for a while;
>contain yourself within the bounds of patience.
>While you were lying here, overwhelmed with your grief
90   (in a fit most unworthy of a man like yourself),
>Cassio came along. I got him away on some pretext
>and came up with a good excuse for the trance you were in.
>I told him to come back soon and to speak with me here;
>he promised that he would. Go hide yourself
95   and observe the sneers, the contempt, and the obvious scorn
>which you can see all over his face.
>I'll make him tell the story all over again—
>where, how, how often, how long ago, and when
>he has, and will again, encounter your wife.
100 I tell you, just watch how he acts. Please, be patient!
>Or I'll have to conclude that you're overwhelmed by rage
>and not a man at all.

OTHELLO
>Do you hear me, Iago?
>I will prove to be very cleverly patient
105 but (do you hear me?) very vengeful.

IAGO
>That's quite appropriate;
>but still, think before you act. Won't you hide yourself?
>   *(OTHELLO hides himself.)*
>Now I'll ask Cassio about Bianca,
>a hussy who, by selling herself to him,
>buys herself bread and clothes. She's a creature
>who loves Cassio. It's the typical curse of whores
>to gain the love of many men and only love one.
>When a man hears about her love, he can't help
>but laugh uncontrollably. Here he comes.
>   *Enter* CASSIO.
115 When he smiles, Othello will go mad;
>and his naive jealousy will interpret

Poor Cassio's smiles, gestures, and light behaviours
Quite in the wrong. How do you, Lieutenant?

CASSIO
The worser that you give me the addition
120 Whose want even kills me.

IAGO
Ply Desdemona well, and you are sure on't.
[*Speaking lower.*] Now, if this suit lay in Bianca's power.
How quickly should you speed!

CASSIO
                            Alas, poor caitiff!

OTHELLO
125 Look how he laughs already!

IAGO
I never knew woman love man so.

CASSIO
Alas, poor rogue! I think, indeed, she loves me.

OTHELLO
Now he denies it faintly, and laughs it out.

IAGO
Do you hear, Cassio?

OTHELLO
130 Now he importunes him
To tell it o'er. Go to; well said, well said.

IAGO
She gives it out that you shall marry her.
Do you intend it?

CASSIO
Ha, ha, ha!

OTHELLO
135 Do ye triumph, Roman? Do you triumph?

CASSIO
I marry her!! What? a customer! Prithee, bear some charity to
my wit; do not think it so unwholesome. Ha, ha, ha!

---

136 *customer* was "one who sold goods"; here a harlot is specifically meant.

poor Cassio's smiles, gestures, and frivolous behavior
quite the wrong way. How are you doing, lieutenant?

CASSIO
120   All the worse since you call me by that title,
the lack of which is killing me.

IAGO
Work on Desdemona well, and you're sure to get it back.
(Speaking lower.) Now if this appeal were something Bianca had
    charge of,
everything would be taken care of quickly!

CASSIO
Oh, the poor wretch!

OTHELLO
125   Look! He's laughing already!

IAGO
I never knew a woman to be so in love with a man.

CASSIO
Oh, the poor rascal! I really do believe she loves me.

OTHELLO
Now he's feebly denying it and laughing about it.

IAGO
Haven't you heard, Cassio?

OTHELLO
130   Now he's begging him
to tell it over again. Go on! Well said, well said!

IAGO
She's spreading it around that you're going to marry her.
Do you really intend to?

CASSIO
Ha, ha, ha!

OTHELLO
135   Are you gloating, conqueror? Are you gloating?

CASSIO
I, marry her? What, a prostitute? Please give me credit for
some intelligence; don't think I'm that stupid. Ha, ha, ha!

OTHELLO
So, so so, so; they laugh that win.

IAGO
Why, the cry goes that you shall marry her.

CASSIO
140   Prithee, say true.

IAGO
I am a very villain else.

OTHELLO
Have you scor'd me? Well.

CASSIO
This is the monkey's own giving out. She is persuaded I will marry her, out of her own love and flattery, not out of my promise.

OTHELLO
145   Iago beckons me; now he begins the story.

CASSIO
She was here even now; she haunts me in every place. I was the other day talking on the sea-bank with certain Venetians; and thither comes the bauble, and, falls me thus about my neck—

OTHELLO
Crying, "O dear Cassio!" as it were; his gesture imports it.

CASSIO
150   So hangs, and lolls, and weeps upon me; so shakes and pulls me. Ha, ha, ha!

OTHELLO
Now he tells how she pluck'd him to my chamber. Oh, I see that nose of yours, but not that dog I shall throw it to.

CASSIO
Well, I must leave her company.

IAGO
155   Before me! look, where she comes.
    Enter BIANCA.

OTHELLO
So, so, so, so. Let the winner laugh!

IAGO
Really, rumor has it that you will marry her.

CASSIO
140   Come, tell the truth.

IAGO
I'm a true villain otherwise.

OTHELLO
Have you branded me? Well.

CASSIO
This is the monkey's own idea. Out of her own love and vanity,
she thinks that I'll marry her, not because of any promise I've made.

OTHELLO
145   Iago's signaling me. Now Cassio's starting the story.

CASSIO
She was here just now; she follows me everywhere. The other
    day I was
talking on the sea bank with some Venetians, and
there came the little plaything and threw her arms around my neck—

OTHELLO
Crying, "Oh, dear Cassio!" as it were. His gestures say as much.

CASSIO
150   She hangs and droops and weeps all over me; she calls and
    pulls at me.
Ha, ha, ha!

OTHELLO
Now he's telling how she took him to my bedroom. Oh, I see that
nose of yours but not yet the dog I'll throw it to.

CASSIO
Well, I must get rid of her company.

IAGO
155   Well look! Here she comes.
        Enter BIANCA.

CASSIO

'Tis such another fitchew! Marry, a perfum'd one.—What do you mean by this haunting of me?

BIANCA

Let the devil and his dam haunt you! What did you mean by that same handkerchief you gave me even now? I was a fine fool to

160   take it. I must take out the work?—A likely piece of work, that you should find it in your chamber, and know not who left it there! This is some minx's token, and I must take out the work? There; give it your hobby-horse. Wheresoever you had it, I'll take out no work on't.

CASSIO

165   How now, my sweet Bianca! how now! how now!

OTHELLO

By heaven, that should be my handkerchief!

BIANCA

If you'll come to supper to-night, you may; if you will not, come when you are next prepar'd for.
        [*Exit.*]

IAGO

After her, after her.

CASSIO

170   Faith, I must; she'll rail in the streets else.

IAGO

Will you sup there?

CASSIO

Yes, I intend so.

IAGO

Well, I may chance to see you; for I would very fain speak with you.

CASSIO

175   Prithee, come; will you?

IAGO

Go to; say no more.
        [*Exit Cassio.*]

---

156 *fitchew*   or a polecat, is a strong-smelling animal.   167-68 *come . . . for*   Bianca means Cassio will never again be welcome if he doesn't come to supper that night.

CASSIO
What a polecat!—though she tries to hide it. What are you
doing, chasing after me?

BIANCA
Let the devil and his mother chase you! What was the idea,
giving me that handkerchief just now? I was a fine fool to
160   take it. I'm supposed to copy the embroidery? A likely story that
you found it in your bedroom and don't know who left it
there! Some hussy gave it to you, and I'm supposed to copy
      the embroidery?
There! Give it to your whore. Wherever it came from, I'm
not copying the embroidery.

CASSIO
165   What is this, my sweet Bianca? What is this? What is this?

OTHELLO
By heaven, that looks like my handkerchief!

BIANCA
If you want to come to supper tonight, you may. If you don't, then
come back again when you're invited.
      Exit BIANCA.

IAGO
After her, after her!

CASSIO
170   Really, I'd better; she'll be yelling in the streets otherwise.

IAGO
Will you have supper there?

CASSIO
Yes, I intend to.

IAGO
Well, I might see you; for I am really eager to talk to you.

CASSIO
175   Please come. Will you?

IAGO
Certainly! Say no more.
      Exit CASSIO.

OTHELLO
[*Advancing.*] How shall I murder him, Iago?

IAGO
Did you perceive how he laugh'd at his vice?

OTHELLO
O Iago!

IAGO
180 And did you see the handkerchief?

OTHELLO
Was that mine?

IAGO
Yours, by this hand. And to see how he prizes the foolish woman
your wife! She gave it him, and he hath given it his whore.

OTHELLO
I would have him nine years a-killing.
185 A fine woman! a fair woman! a sweet woman!

IAGO
Nay, you must forget that.

OTHELLO
Ay, let her rot, and perish, and be damn'd to-night; for she shall
not live. No, my heart is turn'd to stone; I strike it, and it hurts
my hand. O, the world hath not a sweeter creature! She might
190 lie by an emperor's side and command him tasks.

IAGO
Nay, that's not your way.

OTHELLO
Hang her! I do but say what she is. So delicate with her needle!
an admirable musician! O! she will sing the savageness out of a
bear. Of so high and plenteous wit and invention!

IAGO
195 She's the worse for all this.

OTHELLO
O, a thousand thousand times. And then, of so gentle a condition!

OTHELLO *(Coming forward)*
How shall I murder him, Iago?

IAGO
Did you see how he laughed at his sin?

OTHELLO
Oh, Iago!

IAGO
180 And did you see the handkerchief?

OTHELLO
Was that mine?

IAGO
Yours, I swear! And look how much he values that foolish woman,
your wife! She gave it to him, and he's given it to his whore.

OTHELLO
I wish I could spend nine years killing him!
185 A fine woman! A lovely woman! A sweet woman!

IAGO
No, you must forget all that.

OTHELLO
Yes, let her rot and perish and be damned tonight, for she's
not going to live. No, my heart has been turned to stone:
when I strike it, it hurts
my hand. Oh, there's not a sweeter creature in the world! She could
190 lie beside an emperor and give him commands.

IAGO
No, that's not the right attitude.

OTHELLO
Hang her! I'm only saying what she's like. So skillful with
her needle!
An admirable musician! Oh, she could sing the savageness
right out of a
bear! Such lofty and abundant intelligence and imagination!

IAGO
195 She's all the worse because of this.

OTHELLO
Oh, a thousand, thousand times! And then she has such a gentle
temperament!

IAGO
Ay, too gentle.

OTHELLO
Nay, that's certain. But yet the pity of it, Iago! O Iago, the pity of it, Iago!

IAGO
200   If you are so fond over her iniquity, give her patent to offend; for if it touch not you, it comes near nobody.

OTHELLO
I will chop her into messes. Cuckold me!

IAGO
O, 'tis foul in her.

OTHELLO
With mine officer!

IAGO
205   That's fouler.

OTHELLO
Get me some poison, Iago; this night. I'll not expostulate with her, lest her body and beauty unprovide my mind again. This night, Iago.

IAGO
Do it not with poison; strangle her in her bed, even the bed she
210   hath contaminated.

OTHELLO
Good, good; the justice of it pleases; very good.

IAGO
And for Cassio, let me be his undertaker. You shall hear more by midnight.
    [*A trumpet.*]
    Enter LODOVICO, DESDEMONA, *and Attendants.*

OTHELLO
Excellent good. What trumpet is that same?

IAGO
215   I warrant, something from Venice. 'Tis Lodovico, this, comes from the Duke. See, your wife's with him.

IAGO
    Yes, too gentle.

OTHELLO
    Yes, that's for certain. But what a pity, Iago! Oh, Iago, what a pity, Iago!

IAGO
200   If you're going to be so foolish about her crime, why don't you give her a license to sin?
    If it doesn't bother you, it won't bother anyone.

OTHELLO
    I'll chop her up in little bits! Cuckold me!

IAGO
    Oh, it's evil of her.

OTHELLO
    With my officer!

IAGO
205   That's even worse.

OTHELLO
    Get some poison for me tonight, Iago. I won't discuss this with her for fear that her body and beauty might weaken my resolve again.
    Tonight, Iago!

IAGO
    Don't do it with poison. Strangle her in her bed, the very bed she
210   has contaminated.

OTHELLO
    Good, good! The justice of that pleases me. Very good!

IAGO
    As for Cassio, let me take care of him. You'll know more by midnight.
        (A trumpet blows offstage.)
        Enter LODOVICO, DESDEMONA, *and* ATTENDANTS.

OTHELLO
    Very good! What was that trumpet?

IAGO
215   Surely someone from Venice. It's Lodovico; he's come from the duke. Look, your wife's with him.

LODOVICO
Save you, worthy General!

OTHELLO

                    With all my heart, sir.

LODOVICO
The Duke and Senators of Venice greet you. [*Gives him a letter.*]

OTHELLO
220   I kiss the instrument of their pleasures. [*Opens the letter and reads.*]

DESDEMONA
And what's the news, good cousin Lodovico?

IAGO
I am very glad to see you, signior;
Welcome to Cyprus.

LODOVICO
I thank you. How does Lieutenant Cassio?

IAGO
225   Lives, sir.

DESDEMONA
Cousin, there 's fall'n between him and my lord
An unkind breach; but you shall make all well.

OTHELLO
Are your sure of that?

DESDEMONA
My lord?

OTHELLO
230   [*Reads.*] "This fail you not to do, as you will."—

LODOVICO
He did not call; he's busy in the paper.
Is there division 'twixt my lord and Cassio?

DESDEMONA
A most unhappy one. I would do much
T' atone them, for the love I bear to Cassio.

LODOVICO
God save you, worthy general!

OTHELLO
I welcome you with all my heart, sir.

LODOVICO *(Giving Othello a letter)*
The duke and senators of Venice send greetings.

OTHELLO
220 I kiss this letter. *(He opens the letter and reads it.)*

DESDEMONA
So what's the news, good cousin Lodovico?

IAGO
I am very glad to see you, signior.
Welcome to Cyprus.

LODOVICO
Thank you. How's Lieutenant Cassio doing?

IAGO
225 He lives, sir.

DESDEMONA
Cousin, there has occurred between him and my lord
an unfortunate quarrel. But you will make all that well.

OTHELLO
Are you sure of that?

DESDEMONA
My lord?

OTHELLO *(Reading)*
230 "Don't fail to do this, as soon as you can—"

LODOVICO
He wasn't speaking to you; he's busy with his letter.
Has there been a falling out between my lord and Cassio?

DESDEMONA
A very unfortunate one. I'd do a great deal
to reconcile them because of the love I feel for Cassio.

OTHELLO
235   Fire and brimstone!

DESDEMONA
                My lord?

OTHELLO
                        Are you wise?

DESDEMONA
    What, is he angry?

LODOVICO
              May be the letter mov'd him;
240   For, as I think, they do command him home,
    Deputing Cassio in his government.

DESDEMONA
    Trust me, I am glad on't.

OTHELLO
                Indeed!

DESDEMONA
                My lord?

OTHELLO
245   I am glad to see you mad.

DESDEMONA
             Why, sweet Othello,—

OTHELLO
    [*Striking her.*] Devil!

DESDEMONA
    I have not deserv'd this.

LODOVICO
    My lord, this would not be believ'd in Venice
250   Though I should swear I saw 't. 'Tis very much.
    Make her amends: she weeps.

OTHELLO
             O devil, devil!
    If that the earth could teem with woman's tears,

OTHELLO
235   Fire and brimstone!

DESDEMONA
    My lord?

OTHELLO
    Are you sane?

DESDEMONA
    What, is he angry?

LODOVICO
    Maybe the letter has upset him.
240   I think they have commanded him to go home
    and turn his position here over to Cassio.

DESDEMONA
    Well really, I'm glad to hear it.

OTHELLO
    Indeed?

DESDEMONA
    My lord?

OTHELLO
245   I'm glad to see you've gone mad.

DESDEMONA
    Why, sweet Othello!

OTHELLO *(Striking her)*
    Devil!

DESDEMONA
    I've done nothing to deserve this.

LODOVICO
    My lord, no one would believe this in Venice,
250   even if I swore I saw it. This is too much.
    Apologize to her; she's weeping.

OTHELLO
    Oh, devil, devil!
    If the earth could be sown by a woman's tears,

Each drop she falls would prove a crocodile.
255 Out of my sight!

DESDEMONA
      I will not stay to offend you. [*Going.*]

LODOVICO
Truly, an obedient lady:
I do beseech your lordship, call her back.

OTHELLO
Mistress!

DESDEMONA
260   My lord?

OTHELLO
      What would you with her, sir?

LODOVICO
Who, I, my lord?

OTHELLO
Ay; you did wish that I would make her turn.
Sir, she can turn, and turn, and yet go on,
265 And turn again; and she can weep, sir, weep;
And she's obedient, as you say, obedient,
Very obedient. Proceed you in your tears.
Concerning this, sir,—O well-painted passion!—
I am commanded home.—Get you away;
270 I'll send for you anon.—Sir, I obey the mandate,
And will return to Venice.—Hence, avaunt!—
    [*Exit Desdemona.*]
Cassio shall have my place. And, sir, to-night
I do entreat that we may sup together.
You are welcome, sir, to Cyprus.—Goats and monkeys!
    [*Exit.*]

LODOVICO
275 Is this the noble Moor whom our full Senate
Call all in all sufficient? Is this the nature
Whom passion could not shake? whose solid virtue
The shot of accident nor dart of chance
Could neither graze nor pierce?

---

254 *crocodile*   according to legend, crocodiles wept false tears to entrap prey.

255

every drop that falls from her eyes would become a crocodile.
Out of my sight!

DESDEMONA *(Starting to go)*
I won't stay to offend you.

LODOVICO
Really, she's an obedient lady.
I beg your lordship to call her back.

OTHELLO
Lady!

DESDEMONA
260 My lord?

OTHELLO
What do you want with her, sir?

LODOVICO
Who? I, my lord?

OTHELLO
Yes! You wanted me to make her turn back.
Sir, she can twist and turn and yet keep moving ahead
265 and continue to deceive you. And she can weep, sir, weep.
And she's obedient; just as you said, obedient,
very obedient. *(To Desdemona)* Go ahead and cry.
(To Lodovico) Concerning this letter, sir. *(To Desdemona)*
Oh, well-acted grief!
(To Lodovico) I've been commanded home. *(To Desdemona)* Go away;
270 I'll send for you soon. *(To Lodovico)* Sir, I'll obey this command
and go back to Venice. *(To Desdemona)* Go, get away from me!
          Exit DESDEMONA.
Cassio will take my place. And, sir, tonight
I hope we can have supper together.
Sir, you are welcome to Cyprus.—Goats and monkeys!
          Exit OTHELLO.

LODOVICO
275 Is this the same noble Moor whom our senate unanimously
called completely capable? Is this the man
who could not be shaken by anger? Whose solid virtue
an accidental shot or a chance arrow
could neither graze or pierce?

IAGO

280   He is much chang'd.

LODOVICO
   Are his wits safe? Is he not light of brain?

IAGO
   He's that he is; I may not breathe my censure
   What he might be. If what he might he is not,
   I would to heaven he were!

LODOVICO

285   What, strike his wife!

IAGO
   Faith, that was not so well; yet would I knew
   That stroke would prove the worst!

LODOVICO
                          Is it his use?
   Or did the letters work upon his blood

290   And new-create this fault?

IAGO
                          Alas, alas!
   It is not honesty in me to speak
   What I have seen and known. You shall observe him,
   And his own courses will denote him so

295   That I may save my speech. Do but go after,
   And mark how he continues.

LODOVICO
   I am sorry that I am deceiv'd in him.
      [*Exeunt.*]

Scene ii: [*A room in the castle.*] *Enter* OTHELLO *and*
EMILIA.

OTHELLO
   You have seen nothing then?

EMILIA
   Nor ever heard, nor ever did suspect.

IAGO

280   He is much changed.

LODOVICO

Is his mind all right? Has he gone mad?

IAGO

He's what he seems to be. I mustn't pass judgment.
The man he could be—if he is not such a man—
I wish to heaven he really were!

LODOVICO

285   And he struck his wife?

IAGO

Really, that wasn't so good; yet I wish I knew
that blow would prove to be his worst action.

LODOVICO

Is he usually like this?
Or did the letter make him angry
290   and just create this fault?

IAGO

Oh, no, no!
It would not be honorable of me to speak
of the things I've seen and known. Observe him for yourself,
and his own actions will tell you enough about him
295   so that I can remain silent. Just follow him
and watch what he does.

LODOVICO

I'm sorry that I was wrong about him.
      They exit.

Act IV, Scene ii: Inside the castle. Enter OTHELLO
and EMILIA.

OTHELLO

You haven't seen anything, then?

EMILIA

Nor ever heard or even suspected anything.

OTHELLO
Yes, you have seen Cassio and she together.

EMILIA
But then I saw no harm, and then I heard
5   Each syllable that breath made up between them.

OTHELLO
What, did they never whisper?

EMILIA
                    Never, my lord.

OTHELLO
Nor send you out o' th' way?

EMILIA
Never.

OTHELLO
10   To fetch her fan, her gloves, her mask, nor nothing?

EMILIA
Never, my lord.

OTHELLO
That's strange.

EMILIA
I durst, my lord, to wager she is honest,
Lay down my soul at stake. If you think other,
15   Remove your thought; it doth abuse your bosom.
If any wretch have put this in your head,
Let Heaven requite it with the serpent's curse!
For, if she be not honest, chaste, and true,
There's no man happy; the purest of their wives
20   Is foul as slander.

OTHELLO
                    Bid her come hither; go.
    [*Exit Emilia.*]
She says enough; yet she's a simple bawd
That cannot say as much. This is a subtle whore,

---

10 *mask* in public, some Elizabethan women wore masks which covered their eyes.
17 *serpent's curse* the curse God laid on the serpent who tempted Eve in the Garden of Eden.

OTHELLO
    Yes, but you have seen Cassio and her together.

EMILIA
    But I saw no harm in it, and I heard
5   every syllable that they said to each other.

OTHELLO
    What, didn't they ever whisper?

EMILIA
    Never, my lord.

OTHELLO
    Nor tell you to go away?

EMILIA
    Never.

OTHELLO
10   To get her fan, her gloves, her mask, or some other trifle?

EMILIA
    Never, my lord.

OTHELLO
    That's strange.

EMILIA
    My lord, I would dare wager that she is faithful—
    I'd bet my very soul on that. If you think otherwise,
15   then get that thought out of your head; it troubles you to no
        purpose.
    If some villain has put this idea in your head,
    let heaven repay him with the curse laid on the serpent!
    If she isn't faithful, chaste, and true,
    there's not a lucky man in the world; the most innocent of wives
20   is as wicked as any rumor says.

OTHELLO
    Tell her to come here. Go.
        Exit EMILIA.
    What she says sounds good; yet it would be a stupid procuress
    who couldn't make up such a story. This is a sly whore,

A closet lock and key of villanous secrets;
25   And yet she'll kneel and pray; I have seen her do't.
   Enter DESDEMONA *with* EMILIA.

DESDEMONA
My lord, what is your will?

OTHELLO
     Pray, chuck, come hither.

DESDEMONA
What is your pleasure?

OTHELLO
     Let me see your eyes;
30   Look in my face.

DESDEMONA
     What horrible fancy's this?

OTHELLO
[*To Emilia.*] Some of your function, mistress;
Leave procreants alone and shut the door;
Cough, or cry "hem," if anybody come.
35   Your mystery, your mystery; nay, dispatch.
   [*Exit Emilia.*]

DESDEMONA
Upon my knee, what doth your speech import?
I understand a fury in your words,
But not the words.

OTHELLO
Why, what art thou?

DESDEMONA
40   Your wife, my lord; your true
And loyal wife.

OTHELLO
     Come, swear it, damn thyself,
Lest, being like one of heaven, the devils themselves
Should fear to seize thee; therefore be double damn'd,
45   Swear thou art honest.

32-35 *Some of your function . . . mystery* Othello is suggesting that Desdemona is a
prostitute and Emilia her procurer.

a locked room and key with all kinds of villainous secrets;
25   but still, she kneels and prays; I've seen her do it.
          Enter DESDEMONA *and* EMILIA.

DESDEMONA
My lord, what do you wish?

OTHELLO
Please, my dear, come here.

DESDEMONA
What do you desire?

OTHELLO
Let me see your eyes.
30   Look at my face.

DESDEMONA
What horrible ideas do you have?

OTHELLO *(To Emilia)*
See to your duty, madam.
Leave the lovers alone and shut the door;
cough or cry "ahem" if anybody comes.
35   Your trade, your trade! Come on, get to it!
          Exit EMILIA.

DESDEMONA
I ask you on my knees, what did you mean by that?
I understood the fury in your words
but not the words themselves.

OTHELLO
Tell me, what are you?

DESDEMONA
40   Your wife, my lord; your true
and loyal wife.

OTHELLO
Come, swear it, and damn yourself
for fear that, since you look like an angel, the devils
   themselves
will be afraid to seize you. So damn yourself a second time—
45   swear you are faithful.

DESDEMONA

> Heaven doth truly know it.

OTHELLO

Heaven truly knows that thou art false as hell.

DESDEMONA

To whom, my lord? With whom? How am I false?

OTHELLO

Ah, Desdemona! Away! away! away!

DESDEMONA

50 Alas the heavy day! Why do you weep?
Am I the motive of these tears, my lord?
If haply you my father do suspect
An instrument of this your calling back,
Lay not your blame on me. If you have lost him,
55 Why, I have lost him too.

OTHELLO

> Had it pleas'd Heaven
To try me with affliction; had they rain'd
All kind of sores and shames on my bare head,
Steep'd me in poverty to the very lips,
60 Given to captivity me and my utmost hopes,
I should have found in some place of my soul
A drop of patience; but, alas, to make me
The fixed figure for the time of scorn
To point his slow and moving finger at!
65 Yet could I bear that too, well, very well;
But there, where I have garner'd up my heart,
Where either I must live or bear no life;
The fountain from the which my current runs
Or else dries up; to be discarded thence!
70 Or keep it as a cistern for foul toads
To know and gender in! Turn thy complexion there,
Patience, thou young and rose-lipp'd cherubin,
Ay, there look grim as hell!

DESDEMONA

I hope my noble lord esteems me honest.

DESDEMONA
Heaven truly knows I am.

OTHELLO
Heaven truly knows that you are as unfaithful as hell.

DESDEMONA
To whom, my lord? With whom? How am I unfaithful?

OTHELLO
Ah, Desdemona! Get away from me! Away! Away!

DESDEMONA
50   Oh, what a sad day! Why are you weeping?
Am I the cause of these tears, my lord?
If you perhaps suspect that my father
might have had something to do with your recall,
don't blame me for it. If you have lost his affection,
55   then I have lost it too.

OTHELLO
Had it been heaven's wish
to persecute me with illness, if it had rained
all kinds of sores and shames on my bare head,
buried me in poverty up to the lips,
60   or given me and my highest hopes over to captivity,
I would have found in some part of my soul
a drop of patience. But to turn me into
a kind of target for scornful time
to point his slowly moving finger at!
65   Yet I could bear that too; and well, very well.
But that place that I have gathered up my heart,
that place that gives me reason to live or not live at all,
that fountain from which my life flows
70   or else dries up—to be driven away from there,
or to have it used as a reservoir for horrible toads
to churn and mate in, that would even turn
Patience, that young and rosy-lipped angel, pale!
This makes me grim as hell!

DESDEMONA
My noble lord, I hope you think me faithful.

OTHELLO

75   O, ay; as summer flies are in the shambles,
That quicken even with blowing. O thou weed,
Who art so lovely fair and smell'st so sweet
That the sense aches at thee, would thou hadst ne'er been
      born!

DESDEMONA

Alas, what ignorant sin have I committed?

OTHELLO

80   Was this fair paper, this most goodly book,
Made to write "whore" upon? What committed!
Committed! O thou public commoner!
I should make very forges of my cheeks,
That would to cinders burn up modesty,

85   Did I but speak thy deeds. What committed!
Heaven stops the nose at it, and the moon winks;
The bawdy wind, that kisses all it meets,
Is hush'd within the hollow mine of earth
And will not hear it. What committed!

90   Impudent strumpet!

DESDEMONA

                    By heaven, you do me wrong.

OTHELLO

Are not you a strumpet?

DESDEMONA

                    No, as I am a Christian.
If to preserve this vessel for my lord

95   From any other foul unlawful touch
Be not to be a strumpet, I am none.

OTHELLO

What, not a whore?

DESDEMONA

                    No, as I shall be sav'd.

OTHELLO

Is't possible?

---

88 *hollow mine of earth*   the winds were assumed to have originated in the hollow interior
of the earth.

OTHELLO

75 Oh, yes! Just like flies near a slaughterhouse,
 which conceive even while they lay their eggs. Oh, you weed,
 who are so beautifully lovely and smell so sweet
 that you make the senses ache, I wish you'd never been born!

DESDEMONA

 Oh, what kind of sin have I unknowingly committed?

OTHELLO

80 Was this fine paper, this handsome book,
 made to write "whore" upon? What have you committed?
 Committed? Oh, you common whore!
 It would make my cheeks into furnaces
 to burn up modesty into cinders
85 if I even spoke of your deeds. What have you committed?
 Heaven holds its nose at it, and the moon closes its eyes;
 the promiscuous wind, which kisses everything it meets,
 hides itself inside the earth
 and refuses to hear of it. What have you committed?
90 You impudent harlot!

DESDEMONA

 By God, you do me wrong.

OTHELLO

 Are you not a harlot?

DESDEMONA

 No, I swear to you as I am a Christian!
 If keeping this body for my lord
95 from any other wicked, improper touch
 means not to be a harlot, then I am not one.

OTHELLO

 What, you're not a whore?

DESDEMONA

 No, I swear by my salvation!

OTHELLO

 Is it possible?

DESDEMONA

100   O, Heaven forgive us!

OTHELLO

I cry you mercy, then.
I took you for that cunning whore of Venice
That married with Othello. [*Raising his voice.*]
    You, mistress,
        Re-enter EMILIA.

105   That have the office opposite to Saint Peter,
And keeps the gate of hell! You, you, ay, you!
We have done our course; there's money for your pains.
I pray you, turn the key and keep our counsel.
        [*Exit.*]

EMILIA

Alas, what does this gentleman conceive?

110   How do you, madam? How do you, my good lady?

DESDEMONA

Faith, half asleep.

EMILIA

Good madam, what's the matter with my lord?

DESDEMONA

With who?

EMILIA

Why, with my lord, madam.

DESDEMONA

115   Who is thy lord?

EMILIA

He that is yours, sweet lady.

DESDEMONA

I have none. Do not talk to me, Emilia;
I cannot weep, nor answers have I none
But what should go by water. Prithee, tonight

120   Lay on my bed my wedding sheets, remember;
And call thy husband hither.

DESChild...

DESDEMONA
100   Oh, heaven help us!

OTHELLO
I ask your pardon, then.
I thought you were that conniving whore of Venice
who married Othello. *(Shouting)*
You, woman,
              Enter EMILIA.
105   who has the opposite job of Saint Peter's
and keeps the gate of hell! You, you, yes, you!
We're finished with our business. Here's money for your
    trouble.
Please, lock up your lips and keep this meeting secret.
              Exit OTHELLO.

EMILIA
My God, what is this gentleman thinking?
110   Are you all right, madam? Are you all right, my good lady?

DESDEMONA
Really, I'm in a daze.

EMILIA
Good lady, what's the matter with my lord?

DESDEMONA
With whom?

EMILIA
Why, with my lord, madam.

DESDEMONA
115   Who is your lord?

EMILIA
The man who is yours too, sweet lady.

DESDEMONA
I have none. Don't talk to me, Emilia.
I can't weep; and I can't say anything
that shouldn't be said with tears. Please, tonight
120   make up my bed with my wedding sheets; remember to do it.
And call your husband here.

EMILIA

                    Here's a change indeed!
        [*Exit.*]

DESDEMONA
    'Tis meet I should be us'd so, very meet.
    How have I been behav'd, that he might stick
125 The small'st opinion on my least misuse?
            Re-enter EMILIA *with* IAGO.

IAGO
    What is your pleasure, madam? How is't with you?

DESDEMONA
    I cannot tell. Those that do teach young babes
    Do it with gentle means and easy tasks.
    He might have chid me so; for, in good faith,
130 I am a child to chiding.

IAGO
                    What's the matter, lady?

EMILIA
    Alas, Iago, my lord hath so bewhor'd her,
    Thrown such despite and heavy terms upon her,
    That true hearts cannot bear it.

DESDEMONA
135 Am I that name, Iago?

IAGO
                    What name, fair lady?

DESDEMONA
    Such as she said my lord did say I was.

EMILIA
    He call'd her whore. A beggar in his drink
    Could not have laid such terms upon his callet.

IAGO
140 Why did he so?

DESDEMONA
    I do not know; I am sure I am none such.

EMILIA
    Things are certainly changed!
        Exit EMILIA.

DESDEMONA
    It's proper that I should be treated this way, very proper.
    What have I done that he could find
125   the slightest reason to think me unfaithful?
        Enter IAGO *and* EMILIA.

IAGO
    What can I do for you, madam? How are you?

DESDEMONA
    I don't know. Those who teach young babies
    do it by gentle means and easy lessons.
    He should have scolded me that way since, really,
130   I'm a child when it comes to scolding.

IAGO
    What's the matter, lady?

EMILIA
    Oh, Iago, my lord has so cruelly called her a whore
    and thrown such spiteful and horrible names
    that innocent hearts can't bear it.

DESDEMONA
135   Do I deserve that name, Iago?

IAGO
    What name, lovely lady?

DESDEMONA
    The one Emilia said my lord called me by.

EMILIA
    He called her a whore. A drunken beggar
    wouldn't have called his slut by those names.

IAGO
140   Why did he do this?

DESDEMONA
    I don't know. I'm sure I am not that.

IAGO
Do not weep, do not weep. Alas the day!

EMILIA
Hath she forsook so many noble matches,
Her father and her country and her friends,
145   To be call'd whore? Would it not make one weep?

DESDEMONA
It is my wretched fortune.

IAGO
                Beshrew him for't!
How comes this trick upon him?

DESDEMONA
             Nay, Heaven doth know.

EMILIA
150   I will be hang'd if some eternal villain,
Some busy and insinuating rogue,
Some cogging, cozening slave, to get some office,
Have not devis'd this slander. I'll be hang'd else.

IAGO
Fie, there is no such man; it is impossible.

DESDEMONA
155   If any such there be, Heaven pardon him!

EMILIA
A halter pardon him! and hell gnaw his bones!
Why should he call her whore? Who keeps her company?
What place? what time? what form? what likelihood?
The Moor's abus'd by some most villanous knave,
160   Some base notorious knave, some scurvy fellow.
O heavens, that such companions thou'dst unfold,
And put in every honest hand a whip
To lash the rascals naked through the world
Even from the east to th' west!

IAGO
165   Speak within door.

IAGO
>Don't weep, don't weep. Oh, what a sad day!

EMILIA
>Has she refused so many noble matches,
>her father, her country, and all her friends
145 >to be called a whore? Doesn't she have a right to weep?

DESDEMONA
>This is my awful fortune.

IAGO
>Curse him for it!
>What made him say this?

DESDEMONA
>Heaven knows.

EMILIA
150 >You can hang me if some thoroughgoing villain,
>some nosy, gossiping rascal,
>some cheating, conniving scoundrel hasn't come up with this lie
>to get himself ahead. You can hang me otherwise.

IAGO
>Nonsense, there's no such man as that! It's impossible.

DESDEMONA
155 >If there is, let heaven forgive him!

EMILIA
>May a noose forgive him! And may hell gnaw on his bones!
>Why would he call her a whore? Who's been keeping her company?
>Where did it happen? When? In what way? And how likely is it?
>The Moor has been misled by some villainous rascal,
160 >some low, infamous rascal, some low-life character.
>Oh, heaven, I wish you'd expose such villains
>and put a whip in the hand of every honest person
>to whip these naked rascals around the world
>all the way from the East to the West!

IAGO
165 >Watch your tongue.

EMILIA

O, fie upon them! Some such squire he was
That turn'd your wit the seamy side without,
And made you to suspect me with the Moor.

IAGO

You are a fool; go to.

DESDEMONA

170 　　　　　　　　Alas, Iago,
What shall I do to win my lord again?
Good friend, go to him; for, by this light of heaven,
I know not how I lost him. Here I kneel:
If e'er my will did trespass 'gainst his love,
175 Either in discourse of thought or actual deed,
Or that mine eyes, mine ears, or any sense
Delighted them in any other form;
Or that I do not yet, and ever did,
And ever will—though he do shake me off
180 To beggarly divorcement—love him dearly,
Comfort forswear me! Unkindness may do much;
And his unkindness may defeat my life,
But never taint my love. I cannot say "whore."
It does abhor me now I speak the word;
185 To do the act that might the addition earn
Not the world's mass of vanity could make me.

IAGO

I pray you, be content; 'tis but his humour.
The business of the state does him offence,
And he does chide with you.

DESDEMONA

190 If 'twere no other,—

OTHELLO

　　　　　　　　It is but so, I warrant.
[*Trumpets within.*]
Hark, how these instruments summon to supper!
The messengers of Venice stay the meat.
Go in, and weep not; all things shall be well.
[*Exeunt Desdemona and Emilia.*]

EMILIA

    Oh, to hell with them! It was just this kind of man
    that turned your thoughts to foul ideas
    and made you think I was the Moor's lover.

IAGO

    You are a fool. Watch yourself.

DESDEMONA

170   Oh, good Iago,
    what should I do to win back the trust of my lord again?
    Good friend, go talk with him; I tell you, by the light of heaven,
    I don't know how I lost his affection. I'm on my knees.
    If I ever deliberately did anything to betray his love,
175   either in thought or in action,
    or if my eyes, my ears, or any of my other senses
    were ever attracted to any other man,
    or if I don't now, and always have,
    and always will (even if he force me into
180   a penniless divorce) very dearly love him,
    let me never know peace again! Unkindness may do much harm,
    and his unkindness may destroy my life,
    but it will not affect my love. I can't say the word "whore."
    It disgusts me even now that I've said that word.
185   To actually do the act that would earn me that title—
    not all the hollow treasure in the world could make me do it.

IAGO

    Please, don't get upset. It's just a mood of his.
    Business of state has made him angry,
    and he's taking it out on you.

DESDEMONA

190   If it's just that—

IAGO

    It's just that, I guarantee you.
      (Trumpets blow offstage.)

    Listen. The trumpets are calling you to supper.
    The Venetian messengers are staying to eat.
    Go in, and stop crying. Everything will be all right.
      Exit DESDEMONA *and* EMILIA.

Enter RODERIGO.

195   How now, Roderigo!

RODERIGO
I do not find that thou deal'st justly with me.

IAGO
What in the contrary?

RODERIGO
Every day thou daff'st me with some device, Iago; and rather, as it seems to me now, keep'st from me all conveniency than
200   suppliest me with the least advantage of hope. I will indeed no longer endure it, nor am I yet persuaded to put up in peace what already I have foolishly suff'red.

IAGO
Will you hear me, Roderigo?

RODERIGO
I have heard too much, and your words and performances are
205   no kin together.

IAGO
You charge me most unjustly.

RODERIGO
With nought but truth. I have wasted myself out of my means. The jewels you have had from me to deliver Desdemona would half have corrupted a votarist. You have told me she hath receiv'd
210   them and return'd me expectations and comforts of sudden respect and acquaintance, but I find none.

IAGO
Well; go to; very well.

RODERIGO
Very well! go to! I cannot go to, man; nor 'tis not very well. Nay, I think it is scurvy, and begin to find myself fopp'd in it.

IAGO
215   Very well.

RODERIGO
I tell you 'tis not very well. I will make myself known to

Enter RODERIGO.

195   What is it, Roderigo?

RODERIGO
I've found out that you haven't been dealing with me honestly.

IAGO
In what way?

RODERIGO
Every day you've put me off with some excuse, Iago, and it
seems to me now that you've been trying to cheat me out of
    every opportunity, rather than
200   give me the smallest reason for hope. I won't
put up with this anymore; and I'm not going to peacefully
    accept what I've
already foolishly suffered.

IAGO
Will you just listen to me, Roderigo?

RODERIGO
I've been listening to you too much. What you say and what you do
205   are not connected.

IAGO
You're accusing me unjustly.

RODERIGO
Only with the truth. I've wasted everything I have.
The jewels you've received from me to give to Desdemona
    would have
half-corrupted a nun. You've told me that she's received
210   them, and led me to have hopes to the comfort of speedy
    consideration
and acquaintance. But it hasn't happened.

IAGO
Well, take it easy; things are all right.

RODERIGO
All right! Take it easy! I can't take it easy, man; and things
    aren't all right. No,
I think it's a rotten business, and I'm starting to feel like
    I've been duped.

IAGO
215   All right, then.

RODERIGO
I'm telling you, it's not all right. I'm going to confront

Desdemona. If she will return me my jewels, I will give over my suit and repent my unlawful solicitation; if not, assure yourself I will seek satisfaction of you.

IAGO

220   You have said now.

RODERIGO

Ay, and said nothing but what I protest intendment of doing.

IAGO

Why, now I see there's mettle in thee, and even from this instant do build on thee a better opinion than ever before. Give me thy hand, Roderigo. Thou hast taken against me a most just excep-
225   tion; but yet, I protest, I have dealt most directly in thy affair.

RODERIGO

It hath not appear'd.

IAGO

I grant indeed it hath not appear'd, and your suspicion is not without wit and judgement. But, Roderigo, if thou hast that in thee indeed, which I have greater reason to believe now than ever,
230   I mean purpose, courage, and valour, this night show it. If thou the next night following enjoy not Desdemona, take me from this world with treachery and devise engines for my life.

RODERIGO

Well, what is it? Is it within reason and compass?

IAGO

Sir, there is especial commission come from Venice to depute
235   Cassio in Othello's place.

RODERIGO

Is that true? Why, then Othello and Desdemona return again to Venice.

IAGO

O, no; he goes into Mauritania and taketh away with him the fair Desdemona, unless his abode be ling'red here by some accident;
240   wherein none can be so determinate as the removing of Cassio.

Desdemona. If she'll give me back my jewels, I'll give up
wooing her and apologize for my improper proposal. If not, you
   can be sure
that I'll make you pay.

IAGO
You've had your say now.

RODERIGO
Yes, and I haven't said anything I don't intend to carry out.

IAGO
Well, now I can see that you've got some grit; and from this
   moment on,
I have a better opinion of you than ever before. Give me your
hand, Roderigo. You have good cause to say all this.
Still, I assure you, I've been very straightforward with you.

RODERIGO
It doesn't look like it.

IAGO
I'll admit that it doesn't, and your suspicions are not
foolish or improbable. But, Roderigo, if you've got some of
that stuff in you which I'm more convinced than ever that you
   really have
(I mean determination, courage, and valor), show it tonight. If
Desdemona isn't yours tomorrow night, you can
treacherously kill me and plot against my life.

RODERIGO
Well, what do you want me to do? Is it reasonable and possible?

IAGO
Sir, there's been an official order from Venice for
Cassio to take Othello's place.

RODERIGO
Is that true? Why, then Othello and Desdemona will be
   returning to
Venice.

IAGO
Oh, no. He'll go to Mauritania and take the lovely
Desdemona with him—unless he has to stay here because of
   some accident.
Nothing can be more certain to bring that about than getting
   rid of Cassio.

RODERIGO
How do you mean, removing him?

IAGO
Why, by making him uncapable of Othello's place; knocking out his brains.

RODERIGO
And that you would have me to do?

IAGO
245   Ay, if you dare do yourself a profit and a right. He sups to-night with a harlotry, and thither will I go to him; he knows not yet of his honourable fortune. If you will watch his going thence, which I will fashion to fall out between twelve and one, you may take him at your pleasure. I will be near to second your attempt,
250   and he shall fall between us. Come, stand not amaz'd at it, but go along with me; I will show you such a necessity in his death that you shall think yourself bound to put it on him. It is now high suppertime, and the night grows to waste. About it.

RODERIGO
I will hear further reason for this.

IAGO
255   And you shall be satisfi'd.
        [*Exeunt.*]

Scene iii: [*Another room in the castle.*] *Enter* OTHELLO, LODOVICO, DESDEMONA, EMILIA, *and Attendants.*

LODOVICO
I do beseech you, sir, trouble yourself no further.

OTHELLO
O, pardon me; 'twill do me good to walk.

LODOVICO
Madam, good-night; I humbly thank your ladyship.

DESDEMONA
Your honour is most welcome.

RODERIGO
What do you mean, getting rid of him?

IAGO
Why, by making him unable to take Othello's place—by beating out
his brains.

RODERIGO
And that's what you want me to do?

IAGO
245   Yes, if you dare to do the best and most profitable thing for
yourself. He's eating tonight
with a harlot, and I'm going to meet him there. He hasn't heard the news
of his good luck yet. If you'll wait for him to leave,
which I'll arrange to have happen between twelve and one, you can
finish him off at your leisure. I'll be nearby to back you up,
250   and between the two of us, he'll die. Come on, don't stand there dumbfounded, but
come with me. I'll give you such good reasons for killing him
that you'll feel obligated to slay him. It's
suppertime now, and the night is going to waste. Let's get to it!

RODERIGO
I want to hear more reasons for this.

IAGO
255   You'll hear them.
       They exit.

Act IV, Scene iii: Another room in the castle. Enter OTHELLO,
LODOVICO, DESDEMONA, EMILIA, *and* ATTENDANTS.

LODOVICO
Please, sir, don't trouble yourself any further.

OTHELLO
No, allow me; the walk will do me good.

LODOVICO
Good night, madam. Thank you for the lovely evening.

DESDEMONA
You are very welcome, your honor.

OTHELLO

₅   Will you walk, sir?
O,—Desdemona,—

DESDEMONA
My lord?

OTHELLO
Get you to bed on th' instant; I will be return'd forthwith. Dismiss
your attendant there. Look 't be done.

DESDEMONA
₁₀   I will my lord.
          [*Exeunt Othello, Lodovico, and Attendants.*]

EMILIA
How goes it now? He looks gentler than he did.

DESDEMONA
He says he will return incontinent;
And hath commanded me to go to bed,
And bid me to dismiss you.

EMILIA
₁₅   Dismiss me!

DESDEMONA
It was his bidding; therefore, good Emilia,
Give me my nightly wearing, and adieu.
We must not now displease him.

EMILIA
I would you had never seen him!

DESDEMONA
₂₀   So would not I. My love doth so approve him,
That even his stubbornness, his checks, his frowns,—
Prithee, unpin me,—have grace and favour in them.

EMILIA
I have laid those sheets you bade me on the bed.

DESDEMONA
All's one. Good faith, how foolish are our minds!
₂₅   If I do die before, prithee, shroud me
In one of these same sheets.

OTHELLO
5 Will you walk with me, sir?
 Oh, Desdemona—

DESDEMONA
 Yes, my lord?

OTHELLO
 Go to bed at once. I'll be back soon. Send
 your servant away. Be sure to do it.

DESDEMONA
10 I will, my lord.
    Exit OTHELLO, LODOVICO, *and* ATTENDANTS.

EMILIA
 How is it going now? He seems to be in a better mood than before.

DESDEMONA
 He says he'll be back immediately.
 He's commanded me to go to bed
 and to send you away.

EMILIA
15 Send me away?

DESDEMONA
 That's what he told me to do. So, good Emilia,
 give me my night clothes, and goodbye.
 We must be careful not to displease him now.

EMILIA
 I wish you had never seen him!

DESDEMONA
20 But I don't. I love him so much
 that even his roughness, his criticisms, and his frowns
 (please unpin me) have something graceful and good about them.

EMILIA *(Helping her change for bed)*
 I've put those sheets on the bed which you told me to.

DESDEMONA
 It doesn't matter. My goodness, how foolish we are!
25 If I die before you do, please wrap me
 in one of these sheets.

EMILIA

Come, come, you talk.

DESDEMONA

My mother had a maid call'd Barbary;
She was in love, and he she lov'd prov'd mad

30 And did forsake her. She had a song of "Willow";
An old thing 'twas, but it express'd her fortune,
And she died singing it. That song to-night
Will not go from my mind; I have much to do
But to go hang my head all at one side

35 And sing it like poor Barbary. Prithee, dispatch.

EMILIA

Shall I go fetch your night-gown?

DESDEMONA

No, unpin me here.
This Lodovico is a proper man.

EMILIA

A very handsome man.

DESDEMONA

40 He speaks well.

EMILIA

I know a lady in Venice would have walk'd barefoot to Palestine
for a touch of his nether lip.

DESDEMONA

[*Singing.*]
"The poor soul sat sighing by a sycamore tree,
  Sing all a green willow;

45 Her hand on her bosom, her head on her knee,
  Sing willow, willow, willow.
The fresh streams ran by her, and murmur'd her moans;
  Sing willow, willow, willow;
Her salt tears fell from her, and soft'ned the stones;

50 Sing willow, willow, willow;"
Lay by these;—
[*Singing.*] "Willow, willow;"—

EMILIA
Come, come! What kind of talk is that?

DESDEMONA
My mother had a maid named Barbary.
She was in love; and the man she was in love with turned out
    to be mad
30 and left her. She sang a song called "Willow."
It was an old song, but it told her sad story,
and she died singing it. I can't get that song
out of my mind tonight. I can barely stop myself
from hanging my head to one side
35 and singing it like poor Barbary. Please hurry.

EMILIA
Should I go get your nightgown?

DESDEMONA
No, unpin me here.
That Lodovico is a fine man.

EMILIA
A very handsome man.

DESDEMONA
40 He speaks well.

EMILIA
I know a Venetian lady who would walk barefoot to Palestine
for just one kiss.

DESDEMONA (*Singing*)
A poor soul sighing sat by a sycamore tree;
    Let's all sing of a green willow.
45 Her hand was on her bosom and her head was on her knee;
    Sing of a willow, willow, willow.
The fresh stream ran by her and echoed her moans;
    Sing of a willow, willow, willow.
Her salt tears fell from her eyes and softened the stones;
50   Sing of a willow—
(*Handing Emilia her clothes.*) Put these away.
(*Singing*)—willow, willow—

Prithee, hie thee; he'll come anon;—
[*Singing.*]
"Sing all a green willow must be my garland.
55　　Let nobody blame him, his scorn I approve,"—
Nay, that's not next.—Hark! who is't that knocks?

EMILIA
It's the wind.

DESDEMONA
[*Singing.*]
"I call'd my love false love; but what said he then?
　　Sing willow, willow, willow.
60　If I court moe women, you'll couch with moe men."—
So, get thee gone; good-night. Mine eyes do itch;
Doth that bode weeping?

EMILIA
　　　　　　　'Tis neither here nor there.

DESDEMONA
I have heard it said so. O, these men, these men!
65　Dost thou in conscience think,—tell me, Emilia,—
That there be women do abuse their husbands
In such gross kind?

EMILIA
　　　　　　There be some such, no question.

DESDEMONA
Wouldst thou do such a deed for all the world?

EMILIA
70　Why, would not you?

DESDEMONA
　　　　　　No, by this heavenly light!

EMILIA
Nor I neither by this heavenly light;
I might do't as well i' th' dark.

DESDEMONA
Wouldst thou do such a deed for all the world?

Please go; he'll be coming soon.
(Singing)
Let's all sing of a green willow, which will be my funeral wreath.
55 Let nobody blame him; I understand his scorn for me—
No, that's not what comes next. Listen! Who is that knocking?

EMILIA
It's just the wind.

DESDEMONA *(Singing)*
I called my lover unfaithful; but what did he say to that?
Sing of a willow, willow, willow.
60 If I pursue other women, you'll sleep with other men.
(To Emilia) Well, get going; good night. My eyes are itching.
Does that mean I'll soon cry?

EMILIA
That has nothing to do with it one way or the other.

DESDEMONA
I've heard it did. Oh, these men, these men!
65 Do you honestly think—tell me the truth, Emilia—
that there are women who mistreat their husbands
in such an awful way?

EMILIA
There are some; there's no question about it.

DESDEMONA
Would you do such a thing for all the world?

EMILIA
70 Why, wouldn't you?

DESDEMONA
No, I swear by the light of the stars I wouldn't!

EMILIA
Well, I wouldn't do it by the light of the stars.
It would be easier to do in the dark.

DESDEMONA
Would you really do such a thing for all the world?

EMILIA

75　The world's a huge thing; it is a great price
For a small vice.

DESDEMONA

　　　　　In troth, I think thou wouldst not.

EMILIA

In troth, I think I should; and undo't when I had done. Marry,
I would not do such a thing for a joint-ring, nor for measures
80　of lawn, nor for gowns, petticoats, nor caps, nor any petty
exhibition; but, for all the whole world,—'ud's pity, who would
not make her husband a cuckold to make him a monarch? I should
venture purgatory for't.

DESDEMONA

Beshrew me, if I would do such a wrong
85　For the whole world.

EMILIA

Why, the wrong is but a wrong i' th' world; and having the world
for your labour, 'tis a wrong in your own world, and you might
quickly make it right.

DESDEMONA

I do not think there is any such woman.

EMILIA

90　Yes, a dozen; and as many to th' vantage as would store
the world they play'd for.
But I do think it is their husbands' faults
If wives do fall. Say that they slack their duties
And pour our treasures into foreign laps,
Or else break out in peevish jealousies,
95　Throwing restraint upon us; or say they strike us,
Or scant our former having in despite;
Why, we have galls, and though we have some grace,
Yet have we some revenge. Let husbands know
Their wives have sense like them; they see and smell
100　And have their palates both for sweet and sour
As husbands have. What is it that they do
When they change us for others? Is it sport?

---

79 *joint-ring*　a ring with two interlocking halves traditionally given as a love token.

EMILIA

75   The world's a huge thing. It would be a great payment
for a little sin.

DESDEMONA

Really, I don't think you would.

EMILIA

Really, I think I would; and I'd make up for it once it was
done. Of course,
I wouldn't do such a thing for a little ring, or for a
great deal
80   of linen, or for dresses, petticoats, or caps, or any trivial
gift. But for the whole world? For God's sake! Who wouldn't
be unfaithful to her husband to make him a king? I'd risk
going to purgatory for that.

DESDEMONA

Curse me if I would do a wrong like that
85   for the whole world.

EMILIA

Why, that wrong is just one of many in the world. And if you
got the whole world
for your trouble, then it's wrong in your own world, and you can
quickly make everything right again.

DESDEMONA

I don't really think there is such a woman.

EMILIA

90   Yes, there are at least a dozen—and enough others
to fill up the world they schemed to get.
But I really think it's the fault of the husbands
if wives do wrong. Suppose they sluff off their duties,
or give our valuables to other women,
or else have a fit of foolish jealousy
95   and restrain our comings and goings. Or suppose they hit us,
or deprive us of things we usually have out of spite—
Well, we can become resentful too; and while we are ladylike,
we can be vengeful as well. So let all husbands know
their wives have feelings like them. They see, smell,
100   and have a taste for both sweet and sour things
just like their husbands. What's behind their actions
when they reject us for other women? Is it an amusement?

I think it is. And doth affection breed it?
I think it doth. Is't frailty that thus errs?
105   It is so too. And have not we affections,
Desires for sport, and frailty, as men have?
Then let them use us well; else let them know,
The ills we do, their ills instruct us so.

DESDEMONA
Good-night, good-night. Heaven me such uses send,
110   Not to pick bad from bad, but by bad mend.
          [*Exeunt.*]

Act V, Scene i: [*Cyprus. A street.*] *Enter* IAGO *and* RODERIGO.

IAGO
Here, stand behind this bulk; straight will he come.
Wear thy good rapier bare, and put it home.
Quick, quick; fear nothing; I'll be at thy elbow.
It makes us, or it mars us; think on that,
5   And fix most firm thy resolution.

RODERIGO
Be near at hand; I may miscarry in't.

IAGO
Here, at thy hand; be bold, and take thy stand. [*Retires.*]

RODERIGO
I have no great devotion to the deed,
And yet he hath given me satisfying reasons.
10   'Tis but a man gone. Forth, my sword: he dies.

IAGO
I have rubb'd this young quat almost to the sense,
And he grows angry. Now, whether he kill Cassio,
Or Cassio him, or each do kill the other,
Every way makes my gain. Live Roderigo,
15   He calls me to a restitution large
Of gold and jewels that I bobb'd from him
As gifts to Desdemona;
It must not be. If Cassio do remain,

---

1 *bulk*   a part of a building that juts out.

I think so. And does it result from desire?
I think it does. Is it frailty that leads them to sin?
105   It certainly is. And don't we have longings,
a desire for amusement, and frailties just like men?
Then they'd better treat us well; otherwise, let them know
the bad things we do are things we learned from them.

DESDEMONA
Good night, good night. I hope that heaven teaches me
110   how not to return evil with evil but to make myself better
    by it!
       They exit.

Act V, Scene i: Cyprus. A street. Enter IAGO *and* RODERIGO.

IAGO
Here, hide behind this corner; he'll be here any minute.
Keep your sword out, and be ready to use it.
Quick, quick! Don't be afraid; I'll be right at your elbow.
This will either bring us success or ruin us—remember that,
5   and resolve yourself to it.

RODERIGO
Stay close by. I might make a mistake.

IAGO
I'll be right here. Be bold, and be ready to fight.
       *(*IAGO *hides himself.)*

RODERIGO
My heart really isn't in doing this;
but still, he's given me good reasons for it.
10   It will be just another man dead. My sword is drawn! He'll die!

IAGO
I've rubbed this young pimple almost raw,
and he's getting angry. It doesn't matter if he kills Cassio
or if Cassio kills him or if they kill each other—
it'll be good for me in any case. If Roderigo lives,
15   he'll expect me to give back
all the gold and jewels I swindled him out of
as gifts to Desdemona.
That must not happen. If Cassio survives,

He hath a daily beauty in his life
20   That makes me ugly; and, besides, the Moor
May unfold me to him; there stand I in much peril.
No, he must die. But so; I heard him coming.
    Enter CASSIO.

RODERIGO
I know his gait, 'tis he.—Villain, thou diest!
    [*Makes a pass at Cassio.*]

CASSIO
That thrust had been mine enemy indeed,
25   But that my coat is better than thou know'st.
I will make proof of thine.
    [*Draws, and wounds Roderigo.*]

RODERIGO
                    O, I am slain.
    [*Iago from behind wounds Cassio in the leg, and exit.*]

CASSIO
I am maim'd for ever. Help, ho! murder! murder! [*Falls.*]
    Enter OTHELLO.

OTHELLO
The voice of Cassio! Iago keeps his word.

RODERIGO
30   O, villain that I am!

OTHELLO
                    It is even so.

CASSIO
O, help, ho! light! a surgeon!

OTHELLO
'Tis he!—O brave Iago, honest and just,
That hast such noble sense of thy friend's wrong!
35   Thou teachest me. Minion, your dear lies dead,
And your unblest fate hies; strumpet, I come.
Forth of my heart those charms, thine eyes, are blotted;
Thy bed, lust-stain'd, shall with lust's blood be spotted.
    [*Exit.*]

20
he has such an everyday beauty in his life
that he makes me look ugly. And besides, the Moor
might reveal my lies to him; that's a very great risk for me.
No, he has to die. But I hear him coming.
    Enter CASSIO.

RODERIGO
I know his walk. It's him. Villain, get ready to die!
    *(*RODERIGO *attacks Cassio with a sword.)*

CASSIO
That thrust would have really done me in
25
if my armor weren't better than you expected.
I'll see how good yours is.
    *(*CASSIO *draws his sword and wounds Roderigo.)*

RODERIGO
Oh, I've been killed!
    *(*IAGO *comes forward, wounds Cassio from behind, and*
      exits.)

CASSIO
I've been badly wounded. Help! Murder! Murder! *(He falls.)*
    Enter OTHELLO.

OTHELLO
That's Cassio's voice. Iago has kept his promise.

RODERIGO
30
Oh, what a villain I am!

OTHELLO
It's really been done.

CASSIO
Oh, help! Give me some light! Bring me a surgeon!

OTHELLO
It's really him. Oh, noble Iago, you honest and just man,
you really feel for a friend who has suffered a wrong!
35
You're my teacher. Hussy, your lover lies dead
and your own death is near. Harlot, I'm coming.
Those charming eyes of yours are blotted out of my heart.
Your lust-stained bed will soon be stained with your lustful blood.
    Exit OTHELLO.

Enter LODOVICO *and* GRATIANO.

CASSIO
What, ho! no watch? no passage? Murder! murder!

GRATIANO
40   'Tis some mischance; the voice is very direful.

CASSIO
O, help!

LODOVICO
Hark!

RODERIGO
O wretched villain!

LODOVICO
Two or three groan. 'Tis heavy night,
45   These may be counterfeits; let's think 't unsafe
To come in to the cry without more help.

RODERIGO
Nobody come? Then shall I bleed to death.
Re-enter IAGO, *with a light.*

LODOVICO
Hark!

GRATIANO
Here's one comes in his shirt, with light and weapons.

IAGO
50   Who's there? Whose noise is this that cries on murder?

LODOVICO
We do not know.

IAGO
                    Do not you hear a cry?

CASSIO
Here, here! for Heaven's sake, help me!

IAGO
                    What's the matter?

Enter LODOVICO *and* GRATIANO.

CASSIO
What's this? No one on watch? No passers-by? Murder! Murder!

GRATIANO
40   Something terrible has happened. That's a very frightening cry.

CASSIO
Oh, help!

LODOVICO
Listen!

RODERIGO
Miserable villain!

LODOVICO
There are two or three men groaning. It's a very dark night.
45   They might be faking in order to trap us. We'd better not try
to approach the ones who are crying without others to help us.

RODERIGO
Won't anybody come? Then I'll bleed to death.
Enter IAGO *with a light.*

LODOVICO
Listen!

GRATIANO
A man is coming in his nightshirt, with a lamp and weapons.

IAGO
50   Who's there? Whose voice is it that's crying out murder?

LODOVICO
We don't know.

IAGO
Didn't you hear a cry?

CASSIO
Over here, over here! For heaven's sake, help me!

IAGO
What's the matter?

GRATIANO
55   This is Othello's ancient, as I take it.

LODOVICO
The same indeed; a very valiant fellow.

IAGO
What are you here that cry so grievously?

CASSIO
Iago? O, I am spoil'd, undone by villains!
Give me some help.

IAGO
60   O me, Lieutenant! what villains have done this?

CASSIO
I think that one of them is hereabout
And cannot make away.

IAGO
                    O treacherous villains!
What are you there?—Come in, and give some help.
[*To Lodovico and Gratiano.*]

RODERIGO
65   O, help me there!

CASSIO
That's one of them.

IAGO
                    O murd'rous slave! O villain!
                         [*Thrusts Roderigo in.*]

RODERIGO
O damn'd Iago! O inhuman dog!

IAGO
Kill men i' th' dark!—Where be these bloody thieves?—
70   How silent is this town!—Ho! murder! murder!—
What may you be? Are you of good or evil?

LODOVICO
As you shall prove us, praise us.

GRATIANO

55   This is Othello's ensign, I assume.

LODOVICO

    Yes it is; he's a very noble fellow.

IAGO

    Who is that who's crying so miserably?

CASSIO

    Iago? Oh, I have been mutilated and killed by villains!
    Give me some help.

IAGO

60   Oh, no, lieutenant! What villains have done this?

CASSIO

    I think one of them is nearby
    and can't get away.

IAGO

    Oh, the treacherous villains!
    (To Lodovico and Gratiano) Who's over there? Come and give
      me some help.

RODERIGO

65   Oh, help me here!

CASSIO

    That's one of them.

IAGO

    You murderous scum! You villain! *(He stabs Roderigo.)*

RODERIGO

    Damn you, Iago! You inhuman dog! *(He dies.)*

IAGO

    The idea of killing men in the dark! Where are these
      bloodthirsty thieves?
70   The town is so silent! Hey! Murder! Murder!
    Who are you? Are you good or evil?

LODOVICO

    You can judge us by what we do.

IAGO
Signior Lodovico?

LODOVICO
He, sir.

IAGO
75   I cry you mercy. Here's Cassio hurt by villains.

GRATIANO
Cassio!

IAGO
How is't, brother!

CASSIO
My leg is cut in two.

IAGO
                      Marry, heaven forbid!
80   Light, gentlemen! I'll bind it with my shirt.
    Enter BIANCA.

BIANCA
What is the matter, ho? Who is't that cried?

IAGO
Who is't that cried!

BIANCA
O my dear Cassio! my sweet Cassio!
O Cassio, Cassio, Cassio!

IAGO
85   O notable strumpet! Cassio, may you suspect
Who they should be that have thus mangled you?

CASSIO
No.

GRATIANO
I am sorry to find you thus; I have been to seek you.

IAGO
Lend me a garter. So. O, for a chair,
90   To bear him easily hence!

IAGO
Signior Lodovico?

LODOVICO
That's me, sir.

IAGO
75   I beg your pardon. Here's Cassio, who's been hurt by villains.

GRATIANO
Cassio?

IAGO
How are you, brother?

CASSIO
My leg has been cut in two.

IAGO
Really, heaven forbid!
80   Give me some light, gentlemen. I'll bandage it with my shirt.
      Enter BIANCA.

BIANCA
What's the matter here? Who did I hear crying out?

IAGO
Who did you hear crying out?

BIANCA
Oh, it's my dear Cassio! My sweet Cassio!
Oh, Cassio, Cassio, Cassio!

IAGO
85   You notorious harlot!—Cassio, do you have any idea
who it was that injured you like this?

CASSIO
No.

GRATIANO
I'm sorry to find you like this. I've been looking for you.

IAGO
Somebody lend me a garter. Good. Oh, if only we had a sedan
chair
90   so we could carry him away more easily!

BIANCA
Alas, he faints! O Cassio, Cassio, Cassio!

IAGO
Gentleman all, I do suspect this trash
To be a party in this injury.
Patience a while, good Cassio. Come, come;
95   Lend me a light. Know we this face or no?
Alas, my friend and my dear countryman
Roderigo! No:—yes, sure:—yes, 'tis Roderigo.

GRATIANO
What, of Venice?

IAGO
Even he, sir; did you know him?

GRATIANO
100   Know him! ay.

IAGO
Signior Gratiano? I cry your gentle pardon;
These bloody accidents must excuse my manners
That so neglected you.

GRATIANO
                I am glad to see you.

IAGO
105   How do you, Cassio? O, a chair, a chair!

GRATIANO
Roderigo!

IAGO
He, he, 'tis he. [*A chair brought in.*] O, that's well said;
    the chair.
Some good man bear him carefully from hence;
I'll fetch the General's surgeon. [*To Bianca.*] For you,
    mistress,
110   Save you your labour. He that lies slain here, Cassio,
Was my dear friend. What malice was between you?

BIANCA
Oh, he's fainted! Oh, Cassio, Cassio, Cassio!

IAGO
Gentlemen, I suspect this slut
to have had a hand in this attack.—
Be patient awhile, good Cassio.—Come, come!
95   Give me some light. *(He goes over to Roderigo.)* Do we know
    this man, or not?
Oh, is it my friend and my dear countryman
Roderigo? It can't be. Yes, it surely is. Oh, heavens! Roderigo.

GRATIANO
You mean from Venice?

IAGO
That's the man, sir. Did you know him?

GRATIANO
100   Know him? Yes.

IAGO
Signior Gratiano? I must ask you to pardon me.
These bloody actions have made me forget my manners
and neglect you.

GRATIANO
I'm glad to see you.

IAGO
105   How are you, Cassio? *(To the others)* Oh, get a chair, a chair!

GRATIANO
Roderigo!

IAGO
Yes, it's him, it's him. *(A chair is brought in.)* Yes, well
    done! The chair.
Some good men carry him carefully away from here.
I'll get the general's surgeon. *(To Bianca)* And as for you,
    woman,
110   don't bother to help. *(To Cassio)* The man lying dead here,
    Cassio,
was my dear friend. What kind of quarrel did you have with
    him?

CASSIO
None in the world; nor do I know the man.

IAGO
[*To Bianca*] What, look you pale? O, bear him out o' th' air.
[*Cassio and Roderigo are borne off.*]
Stay you, good gentleman. Look you pale, mistress?
115   Do you perceive the gastness of her eye?
Nay, if you stare, we shall hear more anon.
Behold her well; I pray you, look upon her.
Do you see, gentlemen? Nay, guiltiness will speak,
Though tongues were out of use.
    Enter EMILIA.

EMILIA
120   Alas, what's the matter? What's the matter, husband?

IAGO
Cassio hath here been set on in the dark
By Roderigo and fellows that are scap'd.
He's almost slain, and Roderigo quite dead.

EMILIA
Alas, good gentleman! alas, good Cassio!

IAGO
125   This is the fruits of whoring. Prithee, Emilia,
Go know of Cassio where he supp'd to-night.
[*To Bianca.*] What, do you shake at that?

BIANCA
He supp'd at my house; but I therefore shake not.

IAGO
O, did he so? I charge you, go with me.

EMILIA
130   Oh, fie upon thee, strumpet!

BIANCA
I am no strumpet, but of life as honest
As you that thus abuse me.

CASSIO
>None at all; I don't even know the man.

IAGO *(To Bianca)*
>Why, you're looking very pale. *(To the others)* Carry him away.
>>*(Cassio and Roderigo are carried off.)*
>Wait, gentlemen. *(To Bianca)* Are you looking pale, woman?
>*(To the others)* Don't you see the terror in her eyes?
>*(To Bianca)* Well, if you keep staring like that, we'll soon
>>know more.
>*(To the others)* Take a good look at her; I ask you to look at her.
>Do you see, gentlemen? Guiltiness will speak for itself,
>even if people stop talking altogether.
>>*Enter* EMILIA.

115

EMILIA
>Oh, what's the matter? What's the matter, husband?

120

IAGO
>Cassio was attacked here in the dark
>by Roderigo and some others who escaped.
>He was almost killed, and Roderigo is dead.

EMILIA
>Oh, such a good gentleman! Oh, good Cassio!

IAGO
>This is what comes of whoring. Please, Emilia,
>go ask where Cassio had supper tonight.
>*(To Bianca)* What, does my question cause you to shake?

125

BIANCA
>He had supper at my house; but I'm not shaking because of that.

IAGO
>Oh, he did? I order you to come with me.

EMILIA
>Curses, curses on you, harlot!

130

BIANCA
>I am no harlot; I live as honestly
>as you people who accuse me.

EMILIA

As I? Fie upon thee!

IAGO

Kind gentlemen, let's go see poor Cassio dress'd.
135   Come, mistress, you must tell's another tale.
Emilia, run you to the citadel,
And tell my lord and lady what hath happ'd.
Will you go on afore? [*Aside.*] This is the night
That either makes me or fordoes me quite.
[*Exeunt.*]

Scene ii: [*A bedchamber in the castle:* DESDEMONA *in bed asleep.*] Enter OTHELLO *with a light.*

OTHELLO

It is the cause, it is the cause, my soul,—
Let me not name it to you, you chaste stars!
It is the cause. Yet I'll not shed her blood,
Nor scar that whiter skin of hers than snow,
5   And smooth as monumental alabaster.
Yet she must die, else she'll betray more men.
Put out the light, and then put out the light.
If I quench thee, thou flaming minister,
I can again thy former light restore,
10   Should I repent me; but once put out thy light,
Thou cunning'st pattern of excelling nature,
I know not where is that Promethean heat
That can thy light relume. When I have pluck'd the rose
I cannot give it vital growth again,
15   It needs must wither. I'll smell it on the tree. [*Kisses her.*]
Oh, balmy breath, that dost almost persuade
Justice to break her sword! One more, one more.
Be thus when thou art dead, and I will kill thee
And love thee after. One more, and that's the last;
20   So sweet was ne'er so fatal. I must weep,
But they are cruel tears. This sorrow's heavenly;
It strikes where it doth love. She wakes.

---

7 *put out the light . . . light*   Othello compares the light of the candle he holds to the "light" of Desdemona's life.   12 *Promethean heat* Prometheus was a Greek deity who stole fire from heaven and gave it to humanity.

EMILIA

    As I? Nonsense! Curses on you!

IAGO

    Kind gentlemen, let's go see that poor Cassio is tended to.
135   *(To Bianca)* Come along, woman. You'd better come up with
        another story.—
    Emilia, run to the castle
    and tell my lord and lady what has happened.—
    Won't you go on ahead? *(To himself)* This is a night
    which will either make me or destroy me.
        They exit.

Act V, Scene ii: A bedchamber in the castle. DESDEMONA *is in bed
asleep.* OTHELLO *enters with a candle.*

OTHELLO

    I know the cause of all this; I know the cause, my soul.
    I won't say its name before you, you chaste stars!
    I know the cause. Still, I won't shed her blood
    or scar that skin of hers, which is whiter than snow
5   and as smooth as the alabaster of a monument.
    Still, she has to die or else she'll betray more men.
    I'll put out this light and then put out her light.
    If I extinguish your light, flaming servant,
    I can always relight you again
10   if I regret my action. But once I put out your light,
    you skillfully designed creation of nature,
    I don't know where to find that divine fire
    that can relight you again. When I've picked a rose,
    I can't make it grow again;
15   it's doomed to wither. I'll smell it on the tree. *(He kisses her.)*
    Her sweet breath would almost persuade
    Justice to break her sword! One more kiss, one more!
    Be like this when you're dead, and I'll kill you
    and love you afterwards. One more kiss, and this is the last!
20   Such sweetness has never before been so fatal. I must weep,
    but I cry cruel tears. My sorrow is like that of God
    when punishing his beloved sinners. She's awakening.

DESDEMONA
Who's there? Othello?

OTHELLO
                    Ay, Desdemona.

DESDEMONA
25   Will you come to bed, my lord?

OTHELLO
Have you pray'd to-night, Desdemon?

DESDEMONA
                    Ay, my lord.

OTHELLO
If you bethink yourself of any crime
Unreconcil'd as yet to Heaven and grace,
30   Solicit for it straight.

DESDEMONA
Alack, my lord, what may you mean by that?

OTHELLO
Well, do it, and be brief; I will walk by.
I would not kill thy unprepared spirit;
No; heavens forfend! I would not kill thy soul.

DESDEMONA
35   Talk you of killing?

OTHELLO
                    Ay, I do.

DESDEMONA
                              Then Heaven
Have mercy on me!

OTHELLO
                    Amen, with all my heart!

DESDEMONA
40   If you say so, I hope you will not kill me.

OTHELLO
Hum!

DESDEMONA
Who's there? Othello?

OTHELLO
Yes, Desdemona.

DESDEMONA
25   Won't you come to bed, my lord?

OTHELLO
Have you prayed tonight, Desdemona?

DESDEMONA
Yes, my lord.

OTHELLO
If you can think of any crime
which you haven't yet confessed to heaven,
30   ask forgiveness for it now.

DESDEMONA
Oh, my lord, what do you mean by that?

OTHELLO
Well, get on with it, and be quick; I will wait nearby.
I don't want to kill your unrepentant spirit.
No, heaven forbid! I don't want to kill your soul.

DESDEMONA
35   Do you talk of killing?

OTHELLO
Yes, I do.

DESDEMONA
Then heaven
have mercy on me!

OTHELLO
I say amen, with all my heart!

DESDEMONA
40   If you mean that, I hope you will not kill me.

OTHELLO
Hum!

DESDEMONA

And yet I fear you; for you're fatal then
When your eyes roll so. Why I should fear I know not,
Since guiltiness I know not; but yet I feel I fear.

OTHELLO

45   Think on thy sins.

DESDEMONA

                   They are loves I bear to you.

OTHELLO

Ay, and for that thou diest.

DESDEMONA

That death's unnatural that kills for loving.
Alas, why gnaw you so your nether lip?
50   Some bloody passion shakes your very frame.
These are portents; but yet I hope, I hope,
They do not point on me.

OTHELLO

                Peace, and be still!

DESDEMONA

I will so. What's the matter?

OTHELLO

55   That handkerchief which I so lov'd and gave thee
Thou gav'st to Cassio.

DESDEMONA

              No, by my life and soul!
Send for the man, and ask him.

OTHELLO

                Sweet soul, take heed,
60   Take heed of perjury; thou art on thy deathbed.

DESDEMONA

Ay, but not yet to die.

OTHELLO

             Yes, presently:
Therefore confess thee freely of thy sin;

DESDEMONA
Still, I'm afraid of you; you are dangerous
when your eyes roll like that. I don't know why I fear you,
since I don't know of what I'm guilty. Still, I'm afraid.

OTHELLO
45   Think about your sins.

DESDEMONA
They are all the different loves I've had for you.

OTHELLO
Yes, and that's why you'll die.

DESDEMONA
It's unnatural to kill out of love.
Oh, why are you gnawing on your lower lip like that?
50   Some violent anger is causing you to shake.
These are bad signs. But still I hope, I hope,
they won't mean any harm to me.

OTHELLO
Hold your tongue and be still!

DESDEMONA
I will do so. What's the matter?

OTHELLO
55   The handkerchief I loved so much and gave to you,
you gave to Cassio.

DESDEMONA
No, I swear by my life and soul!
Send for the man and ask him.

OTHELLO
Sweet soul, be careful,
60   be careful of perjury; you're on your deathbed.

DESDEMONA
Yes, but it's not time for me to die.

OTHELLO
Yes, immediately.
Therefore, confess your sins openly,

For to deny each article with oath
65   Cannot remove nor choke the strong conception
That I do groan withal. Thou art to die.

DESDEMONA
O, Heaven, have mercy on me!

OTHELLO
                I say, amen.

DESDEMONA
And have you mercy too! I never did
70   Offend you in my life; never lov'd Cassio
But with such general warranty of heaven
As I might love; I never gave him token.

OTHELLO
By heaven, I saw my handkerchief in 's hand.
O perjur'd woman! thou dost stone my heart,
75   And makes me call what I intend to do
A murder, which I thought a sacrifice.
I saw the handkerchief.

DESDEMONA
              He found it then;
I never gave it him. Send for him hither;
80   Let him confess a truth.

OTHELLO
              He hath confess'd.

DESDEMONA
What, my lord?

OTHELLO
That he hath us'd thee.

DESDEMONA
              How! unlawfully?

OTHELLO
85   Ay.

DESDEMONA
He will not say so.

---

76 *A murder . . . sacrifice* Desdemona's protests have so incensed Othello that his killing of Desdemona will more resemble a murder committed out of heated passion than an execution dispassionately carried out.

since solemnly denying each charge
65   won't lift or kill the set purpose
that causes me to groan like this. You must die.

DESDEMONA
Then may the Lord have mercy on me!

OTHELLO
I say amen.

DESDEMONA
And may you have mercy too! I never
70   offended you in my life. I never loved Cassio
except in such a way that heaven
would find permissible. I never gave him a token of love.

OTHELLO
By heaven, I saw my handkerchief in his hand!
You lying woman! You have turned my heart into stone
75   and make me call what I intend to do
a murder, when I intended it as a sacrifice.
I saw the handkerchief.

DESDEMONA
He must have found it then.
I never gave it to him. Summon him here.
80   Let him confess the truth.

OTHELLO
He has confessed already.

DESDEMONA
To what, my lord?

OTHELLO
That he has had you.

DESDEMONA
How? Improperly?

OTHELLO
85   Yes.

DESDEMONA
He won't say that.

OTHELLO

                      No, his mouth is stopp'd;
Honest Iago hath ta'en order for't.

DESDEMONA

O! my fear interprets. What, is he dead?

OTHELLO

90   Had all his hairs been lives, my great revenge
Had stomach for them all.

DESDEMONA

Alas! he is betray'd and I undone.

OTHELLO

Out, strumpet! weep'st thou for him to my face?

DESDEMONA

O, banish me, my lord, but kill me not!

OTHELLO

95   Down, strumpet!

DESDEMONA

Kill me to-morrow; let me live to-night!

OTHELLO

Nay, if you strive,—

DESDEMONA

But half an hour!

OTHELLO

                   Being done, there is no pause.

DESDEMONA

100   But while I say one prayer!

OTHELLO

                     It is too late.

    [*He smothers her.*]

EMILIA

    [*At the door.*] My lord, my lord! What, ho! my lord,
    my lord!

OTHELLO
No, his mouth has been stopped.
Honest Iago was given orders to see to that.

DESDEMONA
Oh, my fear makes me wonder. Is he dead?

OTHELLO
90 If all of his hairs had been lives, my vengefulness
would have killed them all.

DESDEMONA
Oh, he has been betrayed, and I am finished!

OTHELLO
Enough, harlot! Are you weeping for him to my very face?

DESDEMONA
Oh, banish me, my lord, but don't kill me!

OTHELLO
95 Down with you, harlot!

DESDEMONA
Kill me tomorrow; let me live tonight!

OTHELLO
No, if you even try—

DESDEMONA
Just half an hour!

OTHELLO
Since this is the end, there can be no delay.

DESDEMONA
100 Just let me say one prayer!

OTHELLO
It's too late for that.
  *(*OTHELLO *smothers Desdemona.)*

EMILIA *(At the door)*
My lord, my lord! Can you hear me? My lord, my lord!

OTHELLO

What noise is this? Not dead? not yet quite dead?
I that am cruel am yet merciful;
105   I would not have thee linger in thy pain.
So, so.

EMILIA

[*Within.*] What, ho! my lord, my lord!

OTHELLO

                      Who's there?

EMILIA

[*Within.*] O, good my lord, I would speak a word with you!

OTHELLO

110   Yes:—'tis Emilia.—By and by.—She's dead.
'Tis like she comes to speak of Cassio's death.
The noise was high. Ha! no more moving?
Still as the grave. Shall she come in? Were't good?—
I think she stirs again:—no. What's best to do?
115   If she come in, she'll sure speak to my wife.
My wife! my wife! what wife? I have no wife.
O, insupportable! O heavy hour!
Methinks it should be now a huge eclipse
Of sun and moon, and that th' affrighted globe
120   Did yawn at alteration.

EMILIA

             [*Within.*] I do beseech you
That I may speak with you, O, good my lord!

OTHELLO

I had forgot thee. O, come in, Emilia.
Soft; by and by.—Let me the curtains draw.—
125   Where art thou? [*Unlocks the door.*]
        Enter EMILIA.
What's the matter with thee now?

EMILIA

O, my good lord, yonder's foul murders done!

118-20 *Methinks . . . alteration* the Elizabethans thought nature sometimes echoed major tragedies or other important events that humans experienced.

OTHELLO

What is this noise? Isn't she dead? Not yet quiet dead?
I may be cruel but I'm also merciful;
105   I won't allow you to suffer anymore.
There, there.

EMILIA *(From offstage)*

Can you hear me? My lord, my lord!

OTHELLO

Who's there?

EMILIA *(From offstage)*

Oh, my good lord, I would like to have a word with you!

OTHELLO

110   *(Calling to her)* Yes. *(To himself)* It's Emilia.
    (Calling) In a moment. *(To himself)* She's dead.
It's likely that she's come to tell me of Cassio's death;
she called very loudly. What! Have you stopped moving?
You're as still as the grave. Should I let her in? Is that wise?
I think she's moving again. No. What's the best thing to do?
115   If she comes in, she'll surely speak to my wife.
My wife! My wife! What wife? I do not have a wife.
Oh, this is unbearable! Oh, what a terrible hour!
I think that now a complete eclipse should come
of the sun and moon and the frightened world
120   should gape with an earthquake.

EMILIA *(From offstage)*

I beg you
to let me talk with you, my good lord!

OTHELLO

I'd forgotten you. Oh, come in, Emilia.
Just a moment, I'll be right there. *(To himself)* I'll pull the curtains.
125   *(To Emilia)* Where are you? *(He opens the door.)*
    Enter EMILIA.
What's the matter with you now?

EMILIA

Oh, my good lord, a foul murder has been committed!

OTHELLO
What, now?

EMILIA
But now, my lord.

OTHELLO
130   It is the very error of the moon;
She comes more nearer earth than she was wont,
And makes men mad.

EMILIA
Cassio, my lord, hath kill'd a young Venetian
Call'd Roderigo.

OTHELLO
135   Roderigo kill'd!
And Cassio kill'd!

EMILIA
                   No, Cassio is not kill'd.

OTHELLO
Not Cassio kill'd! Then murder's out of tune,
And sweet revenge grows harsh.

DESDEMONA
140   O, falsely, falsely murder'd!

EMILIA
                   O Lord, what cry is that?

OTHELLO
That! What?

EMILIA
Out, and alas! that was my lady's voice.
Help! help, ho! help! O lady, speak again!
145   Sweet Desdemona! O sweet mistress, speak!

DESDEMONA
A guiltless death I die.

EMILIA
O, who hath done this deed?

OTHELLO
What? Now?

EMILIA
Just now, my lord.

OTHELLO
130   This is due to the irregular course of the moon.
It has come closer to earth than usual
and makes men mad.

EMILIA
My lord, Cassio has killed a young Venetian
named Roderigo.

OTHELLO
135   Has Roderigo been killed?
And Cassio's been killed?

EMILIA
No, Cassio's not been killed.

OTHELLO
Cassio's not been killed? Then the wrong murder has been committed,
and my sweet revenge has turned bitter.

DESDEMONA
140   Wrongly, wrongly murdered!

EMILIA
Oh, lord! What is that cry?

OTHELLO
That? What?

EMILIA
Oh, no! That was my lady's voice.
(Pulling back the bed curtains) Help! Help, somebody!
Help! Oh, lady, speak again!
145   Sweet Desdemona! Oh, sweet lady, speak!

DESDEMONA
I shall die guiltless.

EMILIA
Oh, who has done this deed?

DESDEMONA
　Nobody; I myself. Farewell!
　Commend me to my kind lord. O, farewell! [*Dies.*]

OTHELLO
150　Why, how should she be murd'red?

EMILIA
　　　　　　　Alas, who knows?

OTHELLO
　You hear her say herself, it was not I.

EMILIA
　She said so; I must needs report the truth.

OTHELLO
　She's, like a liar, gone to burning hell.
155　'Twas I that kill'd her.

EMILIA
　　　　　　O, the more angel she,
　And you the blacker devil!

OTHELLO
　She turn'd to folly, and she was a whore.

EMILIA
　Thou dost belie her, and thou art a devil.

OTHELLO
160　She was false as water.

EMILIA
　　　　　　Thou art rash as fire to say
　That she was false: O, she was heavenly true!

OTHELLO
　Cassio did top her; ask thy husband else.
　O, I were damn'd beneath all depth in hell
165　But that I did proceed upon just grounds
　To this extremity. Thy husband knew it all.

EMILIA
　My husband!

---

160 *false as water*　water was said to be false because it holds no shape of its own but shifts to fill whatever container it is in.

DESDEMONA
> Nobody. I, myself. Goodbye.
> Speak well of me to my kind lord. Oh, goodbye! *(She dies.)*

OTHELLO
150   Why, how could she have been murdered!

EMILIA
> Oh, who knows?

OTHELLO
> You heard her say herself, it wasn't me who did it.

EMILIA
> She did say so; I'd testify to that.

OTHELLO
> She's like a liar who's gone to burning hell!
155   It was I who killed her.

EMILIA
> Oh, then she's all the more an angel,
> and you're an even blacker devil!

OTHELLO
> She became an adulteress; she was a whore.

EMILIA
> You are slandering her, and you are a devil.

OTHELLO
160   She was as inconstant as water.

EMILIA
> You are as rash as fire to say
> that she was inconstant. Oh, she was as true as heaven!

OTHELLO
> Cassio made love to her. Ask your husband if that isn't true.
> Oh, I would be damned to the lowest depths of hell
165   if I hadn't proceeded upon just grounds
> to such an extreme action. Your husband knew all about it.

EMILIA
> My husband?

OTHELLO
Thy husband.

EMILIA
That she was false to wedlock?

OTHELLO
170   Ay, with Cassio. Had she been true,
If Heaven would make me such another world
Of one entire and perfect chrysolite,
I'd not have sold her for it.

EMILIA
My husband!

OTHELLO
175   Ay, 'twas he that told me on her first.
An honest man he is, and hates the slime
That sticks on filthy deeds.

EMILIA
My husband!

OTHELLO
What needs this iterance, woman? I say thy husband.

EMILIA
180   O mistress, villainy hath made mocks with love!
My husband say that she was false!

OTHELLO
He, woman;
I say thy husband; dost understand the word?
My friend, thy husband, honest, honest Iago.

EMILIA
185   If he say so, may his pernicious soul
Rot half a grain a day! He lies to the heart.
She was too fond of her most filthy bargain.

OTHELLO
Ha!

EMILIA
Do thy worst!

OTHELLO
Your husband.

EMILIA
That she was unfaithful to her marriage vows?

OTHELLO
170   Yes, with Cassio. No, if she had been true,
heaven could have made me another world
entirely out of perfect topaz,
and I wouldn't have sold her for it.

EMILIA
My husband?

OTHELLO
175   Yes, he told me first.
He's an honest man, and he hates the slime
that sticks to filthy deeds.

EMILIA
My husband?

OTHELLO
Why do you repeat yourself, woman? I said your husband.

EMILIA
180   Oh, my lady, a villain has toyed with your love!
My husband said she was unfaithful?

OTHELLO
It was he, woman.
I said your husband. Do you understand the word?
My friend, your husband; honest, honest Iago.

EMILIA
185   If he said so, I hope his lying soul
rots little by little! He's lying in his heart.
She was all too devoted to her filthy marriage.

OTHELLO
Ha!

EMILIA
Do your worst.

190   This deed of thine is no more worthy heaven
      Than thou wast worthy her.

OTHELLO
                              Peace, you were best.

EMILIA
      Thou hast not half that power to do me harm
      As I have to be hurt. O gull! O dolt!
195   As ignorant as dirt! Thou has done a deed—
      I care not for thy sword; I'll make thee known
      Though I lost twenty lives.—Help! help, ho! help!
      The Moor hath kill'd my mistress! Murder! murder!
          Enter MONTANO, GRATIANO, IAGO, *and others.*

MONTANO
      What is the matter? How now, general!

EMILIA
200   O, are you come, Iago? You have done well,
      That men must lay their murders on your neck.

GRATIANO
      What is the matter?

EMILIA
      Disprove this villain, if thou be'st a man.
      He says thou told'st him that his wife was false.
205   I know thou didst not, thou'rt not such a villain.
      Speak, for my heart is full.

IAGO
      I told him what I thought, and told no more
      Than what he found himself was apt and true.

EMILIA
      But did you ever tell him she was false?

IAGO
210   I did.

EMILIA
      You told a lie, an odious, damned lie;
      Upon my soul, a lie, a wicked lie.
      She false with Cassio!—did you say with Cassio?

190   This deed you've done is no more worthy of heaven
    than you were worthy of her.

OTHELLO
    You'd better be quiet.

EMILIA
    You can only hurt my body;
    you can't harm my soul. You fool! You dolt!
195   You're as ignorant as dirt! You've done a deed—
    I'm not afraid of your sword. I'll make your murder known,
    even if you kill me twenty times. Help! Help, somebody! Help!
    The Moor has killed my lady! Murder! Murder!
        Enter MONTANO, GRATIANO, IAGO, *and others.*

MONTANO
    What's the matter? What is it, general?

EMILIA
200   Oh, you've come too, Iago? You've done very well
    to have other men blame their murders on you.

GRATIANO
    What's the matter?

EMILIA *(To Iago)*
    Prove this villain wrong if you are a man.
    He says you told him that his wife was unfaithful.
205   I know you didn't; you are not such a villain.
    Tell me; my heart is in anguish.

IAGO
    I told him what I thought and told no more
    than what he himself found to be perfectly true.

EMILIA
    But did you ever tell him she was unfaithful?

IAGO
210   I did.

EMILIA
    You told a lie, a foul, damned lie!
    By my very soul, a lie! A wicked lie!
    She, unfaithful with Cassio? Did you say with Cassio?

IAGO
    With Cassio, mistress. Go to, charm your tongue.

EMILIA
215   I will not charm my tongue; I am bound to speak.
    My mistress here lies murdered in her bed,—

ALL
    O heavens forfend!

EMILIA
    And your reports have set the murderer on.

OTHELLO
    Nay, stare not, masters; it is true, indeed.

GRATIANO
220   'Tis a strange truth.

MONTANO
    O monstrous act!

EMILIA
                    Villany, villany, villany!
    I think upon't,—I think I smell 't,—O villany!
    I thought so then,—I'll kill myself for grief—
225   O villany, villany!

IAGO
    What, are you mad? I charge you, get you home.

EMILIA
    Good gentlemen, let me have leave to speak;
    'Tis proper I obey him, but not now.
    Perchance, Iago, I will ne'er go home.

OTHELLO
230   O! O! O!   [*He falls on the bed.*]

EMILIA
                    Nay, lay thee down and roar;
    For thou hast kill'd the sweetest innocent
    That e'er did lift up eye.

OTHELLO
            [*Rising.*] O, she was foul!

IAGO
> With Cassio, woman. Calm down and hold your tongue.

EMILIA
215
> I will not hold my tongue; I have to speak.
> My mistress is lying here, murdered in her bed—

ALL
> Oh, heaven forbid!

EMILIA
> And things you said brought about this murder.

OTHELLO
> Stop staring, gentlemen. It is really the truth.

GRATIANO
220
> It is a terrible truth.

MONTANO
> A monstrous act!

EMILIA
> Villainy, villainy, villainy!
> I sense it—I think I smell it!—Oh, villainy!
> I realize it now—I'll kill myself out of grief!—
225
> Oh, villainy, villainy!

IAGO
> What's the matter? Are you mad? I order you to go home.

EMILIA
> Good gentlemen, just let me speak.
> It's proper that I obey him, but not now.
> Perhaps, Iago, I'll never go home.

OTHELLO
230
> Oh! Oh! Oh!
> *(He falls on the bed.)*

EMILIA
> Go right ahead and lie there roaring!
> You've killed the sweetest, most innocent creature
> who ever looked upward.

OTHELLO
> *(He rises)* Oh, she was wicked!

235 I scarce did know you, uncle; there lies your niece,
Whose breath, indeed, these hands have newly stopp'd.
I know this act shows horrible and grim.

GRATIANO
Poor Desdemona! I am glad thy father's dead.
Thy match was mortal to him, and pure grief
240 Shore his old thread in twain. Did he live now,
This sight would make him do a desperate turn,
Yea, curse his better angel from his side,
And fall to reprobance.

OTHELLO
'Tis pitiful; but yet Iago knows
245 That she with Cassio hath the act of shame
A thousand times committed. Cassio confess'd it;
And she did gratify his amorous works
With that recognizance and pledge of love
Which I first gave her. I saw it in his hand;
250 It was a handkerchief, an antique token
My father gave my mother.

EMILIA
O God! O heavenly God!

IAGO
'Zounds, hold your peace.

EMILIA
'Twill out, 'twill out! I peace!
255 No, I will speak as liberal as the north.
Let Heaven and men and devils, let them all,
All, all, cry shame against me, yet I'll speak.

IAGO
Be wise, and get you home.

EMILIA
I will not.

[*Iago offers to stab Emilia.*]

GRATIANO
Fie!
260 Your sword upon a woman?

235   *(To Gratiano)* I hardly recognized you, uncle. There lies
      your niece,
    whose breath has, indeed, just been stopped by these hands.
    I know this act appears to be horrible and grim.

GRATIANO
    Poor Desdemona! I'm glad your father is already dead.
    Your marriage killed him and sheer grief
240   cut his thread of life in two. If he were still alive,
    this sight would cause him to do something desperate—
    he might even have renounced his better nature
    and given himself up to damnation.

OTHELLO
    It's a pitiful thing; but still, Iago knows
245   that she committed adultery with Cassio
    a thousand times. Cassio confessed it;
    and she rewarded his acts of love
    with a present and token of love
    which I first gave to her. I saw it in his hand.
250   It was a handkerchief, an old gift
    which my father gave to my mother.

EMILIA
    Oh, God! Oh, heavenly powers!

IAGO
    By God, keep quiet!

EMILIA
    It will all come out, it will all come out! I, hold my tongue?
255   No, I'll speak as freely as the north wind.
    Let angels, men, and devils, let all of them—
    all, all—denounce me for it, but I'll still speak.

IAGO
    Be wise and go home.

EMILIA
    I will not.
      (IAGO draws his sword and threatens Emilia.)

GRATIANO
260   For shame!
    Would you use your sword against a woman?

EMILIA

O thou dull Moor! that handkerchief thou speak'st of
I found by fortune and did give my husband;
For often, with a solemn earnestness,
265   More than indeed belong'd to such a trifle,
He begg'd of me to steal 't.

IAGO

Villanous whore!

EMILIA

She give it Cassio! No, alas! I found it,
And I did give't my husband.

IAGO

270   Filth, thou liest!

EMILIA

By heaven, I do not, I do not, gentlemen.
O murd'rous coxcomb! what should such a fool
Do with so good a wife?

OTHELLO

Are there no stones in heaven
275   But what serves for the thunder? Precious villain!
[*He runs at Iago: Iago kills Emilia.*]

GRATIANO

The woman falls; sure, he hath kill'd his wife.

EMILIA

Ay, ay! O, lay me by my mistress' side.
[*Exit Iago.*]

GRATIANO

He's gone, but his wife's kill'd.

MONTANO

'Tis a notorious villain. Take you this weapon
280   Which I have here recover'd from the Moor.
Come, guard the door without; let him not pass,
But kill him rather. I'll after that same villain,
For 'tis a damned slave.
[*Exeunt Montano and Gratiano.*]

EMILIA
 Oh, you stupid Moor, the handkerchief you speak of
 I found by luck, and I gave it to my husband
 because he often, and with deadly earnestness
265 (more than seemed appropriate for such a small thing),
 asked me to steal it.

IAGO
 You villainous whore!

EMILIA
 Did she give it to Cassio? No, sadly, I found it,
 and I gave it to my husband.

IAGO
270 You filthy thing, you lie!

EMILIA
 By heaven, I do not, I do not, gentlemen.
 Oh, you murderous idiot! What was a fool like you
 doing with such a good wife?

OTHELLO
 Aren't there any bolts in the sky
275 except those used for thunder? You clever villain!
  (OTHELLO attacks Iago, but is disarmed by MONTANO.
  IAGO *stabs Emilia.)*

GRATIANO
 The woman has fallen. He has certainly killed his wife.

EMILIA
 Yes, yes. Oh, lay me by my lady's side.
  Exit IAGO.

GRATIANO
 He's gone, but his wife's been killed.

MONTANO
 He's a complete villain. Take this weapon,
280 which I just took away from the Moor.
 Come, guard the outside door. Don't let him pass;
 if he tries, kill him. I'll go after the villain myself;
 he's a damned scoundrel.
  MONTANO *and* GRATIANO *exit with others, leaving*
  Othello and Emilia alone.

OTHELLO

                          I am not valiant neither,
285   But every puny whipster gets my sword.
But why should honour outlive honesty?
Let it go all.

EMILIA

                   What did thy song bode, lady?
Hark, canst thou hear me? I will play the swan,
290   And die in music. [*Singing.*] "Willow, willow, willow!"—
Moor, she was chaste; she lov'd thee, cruel Moor;
So come my soul to bliss, as I speak true;
So speaking as I think, alas, I die. [*Dies.*]

OTHELLO

I have another weapon in this chamber;
295   It was a sword of Spain, the ice-brook's temper,—
O, here it is. Uncle, I must come forth.

GRATIANO

[*Within.*] If thou attempt it, it will cost thee dear:
Thou hast no weapon, and perforce must suffer.

OTHELLO

Look in upon me then and speak with me,
300   Or, naked as I am, I will assault thee.
             Re-enter GRATIANO.

GRATIANO

What is the matter?

OTHELLO

                  Behold, I have a weapon;
A better never did itself sustain
Upon a soldier's thigh. I have seen the day
305   That, with this little arm and this good sword,
I have made my way through more impediments
Than twenty times your stop. But, O vain boast!
Who can control his fate? 'tis not so now.
Be not afraid though you do see me weapon'd;
310   Here is my journey's end, here is my butt
And very sea-mark of my utmost sail.

289-90 *swan . . . music* swans were believed to sing as they died.

OTHELLO

285
My courage is gone along with everything else;
any contemptible fellow can get my sword now.
But why should my good reputation outlive what I really am?
Let me lose it all.

EMILIA

290
What was that song you sang to me, lady?
Listen, can't you hear me? I'll pretend to be a swan
and die with music. *(She sings.)* "Willow, willow, willow."
Moor, she was faithful; she loved you, cruel Moor.
As I hope for eternal happiness, I'm telling the truth.
So, speaking my mind, I die, I die. *(She dies.)*

OTHELLO

295
I have another weapon in this room;
it's a Spanish sword, tempered in ice-cold water.
Oh, here it is. *(Calling outside)* Uncle, I must come out.

GRATIANO *(From offstage)*
If you try it, you'll pay for it dearly.
You don't have a weapon, so you'll undoubtedly suffer.

OTHELLO

300
Come in here, then, and talk to me,
or I'll attack you, even though I'm unarmed.
                    Enter GRATIANO.

GRATIANO
What's the matter?

OTHELLO

305

310
Look, I do have a weapon.
A better sword was never carried
at a soldier's side. I have seen a day
when, with this little arm and this good sword,
I've fought my way past more obstacles
than twenty of your kind. But what a useless boast!
Who can control his fate? It's not like that now.
Don't be afraid, though you see me with a weapon.
This is my journey's end, this is my arrow's target,
the landmark of my ship's final destination.

Do you go back dismay'd? 'Tis a lost fear;
Man but a rush against Othello's breast
And he retires. Where should Othello go?
315   Now, how dost thou look now? O ill-starr'd wench!
Pale as thy smock! when we shall meet at compt,
This look of thine will hurl my soul from heaven,
And fiends will snatch at it. Cold, cold, my girl!
Even like thy chastity. O cursed, cursed slave!
320   Whip me, ye devils,
From the possession of this heavenly sight!
Blow me about in winds! roast me in sulphur!
Wash me in steep-down gulfs of liquid fire!
O Desdemon! dead, Desdemon! dead!
325   Oh! Oh!

Enter LODOVICO, MONTANO, CASSIO *carried in a chair, and* Officers, *with* IAGO *prisoner.*

LODOVICO
Where is this rash and most unfortunate man?

OTHELLO
That's he that was Othello; here I am.

LODOVICO
Where is that viper? Bring the villain forth.

OTHELLO
I look down towards his feet; but that's a fable.
330   If that thou be'st a devil, I cannot kill thee. [*Wounds Iago.*]

LODOVICO
Wrench his sword from him.

IAGO
                    I bleed, sir; but not kill'd.

OTHELLO
I am not sorry neither. I'd have thee live;
For, in my sense, 'tis happiness to die.

LODOVICO
335   O thou Othello, that wast once so good,
Fall'n in the practice of a cursed slave,
What shall be said to thee?

---

329 *I . . . feet*   Othello is looking to see if Iago has cloven feet like Satan.

Are you backing away from me out of fear? No need.
If you attack Othello with only a reed,
he'll retreat. Where should Othello go?

315 *(To Desdemona)* How do you look now? Oh, unfortunate woman!
As pale as your gown! When we meet at the Judgment Day,
this innocent look of yours will cause my soul to be damned,
and devils will snatch at it. Are you cold, cold, my girl?
Just like your good virtue. Oh, what a cursed fool I am!

320 Devils, whip me
the sight of this heavenly vision from my mind!
Blow me about with the wind! Roast me in sulfur!
Wash me down into deep seas of liquid fire!
Oh, Desdemona, Desdemona! Dead!

325 Oh! Oh! Oh!

Enter LODOVICO, MONTANO, CASSIO, *in a*
chair, and OFFICERS *with* IAGO *as a prisoner.*

LODOVICO
Where is this rash and very unfortunate man?

OTHELLO
You're speaking of the man who used to be Othello. Here I am.

LODOVICO
Where is that snake, Iago? Bring the villain forward.

OTHELLO
I'm looking at his feet—but that's only a myth.
330 If you really are a devil, I can't kill you. *(He stabs Iago.)*

LODOVICO
Get that sword away from him.
(Othello is disarmed.)

IAGO
I'm bleeding, sir, but I've not been killed.

OTHELLO
I'm not sorry to hear that. I'd rather you lived on.
From my point of view, it would be happiness to die.

LODOVICO
335 Oh, Othello, you used to be so good,
but you've fallen prey to the plot of a damned villain.
What can I say to you?

OTHELLO
                    Why, anything.
    An honourable murderer, if you will;
340 For nought I did in hate, but all in honour.

LODOVICO
    This wretch hath part confess'd his villainy.
    Did you and he consent in Cassio's death?

OTHELLO
    Ay.

CASSIO
    Dear General, I never gave you cause.

OTHELLO
345 I do believe it, and I ask your pardon.
    Will you, I pray, demand that demi-devil
    Why he hath thus ensnar'd my soul and body?

IAGO
    Demand me nothing; what you know, you know.
    From this time forth I never will speak word.

LODOVICO
350 What, not to pray?

GRATIANO
                    Torments will ope your lips.

OTHELLO
    Well, thou dost best.

LODOVICO
    Sir, you shall understand what hath befall'n,
    Which, as I think, you know not. Here is a letter
355 Found in the pocket of the slain Roderigo,
    And here another. The one of them imports
    The death of Cassio to be undertook
    By Roderigo.

OTHELLO
    O villain!

OTHELLO
Why, anything.
Call me an honorable murderer, if you wish,
340   for I did nothing out of hate but everything out of honor.

LODOVICO
This wretch has partially confessed to his villainy.
Did you and he plot to kill Cassio?

OTHELLO
Yes.

CASSIO
Dear general, I never gave you any cause.

OTHELLO
345   I believe you, and I ask your pardon.
Please, will you ask that half-devil
why he trapped me, soul and body, into this?

IAGO
Don't ask me any questions. You know everything you'll ever know.
I'll never say a word from now on.

LODOVICO
350   What, you won't even pray?

GRATIANO
Torture will make you talk.

OTHELLO
You are right not to speak (of such horrible crimes).

LODOVICO
Sir, I'll try to explain what has happened,
since I don't believe you understand. I have a letter here,
355   which was found in the pocket of the slain Roderigo;
and here is another. One of them orders
that Cassio be killed
by Roderigo.

OTHELLO
Oh, you villain!

CASSIO

360   Most heathenish and most gross!

LODOVICO
    Now here's another discontented paper,
    Found in his pocket too; and this, it seems,
    Roderigo meant t' have sent this damned villain;
    But that, belike, Iago in the interim
365   Came in and satisfi'd him.

OTHELLO
                  O thou pernicious caitiff!—
    How came you, Cassio, by that handkerchief
    That was my wife's?

CASSIO
               I found it in my chamber,
370   And he himself confess'd but even now
    That there he dropp'd it for a special purpose
    Which wrought to his desire.

OTHELLO
             O fool! fool! fool!

CASSIO
    There is besides in Roderigo's letter,
375   How he upbraids Iago, that he made him
    Brave me upon the watch, whereon it came
    That I was cast; and even but now he spake,
    After long seeming dead, Iago hurt him,
    Iago set him on.

LODOVICO
380   You must forsake this room and go with us.
    Your power and your command is taken off,
    And Cassio rules in Cyprus. For this slave,
    If there be any cunning cruelty
    That can torment him much and hold him long,
385   It shall be his. You shall close prisoner rest,
    Till that the nature of your fault be known
    To the Venetian state. Come, bring away.

CASSIO

360   An unholy and horrible villain!

LODOVICO

And here's another disturbing letter
which was found in his pocket too. It seems that this one
Roderigo meant to have sent to this damned villain,
but perhaps before it was delivered,
365   Iago spoke with him and convinced him.

OTHELLO

Oh, you despicable coward!
Cassio, how did you get that handkerchief
that belonged to my wife?

CASSIO

I found it in my room;
370   and he himself confessed just now
that he left it there deliberately
in order to carry out his plan.

OTHELLO

Oh, I am a fool! A fool! A fool!

CASSIO

Also in Roderigo's letter,
375   he angrily criticized Iago for making him
bait me while I was on guard duty, which led
to my dismissal. So even now he speaks,
long after he seemed to be dead. Iago ruined him;
Iago led him on.

LODOVICO

380   You must leave this room and come with us.
Your authority and power have been taken away,
and Cassio is now ruler of Cyprus. As for this scoundrel,
whatever elaborate torture
can be devised to torment him a great deal and for a long time
385   will be used against him. You'll be kept a closely guarded prisoner
until the nature of your crimes is known
by the government of Venice. Come, let's go.

OTHELLO
Soft you; a word or two before you go.
I have done the state some service, and they know 't.
390   No more of that. I pray you, in your letters,
When you shall these unlucky deeds relate,
Speak of me as I am; nothing extenuate,
Nor set down aught in malice. Then must you speak
Of one that lov'd not wisely but too well;
395   Of one not easily jealous, but, being wrought,
Perplex'd in the extreme; of one whose hand,
Like the base Indian, threw a pearl away
Richer than all his tribe; of one whose subdu'd eyes,
Albeit unused to the melting mood,
400   Drops tears as fast as the Arabian trees
Their medicinal gum. Set you down this;
And say besides, that in Aleppo once,
Where a malignant and a turban'd Turk
Beat a Venetian and traduc'd the state,
405   I took by th' throat the circumcised dog,
And smote him—thus. [*Stabs himself.*]

LODOVICO
O bloody period!

GRATIANO
                        All that's spoke is marr'd.

OTHELLO
I kiss'd thee ere I kill'd thee: no way but this,
410   Killing myself, to die upon a kiss.
      [*Falls on the bed, and dies.*]

CASSIO
This did I fear, but thought he had no weapon;
For he was great of heart.

LODOVICO
                  [*To Iago.*] O Spartan dog,
More fell than anguish, hunger, or the sea!
415   Look on the tragic loading of this bed;
This is thy work. The object poisons sight;

---

397 *the base Indian*   this may refer to an ignorant Indian who does not know the value
of a pearl. Some editors prefer to use the word "Judean," which suggests Christian betrayal.
413 *Spartan dog*   the dogs of Sparta were thought to have been very fierce.

OTHELLO
>But wait! Just a word or two before you go.
>I have done some service for the state, and they know it.
390 But leave all that aside. I beg you, in your letters
>telling of these unfortunate deeds,
>speak of me as I am. Don't mitigate anything
>or write anything out of malice. You must describe me
>as one who loved not wisely, but too much;
395 as one not easily made jealous, but, being manipulated,
>became distracted in the extreme; as one whose hand
>(like an ignorant Indian) threw a pearl away
>worth more than all his people; as one whose humbled eyes,
>not normally given to weeping,
400 let drop tears as fast as Arabian trees
>drop their medicinal gum. Write all this;
>and also tell how, in Aleppo once,
>when a vicious Turk wearing a turban
>attacked a Venetian and insulted the state,
405 I took the circumcised dog by the throat
>and stabbed him—like this. *(He stabs himself.)*

LODOVICO
>Oh, what a bloody end!

GRATIANO
>Words can't describe it.

OTHELLO
>I kissed you before I killed you. Now this is the only way:
410 as I kill myself, I'll die with a kiss.
>   *(*OTHELLO *falls on the bed and dies.)*

CASSIO
>I was afraid of this—but I thought he had no weapon—
>for he had a noble heart.

LODOVICO *(To Iago)*
>Oh, you Spartan dog,
>more cruel than anguish, hunger, or the sea!
415 Look at the tragic victims on this bed.
>This is your doing. This sight is too horrible to look at;

Let it be hid. Gratiano, keep the house,
And seize upon the fortunes of the Moor,
For they succeed on you. To you, Lord Governor,
420   Remains the censure of this hellish villain;
The time, the place, the torture. O, enforce it!
Myself will straight aboard; and to the state
This heavy act with heavy heart relate.
     [*Exeunt.*]

let it be hidden. Gratiano, you guard the house
and take possession of the Moor's property,
since you are the heir. *(To Cassio)* Lord governor, it is up to you
420   to see that this hellish villain is punished.
Decide on the time, the place, and the means of torture—make
    sure it is enforced!
As for myself, I'll leave at once and report to the state
these sad acts with a sad heart.
    Everyone exits.

THE PLAY IN REVIEW:

A Teacher and Student Supplement

Between Acts: Study Questions

Act I

1. How does the way Shakespeare begins the play immediately involve the audience?

The tragedy opens with a striking, attention-getting device—Iago and Roderigo arrive onstage in the midst of a heated conversation. Shakespeare does not slowly dole out the expository information the audience needs to understand the conflicts of the play. Instead, the playwright demands that his audience immediately absorb the conversation just to grasp what's going on. (The ploy may have been Shakespeare's way of quieting the frequently unruly and inattentive Elizabethan audience.) And he baits the dramatic hook by leading off the play with intriguing, enigmatic lines beginning with Roderigo's "Tush, never tell me!"

As the scene progresses, we realize that Iago has already told Roderigo of Othello's elopement with Desdemona. The news has quite an effect on the young man, who has been earnestly seeking Desdemona for himself. Iago has brought Roderigo to this particular household in hopes that he can persuade him to help awaken Desdemona's father, Brabantio, and make trouble for Othello.

This expository technique forces our attention on Iago the manipulator. Our confusion as the play opens gives way to fascination as we see how Iago works his will first on Roderigo, then on Desdemona's irate father.

2. What imagery does Iago use to describe Othello and Desdemona's elopement, and what conflict does that imagery develop?

Othello's marriage is described in the most distasteful terms possible, particularly by Iago. In fact, Iago likens

284

the consummation of the marriage to the mating of animals. "Even now, now, very now," he says to Brabantio, "an old black ram / Is tupping your white ewe." This is not the last time that animal imagery will be grotesquely applied to various characters in the play, particularly by Iago.

The animal imagery serves two purposes. First, Iago's comments mirror how society will view the match. The marriage of a dark-skinned Moor and a fair-skinned Venetian is going to cause tension in Venice. We immediately see that Othello's present situation is not a comfortable one.

Second, the animal imagery introduces a major philosophical conflict between two viewpoints. One view states that man is essentially an animal, driven by selfishness, greed, and carnality. As in the first scene, this viewpoint is constantly forwarded by the conniving Iago. The second view is that human beings are capable of true honesty, loyalty, and forgiveness. This outlook will be personified in the character of Desdemona. The thematic tension of the play lies in the audience's concern over which of these two viewpoints will prevail at the end of the tragedy.

3.   **How does Iago enlist the aid and the trust of Roderigo in the first scene?**

First, Iago infuriates Roderigo with news of Othello's elopement with Desdemona. Then he convinces Roderigo that their hatred of Othello is mutual. Iago justifies his hatred by saying that he was rejected as Othello's lieutenant and the "great arithmetician," Michael Cassio, was chosen instead.

Roderigo's susceptibility to Iago's manipulation is almost comic. Iago takes advantage of Roderigo's gullibility, even to the point of speaking quite bluntly of his own double-dealing nature. Explaining his hypocritical tactics to Roderigo, Iago remarks, "I am not what I am." Roderigo, a bit foolishly, takes confidence in this. He assumes that Iago's underhandedness will be used only against Othello. He does not yet realize that he, too, will become Iago's victim.

4. **What impending crisis do the duke and his senators face at the beginning of Scene 3?**

Turkey has sent a fleet to invade the island of Cyprus, a Venetian colony. As the scene opens, a series of messengers bring conflicting messages concerning the reality of this threat. At one point, it seems that the Turkish ships are on their way to Rhodes instead of Cyprus. But the senators quickly realize that this is "a pageant / To keep us in false gaze"—a tactic to cause confusion in Venice. The Turkish ships turn out to be headed for Cyprus after all, and Venice must prepare for war.

These warlike events are a crucial background to the play. Most importantly, they allow us to quickly see Othello's prestige as a military man in Venice. Othello is given charge of Cyprus and sent on his way to the embattled island. Even though he is an outsider, the Moor is a powerful citizen in time of crisis—a man to contend with.

The events also create a climate of political tension and rivalry, which serves as a catalyst for the personal conflicts in the play. The rivalry between Cassio and Iago, for example, would not be nearly so heated in peaceful times. The difficulties of Othello's personal decisions also will be compounded by the uneasy political situation.

5. **Why is Brabantio's suit against Othello balked?**

Brabantio intends to have Othello arrested for the elopement of his daughter and the alleged crime of witchcraft. Brabantio's threat cannot be lightly dismissed. We already have learned that he is a prominent citizen of tremendous power and influence. However, his allegations are ill-timed. Othello is too valuable in wartime to be prosecuted. As Iago notes, "Another of his fathom they have none / To lead their business."

Even the duke is clearly in no position to punish Othello, though he had earlier promised to prosecute the man who stole Brabantio's daughter away. Indeed, in Scene 3, the duke's very first words to Othello are a plea for the Moor's aid against the Turks. By contrast, the duke isn't even aware of Brabantio's presence at first.

6. **How does Brabantio seem to feel about Othello?**

In the past, Brabantio has lavished great attention and affection on the Moor. He has repeatedly invited Othello to his house for dinner and pumped his guest for stories of personal adventures. The two appeared to be close friends.

But Brabantio cannot accept his daughter's marriage to Othello. Ironically, the basis of Brabantio's friendship with Othello seems to be the basis of his objection to the marriage. Othello's exotic personality and his status as a racial and cultural outsider are not suitable characteristics for a son-in-law. Brabantio wants a prominent Venetian to marry Desdemona, not a mysterious foreigner. In fact, after the elopement, Brabantio wishes Desdemona had married the mediocre Roderigo—a suitor Brabantio had previously turned away.

7. **How does Othello defend himself against Brabantio's charges of witchcraft?**

Othello simply relates how an attraction grew between himself and Desdemona. She overheard parts of the many stories Othello told her father and asked Othello to tell them all to her. After that, the two quickly fell in love. "She lov'd me for the dangers I had pass'd, / And I lov'd her that she did pity them," Othello says.

It is clear to everyone who hears Othello's explanation that no witchcraft was involved. This is simply an honest attraction between two good-hearted people. The duke finds Othello's story entirely satisfactory and admits, "I think this tale would win my daughter too."

8. **What kind of impression does Desdemona create in the third scene of the play?**

In Scene 3, Desdemona reveals her determination and firm values by stating her respective loyalties. She says that her principal duty was once to her father. But now her loyalty is due to her husband. Shakespeare's audience would have found nothing callous in Desdemona's decision. She has made the most ethical choice in dedicating her future life to Othello.

The scene also dramatically demonstrates Desdemona's devotion. Instead of remaining safely in Venice during her husband's absence, Desdemona wishes to go with him to the embattled island of Cyprus. "My heart's subdu'd / Even to the very quality of my lord," she says. In other words, she considers herself as much Othello's comrade-at-arms as his spouse. Desdemona is clearly dedicated to Othello and incapable of the infidelity which will be imputed to her later.

9. **How does Iago continue to manipulate Roderigo at the end of the act?**

Roderigo is demoralized by the marriage of Desdemona to Othello and is on the verge (or so he says) of suicide. But Iago quickly persuades him that Desdemona's attraction to the dark-skinned and middle-aged Moor is certain to fade. Desdemona will soon be ready for an adulterous relationship, and Roderigo will have his chance. Iago persuades him to come to Cyprus and bring lots of money. Roderigo prepares to sell all his land, not realizing that Iago is planning to take him for all he's worth.

10. **What sorts of ironies surround Iago in the first act of the play?**

The contrast between Iago's persona and his real personality creates many ironies. Only the audience is fully aware of Iago's villainy. Consequently, the trust which all the principal characters place in Iago seems notably ironic. For example, Othello entrusts Desdemona's care to Iago and Emilia until Desdemona is able to come to Cyprus. And Roderigo believes everything Iago tells him. In fact, Iago actually draws a sword against Roderigo without shaking the fool's trust.

Iago plays with his dual image by frequently saying ironic things about himself. Explaining to Othello why he let Brabantio's insults pass, Iago says, "I lack iniquity / Sometimes to do me service." The audience knows full well that Iago suffers from no shortage of iniquity. These ironies will be compounded as Iago's villainy escalates during the play.

11. **How is Othello's status as a "tragic hero" established in the first act?**

A "tragic hero," at least in classical tragedy, was expected to be of noble disposition and high rank. This person's reversal of fortune was brought about by a tragic flaw in an otherwise excellent character. Usually the character's downfall from happiness and power resulted from some error in judgment.

Othello fits this sketch of the tragic hero, with all the hero's strengths. When we first meet the Moor, he is coping with a difficult situation. His marriage to Desdemona is about to be challenged by Brabantio, and he will be sent to the war in Cyprus on the eve of his honeymoon. The regard others have for Othello is immediately demonstrated by this situation. Othello is obviously a respected general in Venice, and the fact that he is about to be placed in command of Cyprus suggests that his power and influence are very great.

Othello mixes his virtues with modesty. For example, he is reluctant to justify his marriage on the basis of his ancestry until he hears that "beasting is an honor." He readily admits to his shortcomings. "Rude am I in speech," he says as he prepares to counter Brabantio's charge that he has exercised witchcraft in winning Desdemona. Still, his explanation of how he won Desdemona's love is simple, direct, and touching—a sharp contrast to the duplicitous Iago. Before the first act is finished, Shakespeare has impressively sketched Othello's commanding, strong, honest, and noble figure.

Shakespeare also deftly shows us that his hero is not perfect. Othello's elopement indicates that the Moor is naive and unsure of himself in Venetian society. And, in a single line, Shakespeare hints at his fatal flaw of jealousy. When Brabantio suggests to him that Desdemona "has deceiv'd her father, and may thee," Othello swears, perhaps to himself, "My life upon her faith!" He is a bit too anxious to assert Desdemona's fidelity, already unnecessarily defensive about her virtue. This is the first manifestation of the obsessive jealousy which will ultimately destroy Othello.

12. **At the end of Act I, what have we learned about Iago's motives in the play?**

Iago has already set out to ruin most of the central characters in the play. He has tangible, if evil, motives for doing so. Othello has slighted him for promotion; Cassio now holds the rank Iago intended for himself; and Roderigo is merely a fitting dupe for Iago to swindle and manipulate.

But in Iago's soliloquy at the end of the act, we are led to suspect that his malice is much more deeply rooted. Surprisingly, Iago states his own unwarranted suspicion that his wife, Emilia, has been unfaithful with Othello. "I know not if 't be true," he admits, "But I, for mere suspicion in that kind, / Will do as if for surety."

Still, none of Iago's motives fully explain the destruction he will wreak on so many of the characters in the play. But while modern audiences may be baffled by Iago's evil, Elizabethans would not have been puzzled at all. They recognized Iago as a familiar stage type: the "machiavel." The term comes from the Renaissance philosopher Niccolo Machiavelli, whose writings sometimes advocated amoral methods of statesmanship. The machiavel was a character who practiced evil as much for its own sake as for any apparent motive. Shakespeare created a machiavel earlier in his career with the historical character Richard III. Edmund the Bastard in *King Lear* is another Shakespearean machiavel.

Whatever Iago's apparent motives may be, his actions are perhaps best summed up by the poet/critic Samuel Taylor Coleridge. Coleridge suggested that Iago acts out of "motiveless malignity."

Act II

13. What happens to the threat of a Turkish invasion of Cyprus?

A terrible storm brings about the complete destruction of the Turkish fleet, thereby lifting the immediate threat of war. The same storm that wrecks the ships of the Turks spares the Venetians. Othello, Desdemona, Iago, Emilia, Cassio, and Roderigo all arrive safely at Cyprus.

14. What nonliteral purpose does the storm play in the story?

The storm is suggestive of the personal and political conflicts of the play, much like the storms in *Julius Caesar* and *King Lear*. The principal characters have escaped the threat of Turkish invasion and the terrors of the sea, but symbolically they remain in the eye of the play's real "storm." Still greater turmoil is about to break out between these characters in Cyprus. The celebration of the Turkish fleet's destruction is tainted with irony; the audience knows that more trouble will follow.

15. Why does Shakespeare move the action of his play from Venice to Cyprus?

Shakespeare could have presented the conflicts of *Othello* in the single setting of Venice. From a classical standpoint, this might have allowed for a more unified drama. But the Cyprus setting grants him several important possibilities.

First, the highly charged civil and political situation of the embattled island serves to increase the already volatile personal relationships and rivalries in the play. The island has been on the verge of war for quite some time; all its inhabitants are on edge and fearful. This atmosphere of tension lends more credibility to a potentially melodramatic story of jealousy and revenge.

Shakespeare also uses the new setting to create a dichotomy between the worlds of Venice and Cyprus. Venice is very much a Renaissance city, cosmopolitan and sophisticated, where people are guided by their intellects. In contrast, Cyprus is an island teetering toward war and civil anarchy, where violent and savage emotions are loosed.

The shift between the two settings also further reveals Othello's character. We have already seen the Moor's social uncertainty in Venice; he is not the Renaissance sophisticate at all. The consummate warrior should be much more in his element at Cyprus. But there one important factor unbalances Othello: he is utterly unused to matrimony and the domestic uncertainties which he experiences. Cyprus is truly Othello's "world"—except that he has brought a part of Venice with him.

16. **How does Montano react to the news that Othello is about to take his place as governor of Cyprus?**

Montano is not at all displeased to have Othello take over command of Cyprus. "I am glad on't," he declares. " 'Tis a worthy governor." Montano goes on to express his admiration for Othello. "I have serv'd him, and the man commands / Like a full soldier." Montano's reaction serves two purposes. First, it develops Montano's own character, proving him to be a good man who knows how to step down gracefully for a man of greater capabilities. Second, Montano's response reflects on Othello's character. The commander's expression of admiration helps increase Othello's stature as a tragic hero.

17. What do Cassio's actions in Act II, Scene 1, tell us about his character?

Cassio is very much the gallant, with a hint of posturing and artificiality in his nature. His description of Desdemona to Montano is extremely high-flown, and his greetings to Desdemona and Emilia are exaggerated in their chivalry. Indeed, Iago considers him to be blatantly flirtatious. Cassio also enjoys alluding to his refined background. As he kisses Emilia, he says to Iago, " 'Tis my breeding / That gives me this bold show of courtesy." This boast and demonstrative courtesy sharply contrast with Othello's behavior. Othello spoke of his breeding only when pressed, and his declarations of affection are simpler but more moving.

In sum, Cassio is portrayed as a capable, well-meaning, but rather shallow person of somewhat limited sincerity.

18. What judgments does Iago pass on women in his conversation with Desdemona and Emilia? What is the purpose of his statements?

Iago's statements to Emilia and Desdemona concerning women help establish his deep-rooted cynicism. He states that a bright and attractive woman makes the most of both qualities. An unattractive woman will get by on her wits, while a beautiful woman does not need too much cleverness to get her way. He adds that even an ugly and foolish woman can get along quite nicely in the world. The highest praise Iago can muster for a truly good woman is that she is worthy "To suckle fools and chronicle small beer." This scene further clarifies that Iago's view of human nature is mistrustful and contemptuous.

19. What happens during the meeting between Roderigo and Iago at the end of Scene 1?

Iago plants the suspicion in Roderigo's mind that Cassio and Desdemona are in love. "They met so near with their lips that their breaths embrac'd together," he tells Roderigo. This has a powerful effect on the lovelorn Roderigo. He falls even further into Iago's snare, becoming a complete pawn. Primed and persuaded by Iago, Roderigo is ready to pick a fight with Cassio—a fight which will result in the ruin of Cassio's military reputation.

20. How does Iago bring about Cassio's dismissal?

Iago discovers that Cassio has a very low tolerance for wine. During the celebration of the destruction of the Turkish fleet, Iago easily gets Cassio drunk while the lieutenant is supposed to be on watch. Cassio is extremely altered by the wine, and Iago manages to convince Montano and several other gentlemen that this is Cassio's nightly condition.

Shortly afterwards, Roderigo starts an offstage quarrel with Cassio. Montano is severely wounded while trying to break up this fight. A quickly sobered and humiliated Cassio finds himself unable to explain his actions to the angry Othello. The Moor is forced to dismiss his lieutenant. "Cassio, I love thee; / But never more be officer of mine," Othello orders.

21. How does Iago manipulate Cassio after the lieutenant's humiliating dismissal?

Iago quickly persuades Cassio that the best way back into Othello's good favor is through Desdemona; she will appeal to the Moor on Cassio's behalf. "Our general's wife is now the general," Iago explains.

Of course, Iago has an ulterior motive. He will begin to play on Othello's jealousies, hinting that Cassio and Desdemona are in love. Iago will bring Othello to the place where Cassio is meeting Desdemona. All of Desdemona's entreaties for Cassio will serve only to increase the jealous Moor's suspicions.

22. **How does Shakespeare develop the theme of illusion and reality in Act II?**

Shakespeare, like many playwrights before and since, was preoccupied with the difference between how we see things and how they really are. Many of his later characters—King Lear, for instance—suffer from their inability to perceive the reality of their situations.

This theme is explored in *Othello,* where things are not what they seem to be. For example, all the major characters believe Iago to be a trustworthy and honest man. Montano and Othello have been made to believe that Cassio is a chronic and irresponsible drunk. Roderigo has been convinced that Cassio and Desdemona are in love. Cassio has been made to believe that Desdemona's appeal will be his most likely means of restitution. Othello is tormented by images of Desdemona's imagined infidelity.

Superficially, Iago seems to be the orchestrator of all these illusions. But Shakespeare is careful to show us that Iago suffers from illusions of his own. He seems to really believe that Cassio and Desdemona are in love, even if they haven't consummated their relationship. In Act II, Iago reiterates his belief that Othello has gone to bed with his wife Emilia. He even suspects her of infidelity with Cassio. While Iago controls and manipulates much of the play's action, he is no more free of illusions than the other characters.

Act III

23. **What is the purpose of the brief scene with the clown and the musicians?**

Shakespeare lightened even his tragedies with moments of comic relief. The porter's scene in *Macbeth* is a classic example. Shakespeare's audience covered a wide social spectrum, and less educated playgoers had limited patience with sustained poetry and character development. Violence, sensationalism, and moments of broad comedy were needed to hold his audience's attention.

The comedy of the scene between the clown and the musicians is "low" in its obscene and crude references. ("High" comedy, by contrast, involves and evokes the intelligence and sophistication of characters.) The clown crudely jokes about syphilis and about flatulence (in his references to "wind instruments").

The clown serves a subtler purpose as well by making fun of Michael Cassio's affectations and speech. When Cassio makes a somewhat verbose request to see Emilia, the clown responds in kind. "If she will stir hither," he says, "I shall seem to notify unto her." Thus Shakespeare uses the clown to comment on Cassio's character and bring the former lieutenant down a peg.

24. **Analyze how Iago works on Othello's suspicions in Scene 3.**

Iago's tactics in Scene 3 fascinate and horrify the viewer and further prove the genius of this machiavel. Iago cleverly manages to bring Othello to the spot where Desdemona and Cassio have met, just as Cassio is leaving. Iago remarks, seemingly to himself, "Ha! I like not that." Iago then superbly uses reverse psychology, criticizing his own motives and feigning reluctance to speak ill of Cassio. "I confess, it is my nature's plague / To spy into abuses," he says, "and oft my jealousy / Shapes faults that are not." He even warns Othello against the jealousy that Iago is actually trying to instill. Iago's reluctance and self-effacement make his insinuations all the more credible to Othello.

Iago also preys on Othello's racial insecurity and social naivete. He persuades Othello that Desdemona will naturally become inclined to a man of her own age, race, and temperament. He also generalizes to the credulous Moor about the nature of Venetian women. "Their best conscience / Is not to leave 't undone, but keep 't unknown," he says. The socially insecure Othello has no reason to doubt the worldly, yet seemingly honest, humble Iago.

Once Othello's suspicions are bred, they begin to

wildly increase. Desdemona's innocent appeals on behalf of Cassio are now poison to her husband. Iago further fuels Othello's jealousy by obtaining Desdemona's handkerchief—a prized gift from Othello. With that coup, Iago's tactics grow bolder. He tells Othello that Desdemona has given her handkerchief to Cassio. Iago also claims that Cassio has spoken of his love for Desdemona in his sleep. By this time Othello is distraught with paranoia and suspicion. He and Iago both swear revenge on Cassio. "Now art thou my lieutenant," says Othello at the end of the scene. Iago now has the rank he hungered for, though his commission is an obscene contrast to the one honest Cassio was given.

25. What was Cassio's relationship with Othello before the beginning of the play?

In Act III, we find out that Cassio and Othello have been close friends for some time. In fact, Cassio served as a kind of go-between when Othello was wooing Desdemona. Desdemona even suggests that Cassio helped Othello to win her when Othello was out of her favor. This prior friendship of Cassio and Desdemona's gives more credence to Iago's suggestion that the pair were attracted to one another and have had time to develop an intimate relationship.

26. How does the handkerchief serve as a plot device in Act III?

The handkerchief was Othello's first gift to Desdemona. During Scene 3, he causes her to accidentally drop it. Emilia recovers it and passes it along to Iago because he has been imploring her for some time to steal it for him. Iago then plants the handkerchief in Cassio's bedroom. In the meantime, Iago convinces Othello that Desdemona has given the handkerchief to Cassio.

Othello consequently interrogates his wife about the handkerchief. Desdemona fearfully denies that she has lost her husband's gift, though she does not have it with her. Othello tells Desdemona that the handkerchief has magical powers and was given to his mother by a sorceress. The audience is not certain whether the story is true or if Othello has fabricated it in a jealous rage. (In the last scene of the play, Othello says that the handkerchief was a gift to his mother from his father.) The stage is now set for Othello to actually see the handkerchief in Cassio's hand.

The handkerchief serves as more than just a plot device. The confrontation between Othello and Desdemona provoked by the handkerchief further develops Desdemona's character. Desdemona's credulity concerning the powers of the handkerchief and her anguish over its loss are evidence of her innocent, loving, and unassuming nature.

The handkerchief also has symbolic significance. It embodies not so much Desdemona's purity but Othello's image of that purity—a purity which has been lost to him.

27. **How is the theme of jealousy developed in Act III?**

Shakespeare brings the idea of jealousy to the forefront, showing how the "green-eyed monster" preys on humans. Jealousy evokes no positive qualities in *Othello;* its corrosive effects destroy the mind and disrupt relationships.

Shakespeare integrates this view of jealousy into his overall theme of illusion versus reality. Jealousy is always a matter of illusion. A betrayed lover can never be satisfied about the reality of his or her suspicions without enduring still greater misery.

In Scene 3, Othello reveals some awareness of the tragic price he must pay for his jealousy. "O, now, for ever / Farewell the tranquil mind! farewell content!" he cries. This speech is a flash of self-recognition worthy of a true tragic hero. As credulous as he is about Iago's allegations, Othello is beginning to suspect that the demons which are destroying him are really the images in his own mind.

28. How is Emilia characterized?

Emilia is most obviously characterized as a woman of great common sense. She makes insightful and often witty observations about jealousy, marital obligation, and infidelity. She expresses herself in a quite worldly and sometimes cynical fashion.

But much of Emilia's worldliness is a facade; she is quite vulnerable underneath. For example, when she steals Desdemona's handkerchief for her husband, she cannot comprehend the evil Iago is about to perpetrate. Though Emilia is easily deceived, she believes in the essential goodness of human nature, particularly in Desdemona. In fact, Emilia will die defending Desdemona's innocence and virtue—qualities which she seemed to view skeptically earlier in the play. In the philosophical conflict of the play, Emilia speaks for human honesty and faithfulness.

29. How does Emilia's remark about jealousy comment on the themes of the play?

Iago has repeatedly told other characters in the play that reputation is merely an illusion, a matter of appearance. Emilia reiterates that same thought about jealousy. "But jealous souls," she says, "are not ever jealous for the cause, / But jealous for they're jealous. It is a monster / Begot upon itself, born on itself." She echoes Iago's reference to jealousy as a "green-eyed monster."

Emilia thus expands on two central themes of the play: that people are trapped by their limited perceptions of the world around them, and that jealousy is a manifestation of that entrapment.

30. What hope does Desdemona cling to in Scene 4?

After Othello's outburst of anger, Desdemona assures Cassio and Emilia that some political crisis has affected Othello. This has caused him to be upset by little things, such as the missing handkerchief. Desdemona goes on to berate herself for not having been more understanding of her husband's mood.

The audience clearly sees that Desdemona's belief in her husband's goodness is not easily shaken by the anger and even cruelty Othello shows her. Her abiding faithfulness is sharply contrasted with Othello's violent distrust.

31. **What is Cassio's relationship to Bianca?**

Bianca is described in the list of characters as "a courtesan" or a prostitute for well-to-do gentlemen. She apparently has fallen in love with Cassio and perhaps entertains illusions that he will marry her and free her from her present life. Cassio has no such intentions, though he makes some effort to pretend to really care for Bianca.

Cassio's relationship to Bianca also gives another view of jealousy. In Act III, Cassio asks Bianca to copy the embroidery of Desdemona's handkerchief, which he has found in his bedroom. Bianca immediately suspects that it is a gift from another lover. In this instance, the jealous suspicions are more comic in tone than shocking and tragic. However, the keynote that runs throughout *Othello* is repeated again—people often allow illusions to obscure their view of reality.

32. **What has become of Cassio's hope to appeal to Othello through Desdemona by the end of Act III?**

Desdemona's attempts to speak to Othello in favor of Cassio only serve to provoke her husband's jealous anger. By the end of the act, Desdemona's efforts have grown more hopeless and more dangerous than she suspects. Desdemona helplessly recognizes her husband's moodiness. In Scene 4, she admits to Cassio, "My advocation is not now in tune. / My lord is not my lord; nor should I know him, / Were he in favour as in humor alter'd."

Act IV

33. How does Iago continue to provoke Othello's jealousy?

Still concealing his motives and pretending to maintain Desdemona's innocence, Iago nevertheless manages to conjure up images of Desdemona and Cassio in bed together. Othello faints from sheer horror. Iago takes the moment to devise the next stage of his plan—to hide Othello nearby while he gets Cassio to talk about Bianca. Iago's plan works smoothly, and Othello believes that Cassio is speaking of Desdemona. Bianca suddenly comes onstage, but her appearance could not be more opportune for Iago. She angrily returns the handkerchief which Cassio passed along to her earlier. Othello recognizes the handkerchief as belonging to Desdemona and immediately concludes that Cassio received it from her. Othello is now completely convinced of Cassio's and Desdemona's guilt.

34. What does the confrontation between Bianca and Cassio reveal about Cassio's character?

Before Bianca's entrance, Cassio has been snobbishly defending himself against the insinuation that he might actually marry Bianca. Consequently, when Bianca appears while Iago is present, Cassio doesn't greet her with the same pretense of love and consideration as he did in Act III. Instead, he calls Bianca a "fitchew" (polecat) and asks, "What do you mean by this haunting of me?" Cassio is presented in a singularly ungallant light here.

Bianca's inopportune appearance allows Shakespeare to show the essentially good Cassio in a weak and less-than-moral perspective. Here Cassio's behavior is just another example of the dark view of mankind presented in the play—the selfish, manipulative, and carnal part of human nature.

35. Why has Lodovico come to Cyprus, and how does he become a part of Iago's scheming?

Lodovico has brought word that Othello has been called back to Venice. What is more disconcerting to the Moor, Cassio is to be left in charge of Cyprus.

Lodovico falls into Iago's scheme when he witnesses jealous Othello strike Desdemona and send her away. Lodovico, a relative of Desdemona's, is shocked by this behavior. Iago takes the opportunity to suggest, with his usual evasiveness, that Othello's mental state is deteriorating. "He's that he is," Iago ambiguously tells Lodovico. "You shall observe him, / And his own courses will denote him so / That I may save my speech."

36. **How does Emilia react to Othello's initial suggestion of Desdemona's unfaithfulness? How does Othello respond?**

Emilia is appalled by Othello's suggestion of Desdemona's infidelity. She tells the Moor, "I durst, my lord, to wager she is honest, / Lay down my soul at stake."

But Othello has been so soundly convinced by Iago's argument that he believes Emilia is a hypocrite. He even insinuates that Emilia is Desdemona's procurer. When Othello wishes to speak to Desdemona alone, he says to Emilia, "Some of your function, mistress; / Leave procreants alone and shut the door." Othello's image of his own home as a brothel shows how deeply he has been consumed by the illusions of jealousy.

37. **How does Desdemona react to Othello's accusations in Scene 2?**

Desdemona tries as well as she can to defend herself against Othello's accusations. But she suffers from a disadvantage—she is too much the innocent to even comprehend the crimes of which she is accused. Indeed, she does not even seem to fully understand the meaning of the angry words which are hurled at her. When Othello calls her a strumpet, Desdemona can only falteringly reply, "If to preserve this vessel for my lord / From

any other foul unlawful touch / Be not to be a strumpet,
I am none."

Perhaps if Desdemona had a better understanding of
the crimes of which she is accused, she could more
eloquently defend herself. It is highly ironic that
Othello's mistaken suspicions are further compounded
by the very fact of Desdemona's innocence.

Act V

38. **How does Iago intend to dispose of Cassio and
Roderigo? What actually transpires?**

Iago has already promised Othello to kill Cassio. But
the wily villain avoids being connected with the slaying
by talking Roderigo into doing the deed. Iago is
naturally careful to avoid showing the double-edged
nature of this duel. Since he has swindled Roderigo out
of all his money, Iago wishes this fool dead as well. The
consummate machiavel simply waits to see which of the
two combatants manages to kill the other.

However, Roderigo and Cassio only wound each other
in the fight. Othello, walking by in the darkness, hears
Cassio calling for help. The Moor concludes that Iago
has carried out the attack on Cassio. Lodovico and
Gratiano arrive, followed by Iago, who stealthily kills
Roderigo in the darkness.

When Bianca arrives on the scene, Iago accuses her
of complicity in the attack on Cassio. The others
present—including Emilia—are all too willing to believe
him.

39. **How does Iago's treachery finally work itself out?**

After Othello has killed Desdemona, the deed is
discovered by Emilia. She reviles Othello. Othello tries
to explain his actions and tells her of the handkerchief.
Emilia remembers how she stole the handkerchief for
Iago and begins to realize the truth—that her husband
is responsible for the tragedy that has occurred. When
Iago arrives with the others, Emilia accuses him, only

to be slain by Iago. Letters found on the dead Roderigo further reveal Iago's treachery. Othello wounds Iago and then kills himself. Iago is taken away to be tortured and executed. Gratiano is given possession of all Othello's property.

40. **What philosophical viewpoint prevails at the end of the play?**

The play has tested two viewpoints against each other: one, that man is carnal, selfish, and savage; the other, that man is capable of nobility and self-sacrifice. In spite of the tragedy's stark ending, the latter viewpoint prevails at the conclusion of *Othello*. Throughout the fifth act, the theme of sacrifice is developed. Othello believes that he must sacrifice Desdemona so she can pay for her sins. Consequently, he tries to force his wife to pray and confess her sins. When she fails to do so, Othello cries out, "O perjur'd woman! thou dost stone my heart, / And makes me call what I intend to do / A murder, which I thought a sacrifice."

Desdemona's murder is a sacrifice, although not in the way Othello expected. She must die so that Othello can see her innocent and loving nature. Even with her last breath, as she conceals the truth that Othello killed her, Desdemona is revealing her virtue. At last Othello perceives the reality behind the illusion. He understands Desdemona's goodness and his own folly. The noble Moor delivers his own judgment on his actions and sacrifices himself.

The play leaves us with the viewpoint that people have sufficient goodness to outweigh their evil, and that we may perceive that goodness if we dig beneath the layers of worldly illusions. But the price of confronting that reality is sometimes a great sacrifice.

Encore: Vocabulary Words

In each group below, the main word is found in *Othello*. Mark the letter of the word in each group which is unrelated to the other three.

1. abhor
   a. detest
   b. tease
   c. hate

2. cashiered
   a. framed
   b. fired
   c. discharged

3. conjuration
   a. magic
   b. dream
   c. charm

4. deficient
   a. stopped
   b. incomplete
   c. lacking

5. incense
   a. anger
   b. madden
   c. inflate

6. iniquity
   a. sin
   b. trial
   c. wrongdoing

7. insolent
   a. curious
   b. uncivil
   c. rude

8. mandate
   a. order
   b. command
   c. choice

9. pertains
   a. relates
   b. simplifies
   c. applies

10. sated
    a. stuffed
    b. sleepy
    c. glutted

11. discern
    a. notice
    b. show
    c. see

12. citadel
    a. moat
    b. castle
    c. stronghold

13. tainting
    a. polluting
    b. smearing
    c. mocking

14. impediment
    a. obstacle
    b. prejudice
    c. hindrance

15. provocation
    a. spur
    b. motivation
    c. interest

16. infirmity
    a. hospital
    b. frailty
    c. weakness

17. prate
    a. babble
    b. imitate
    c. jabber

18. clamor
    a. uproar
    b. racket
    c. gossip

9. importune
    a. beg
    b. prefer
    c. plead

20. dilatory
    a. unhurried
    b. slow
    c. timid

21. procure
    a. acquire
    b. snatch
    c. gain

22. converse
    a. introduce
    b. talk
    c. visit

23. penitent
    a. angry
    b. regretful
    c. sorry

24. ruminate
    a. ponder
    b. reject
    c. consider

25. vehement
    a. intense
    b. violent
    c. complicated

26. pomp
    a. play
    b. formality
    c. splendor

27. slander
   a. defame
   b. backstab
   c. convict

28. veritable
   a. genuine
   b. true
   c. extreme

29. sanctified
   a. protected
   b. holy
   c. blessed

30. arraigning
   a. confessing
   b. accusing
   c. charging

31. venial
   a. forgivable
   b. lovable
   c. excusable

32. credulous
   a. believing
   b. trusting
   c. impressive

33. strumpet
   a. hussy
   b. slut
   c. witch

34. expostulate
   a. exclaim
   b. debate
   c. argue

35. breach
   a. split
   b. division
   c. cross

36. procreants
   a. reproducers
   b. parents
   c. messengers

37. garnered
   a. concealed
   b. stored
   c. gathered

38. cozening
   a. deceiving
   b. mocking
   c. double-crossing

39. notorious
   a. ill-famed
   b. unforgotten
   c. infamous

40. mettle
   a. spirit
   b. anger
   c. courage

41. restitution
    a. repayment
    b. reward
    c. renewal

42. direful
    a. horrible
    b. moody
    c. shocking

43. balmy
    a. perfumed
    b. tempting
    c. sweet

44. forfend
    a. rescue
    b. forbid
    c. block

45. insupportable
    a. unbearable
    b. enviable
    c. intolerable

46. pernicious
    a. sinister
    b. desperate
    c. poisonous

47. odious
    a. hateful
    b. horrid
    c. dirty

48. puny
    a. feeble
    b. forceless
    c. feminine

49. interim
    a. prayer
    b. interval
    c. pause

50. extenuate
    a. whitewash
    b. pretend
    c. rationalize

Improvisation: Student Enrichment

Research:

1. View two or more productions of *Othello* on videotape or film; the version with Laurence Olivier as Othello, for example, or the version made for *The Shakespeare Plays* television series, directed by Jonathan Miller. How do the versions vary? What different choices did actors and directors make in interpreting the play?

2. Read another one of Shakespeare's later tragedies such as *Hamlet, Coriolanus, King Lear, Antony and Cleopatra,* or *Macbeth.* Compare that play to *Othello* in terms of setting, character, conflict, plot, and theme.

3. Compare Iago to another Shakespearean villian such as Richard III in *Richard III,* Edmund in *King Lear,* or Aaron in *Titus Andronicus.* Analyze why both characters chose their villainous paths. Which character seems the most villainous? Why?

4. Read the passage from the *Hecatommithi* by Giraldi Cinthio from which Shakespeare derived the plot of *Othello.* What did Shakespeare choose to change—and not to change—in the story?

5. Read a tragedy from classical antiquity—Sophocles' *Oedipus Rex,* for example. Compare it to *Othello* in terms of setting, character, conflict, plot, and theme. How are Jacobean and Greek tragedies different in technique and outlook? How are they similar?

6. Two nineteenth-century operas were based upon *Othello,* one by Rossini and the other by Verdi. Both were entitled *Othello.* Listen to a recording of one of these operas. What did the composer do to adapt the story to a different medium?

7. Research the depictions of Othello throughout the centuries of the play's performance. Specifically, study Othello's appearance in some of the various productions. Did Shakespeare mean for Othello to be seen as a black? How have succeeding generations viewed Othello's race?

Reaction:

1. Analyze Othello's speech to Desdemona about the handkerchief. Consider it in the overall context of the play—including Othello's later statement that his mother received it as a gift from his father. Do you think Othello tells the truth in his speech to Desdemona? Why or why not?

2. Does Iago's manipulation of Othello seem truly plausible? Do you think Othello's gullibility is not credible, or do Iago's tactics seem genuinely effective to you? Explain your answer.

3. Examine the use of animal images in *Othello*, beginning with Iago's speeches in the first scene of the play. Start by locating as many references to animals throughout the play as you can. What patterns do you find? What does the animal imagery contribute to the themes of the play?

4. Consider one of the male/female relationships in *Othello*. (The relationship between Othello and Desdemona, Iago and Emilia, or Cassio and Bianca would be a good choice.) Consider the relationship from a modern standpoint. How have behavior and attitudes between the sexes changed since Shakespeare's time? How have behavior and attitudes remained the same?

5. Why do you think Othello originally appointed Cassio his lieutenant instead of Iago? Improvise the scene where Othello announces his decision regarding the appointment, giving the general a chance to explain his

310

choice. Include parts for any characters whom you think might be involved in the scene. (Remember, none or all of Iago's account to Roderigo might be a lie.)

6. Tragic heroes experience a "reversal of fortune"—a moment when their fall from power and happiness becomes inevitable. When does this point occur in *Othello*? Support your arguments with specifics from the play.

Creation/Composition:

1. Select one of the following scenes, then paraphrase it into contemporary dialogue: Act I, Scene 1; Act III, Scene 3; Act IV, Scene 4; Act V, Scene 2 (confrontation between Othello and Desdemona).

2. Write a story based on one of Othello's adventures hinted at in his speech in Act I, Scene 3.

3. Write one of the scenes, previous to the action of the play, in which Cassio appeals to Desdemona on Othello's behalf during the courtship of the lovers. You might choose to depict the occasion when Othello has fallen out of Desdemona's favor.

4. Of the play's principal characters, only Cassio and Iago are still alive at the end of the play. Write a "sequel" to *Othello* focusing on one of these two men. Does the conniving Iago escape execution? What happens between Cassio and Bianca? Most importantly, how have the characters been changed by the events in the play?

5. Consider the plot of *Othello* from the standpoint of modern racial relations. Retell the story in a modern setting of your choice.

6. Describe the plot of *Othello* if there had been no threat of war in Cyprus. How would the story have been different if the action had been set entirely in Venice?

7. Tell Brabantio's story from the time Othello and Desdemona leave for Cyprus to the time of the older man's death.

Between the Lines: Essay Test

Literal Level

1. What role does sheer chance play in Iago's use of the handkerchief to exact revenge?

2. Describe the use of exposition in Act I. What basic information is the audience given concerning the characters of the play and what has happened prior to the play?

3. Figure out the chronology of the play; how many days and nights does the action require? When do the specific incidents take place in relation to each other? The time which transpires while the principal characters travel to Cyprus may only be guessed at; the rest of the play follows a strict chronology.

Interpretive Level

1. Roderigo, Cassio, and Othello are all manipulated by Iago, but how are they different? What weaknesses or virtues does Iago exploit in each character's case? How do the three comment on each other as characters?

2. What purpose do Desdemona's story of Barbary and the song about the "willow maid" in Act IV serve in the play?

3. Describe Emilia and determine what values and characteristics she represents. Discuss her personality with reference to Desdemona's character.

Final Curtain: Objective Test

I. True—False

Mark each statement T for true or F for false.

_____ 1. Iago tries to conceal Othello and Desdemona's marriage from Roderigo.

_____ 2. Brabantio goes to the duke to accuse Othello of witchcraft.

_____ 3. Othello is chosen as governor of Cyprus for his military abilities.

_____ 4. Cyprus is saved because the Turkish ships are attacked by vessels from Rhodes.

_____ 5. Brabantio warns Othello that since Desdemona deceived her father, she may deceive her husband.

_____ 6. Iago suspects his own wife of infidelity with Othello.

_____ 7. Iago tells Cassio to appeal directly to Othello for reinstatement because Iago knows this will irritate Othello.

_____ 8. Iago cautions Othello against the dangers of jealousy and pretends to find excuses for Desdemona.

_____ 9. Emilia claims she would never be unfaithful to her husband under any circumstances.

_____10. Cassio is mortally wounded in a fight with Roderigo.

_____11. Othello is reluctant to kill Desdemona until she confesses her sins.

_____12. On her deathbed, Desdemona says no one is guilty of her death and asks Othello to remember her.

_____13. Emilia does not detect her husband's deception until the final scene.

_____14. Iago repents his villainy at the end of the play and tries to commit suicide.

_____15. Gratiano inherits Othello's property because he is Desdemona's uncle.

II. Multiple Choice

Select the *one false* answer for each statement.

16. Iago shows his manipulativeness by

    a. swindling Roderigo out of all his money.
    b. convincing the duke that Othello is guilty of witchcraft.
    c. telling Othello that Desdemona gave Cassio her handkerchief.
    d. persuading Cassio to drink more wine.

17. In the past, Brabantio

    a. opened his home to Othello on many occasions.
    b. actively encouraged Othello's love for Desdemona.
    c. discouraged Roderigo as a suitor.
    d. listened to Othello's life story.

18. Iago describes Othello's elopement with Desdemona as

    a. the mating of a ewe and ram.
    b. thievery from Brabantio's house.
    c. cross-breeding of horses.
    d. the union of songbirds.

19. In commenting upon his background, Othello claims that he

   a. is related to royalty.
   b. has been a warrior since he was a boy.
   c. possesses a large fortune.
   d. was born of a white father and black mother.

20. Desdemona testifies before the duke that she

   a. now owes her greatest duty to her husband.
   b. will not stay with her father while Othello is gone.
   c. regrets offending her father.
   d. saw Othello's virtues behind his looks.

21. After hearing Othello and Desdemona explain their elopement, the duke

   a. says he thinks his own daughter might have been won by Othello.
   b. suggests that Desdemona stay with her father.
   c. tells Brabantio to make the best of the situation.
   d. postpones passing judgment on Othello.

22. While Desdemona waits for Othello to arrive in Cyprus, she

   a. is warmly greeted by Cassio.
   b. expresses her confidence in Othello's safety.
   c. exchanges clever words with Iago about women.
   d. conceals her fears for her husband's safety.

23. Iago resents Cassio because

   a. Cassio's "beauty" makes Iago seem ugly.
   b. Iago thinks Cassio had an affair with Emilia.
   c. Cassio was promoted over Iago.
   d. Bianca rejected Iago in favor of Cassio.

24. Iago plots Cassio's dismissal by

    a. seducing Bianca.
    b. encouraging Cassio to get drunk.
    c. causing Othello to be wakened so Cassio's actions will be known.
    d. inciting Roderigo to bait Cassio.

25. Cassio is accurately described as

    a. an overly courteous ladies' man.
    b. a loyal lieutenant who worships Othello.
    c. a trusting and accommodating gentleman.
    d. a strong-willed schemer.

26. After his dismissal by Othello, Cassio

    a. curses the nature of drink.
    b. bemoans that he has no way to regain his position.
    c. lets Iago convince him to appeal to Desdemona.
    d. describes in detail his quarrel with Roderigo.

27. An example of a comic interlude in the play is

    a. the clown's conversation with the musicians.
    b. Desdemona's attempt to locate Cassio's lodging.
    c. Cassio's drunken remarks to Roderigo and Montano.
    d. Iago's discussion of the types of women.

28. When Cassio appeals to Desdemona, she says

    a. she would rather die than fail in his behalf.
    b. she will do what she can but must heed Othello's wishes.
    c. he will certainly get his position back.
    d. she won't give Othello peace until Cassio is reinstated.

29. Iago preys on Othello's suspicions by

    a. saying he saw Cassio enter Desdemona's room.
    b. seeming to evade discussing Desdemona's infidelity.
    c. appearing to question his own motives in speaking to Othello.
    d. reminding Othello that Desdemona betrayed her own father.

30. At one point, Othello tells Desdemona to cherish the handkerchief because

    a. it was the first love token he gave to Desdemona.
    b. Othello's father gave it to his mother.
    c. it is a love charm.
    d. Othello's mother gave it to him to present to his wife.

31. The following things happen to Desdemona's handkerchief:

    a. Iago causes Desdemona to drop it.
    b. Emilia picks it up and gives it to her husband.
    c. Cassio finds it in his bedchamber.
    d. Cassio asks Bianca to copy the embroidery.

32. Enraged with jealousy, Othello says that he

    a. wishes all his soldiers had slept with Desdemona, so long as he didn't know.
    b. is finished with soldiering.
    c. wishes to go away to war.
    d. must have proof from Iago.

33. The conversation between Iago, Cassio, and Bianca convinces Othello that

    a. Cassio should be murdered.
    b. Bianca is hiding something.
    c. Desdemona deserves to die.
    d. Desdemona gave Cassio her handkerchief.

34. As Othello prepares to die, he

    a. compares himself to an infidel.
    b. justifies his actions.
    c. asks his witnesses to speak the truth about him.
    d. describes how he once killed a Turk.

35. By the end of the play,

    a. Iago has been slain by Othello.
    b. Brabantio has died of grief.
    c. Cassio has been named governor.
    d. Emilia has been killed by Iago.

III. Matching

A. Match the character with the proper description.

    a. Iago   e. Brabantio
    b. Cassio   f. Othello
    c. Bianca   g. Roderigo
    d. Emilia   h. Desdemona

_____36.   " . . . a maid / That paragons descriptions and wild fame"

_____37.   "O Spartan dog, / More fell than anguish, hunger, or the sea!"

_____38.   " 'Tis such another fitchew! Marry, a perfum'd one."

_____39.   "Mere prattle, without practice / Is all his soldiership"

_____40.   "The magnifico is much belov'd, / And hath in his effect a voice potential / As double as the Duke's."

_____41.   "Sir, would she give you so much of her lips / As of her tongue she oft bestows on me, / You'd have enough."

_____42.   " . . . one that lov'd not wisely, but too well"

_____43. "My sick fool . . . / Whom love hath turn'd almost the wrong side out."

B. Match the character with the statement that expresses his or her philosophy.

a. Emilia   e. Cassio
b. Desdemona f. Othello
c. Iago   g. Roderigo
d. Duke

_____44. "When remedies are past, the griefs are ended / By seeing the worst, which late on hopes depended."

_____45. "Virtue? a fig! 'tis in ourselves that we are thus or thus."

_____46. "The world's a huge thing; it is a great price/ For a small vice."

_____47. "I have no great devotion to the deed, / And yet he hath given me satisfying reasons. / 'Tis but a man gone."

_____48. "O, I have lost my reputation! I have lost the immortal part of myself, and what remains is bestial."

_____49. "Heaven me such uses send, / Not to pick bad from bad, but by bad mend!"

_____50. "He that is robb'd, not wanting what is stolen, / Let him not know 't, and he's not robb'd at all."